ROYAL DOULTON BUNNYKINS

SECOND EDITION

A CHARLTON STANDARD CATALOGUE

By

Jean Dale

Louise Irvine

W.K. Cross

Publisher

The Charlton Press

TORONTO, ONTARIO ❖ PALM HARBOR, FLORIDA

Canadian Catalogue in Publication Data

The National Library of Canada has Catalogued this publication as follow:

The Charlton standard catalogue of Royal Doulton bunnykins

1st ed. ([1999])-
ISSN 1485-1008
ISBN 0-88968-220-8 (2nd edition)

1. Porcelain animals-Catalogs. 2. Royal Doulton figurines-Catalogs.
3. Children's china (Porcelain)-Catalogs. I. Title: Bunnykins.

NK4660.C515   738.8'2'029442   C98-900623-9

Printed in Canada
in the Province of Ontario

The Charlton Press
www.charltonpress.com

EDITORIAL

Editors	W. K. Cross, Jean Dale
Editorial Assistant	Susan Cross
Graphic Technician	Davina Rowan
Colour Technician	Marina Tsourkis
Cover Illustration	Sand Castle Money Box

ACKNOWLEDGEMENTS

The Charlton Press wishes to thank those who have assisted with the second edition of *The Charlton Standard Catalogue of Royal Doulton Bunnykins*. Also, we would like to thank Louise Irvine for her work on this edition. Louise is an independent writer and lecturer on Royal Doulton's history and products and is not in anyway connected with the pricing in this guide.

Special Thanks

We would like to thank the staff of Royal Doulton on both sides of the ocean for all their help and assistance: **Heather Bayliss** (UK), **Paula Bell** (Canada), **Janet Drift** (USA), **Joe Golden** (UK), **Fiona Hawthorne** (UK), **Josie Hunt** (UK), **Joan Jones** (UK), **Kevin Moyer** (USA), **Maria Murtagh** (UK), **Sarah Jane Rowley** (UK).

Contributors to the Second Edition

The publisher would also like to thank the following individuals and companies who graciously supplied photographs or information or allowed us access to their collections for photographic purposes:

Dealers

Ann Burns, Antiquity Ann's, Northbay, Ontario, Canada; **William T. Cross**, William Cross Antiques & Collectibles, Delta, B.C. Canada; **Claire Green**, *Cottontales*, England; **Leah Selig**, *Rabbiting On*, Merrylands, NSW, Australia; **Nick Tzimas**, U.K.I. Ceramics, Woodbridge, Suffolk, England

Collectors

Wendy Bailey, Guildford, Surrey, England; **Joan and Bob Barwick**, Ontario, Canada; **Brenda Bemben**, New Britain, Connecticut, U.S.A.; **Steven Bradley**, P.E.I., Canada; **Nick Claire**, United Kingdom; **Ken Clifton,** Stoke-on-Trent, England; **Mr. R. Davey**, Leicester, England; **Cassie Fletcher**, Stoke-on-Trent, England; **Ray Ford**, Tadcaster, North Yorks, England; **Jane Hodson**, England; **Paul Holder**, Derbyshire, England; **Jemma Hoskin**; **Ann R. H. Lee**, Victoria, Australia; **Joanne Neill**, New Britain, Connecticut, U.S.A.; **Scott Reichenberg**, North Smithfield, RI, U.S.A.; **Julie Sandry**, Sydney, Australia; **John and Maureen Sewell**, Paso Robles, California, U.S.A.; **Pat Sage**, Unionville, Ontario, Canada; **Tracy and John Simpson**, Burlington, Ontario, Canada; **Niki Smith**, Battle, East Sussex, England; **Margaret and Rob Stephens**, Brecon, Wales; **Kylie Webb**, Victoria, Australia; **Sue and Phil Williams**, Halesowen, West Midlands, England.

A SPECIAL NOTE TO COLLECTORS

We welcome and appreciate any comments or suggestions in regard to *The Charlton Standard Catalogue of Royal Doulton Bunnykins*. If any errors or omissions come to your attention, please do not hesitate to write to us, or if you would like to participate in pricing or supply previously unavailable data or information, please contact Jean Dale at (416) 488-1418, or E-mail us at **chpress@charltonpress.com**.

The Charlton Press

Editorial Office
P.O. Box 820, Station Willowdale B
North York, Ontario, Canada. M2K 2R1
Telephone: (416) 488-1418 Fax: (416) 488-4656
Telephone: (800) 442-6042 Fax: (800) 442-1542
E-mail chpress@charltonpress.com   www.charltonpress.com

HOW TO USE THIS CATALOGUE

THE PURPOSE

As with the other catalogues in Charlton's Royal Doulton reference and pricing library, this publication has been designed to serve two specific purposes: first, to furnish collectors with accurate and detailed listings that will provide the essential information needed to build a rich and rewarding collection; second, to provide collectors and dealers with an indication of the current market prices of Bunnykins figurines and tableware items.

The second edition of this price guide is the second attempt to link Bunnykins tableware designs to shapes and to prices. While all designs are more than likely known to collectors, the list of shapes on which they appear is still being compiled.

THE LISTINGS

The *Charlton Standard Catalogue of Royal Doulton Bunnykins* is divided into four chapters, the first being devoted to Bunnykins tableware and the fourth, to modern Bunnykins figurines. It is within these two chapters that we will outline how the listings function.

The tableware chapter has the Bunnykins designs listed in alphabetical order, beginning with the ABC Theme and ending with Xmas Menu. Within the design layout is a shape/price table incorporating, on the left side of the table, a vertical listing of the different shapes on which the design appears. To the right of the shape column is the price column indicating a level at which collectors may expect to see that design/shape trade.

Within these columns are two sub-listings that must be understood to make the catalogue the useful tool that it is intended to be.

The Barbara Vernon designs carried her facsimile signature, unless, of course, the shape was too small and the signature was therefore dropped. These signatures were in continuous use until the early 1950s. As a result, a shape that was in production from 1934 to the mid-1950s will appear in the shape column as with signature and without signature. The demand is much greater for shapes with the facsimile signature and this necessitates a two-tier pricing structure.

The second sub-listing is the copy printed in bold type, indicating a design that is current, on a shape that is current, and that is still being produced by Royal Doulton. The lines that are not bold indicate shapes that have been discontinued.

In the pricing tables of the tableware section, we have listed all the shapes that are known to exist with a specific design. There is a good possibility that more shapes exist, and these will be added to the design table in future editions as they become known.

The list of Bunnykins figurines is simple by comparison. Royal Doulton numbered the Bunnykins figurines in chronological order, as they were issued, starting with DB1 and carrying on to the present, which is above DB265.

STYLES AND VERSIONS

Tableware

All designs are named by the designer and, within any design, modifications may be needed so that the design may better fit the shape. As designs are changed or modified, it is necessary to bring our classifications to bear on Bunnykins tableware.

Styles: If the same design name is used at various times by different designers, the earlier issue then becomes Style One and the latter, Style Two.

Versions: The design may have one or more elements removed from the main design.

Variations: The design has all elements intact but minor modifications have been made to allow the design to better fit the shape

Figurines

All listings include the modeller, where known, and the name of the animal figurine, designer, height, colour, dates of issue and discontinuation, varieties and series.

Styles: If the same design name is used at various times by different designers, the earlier issue then becomes Style One and the latter, Style Two.

Versions: Versions are modifications in a major style element.

Variations: Variations are modifications in a minor style element. A change in colour is a variation

SIGNATURES

A second word about the facsimile signature of Barbara Vernon is needed. Designs discontinued by 1952 should all carry the Barbara Vernon signature. However, there is the possibility that the signature was cut a way from the transfer when the shape was too small to accommodate it, and the piece was issued without it

While the absence of the signature affects the value of a piece, we consider that the value would be in the range of 75 percent of the catalogue price listed.

SHAPES

Some shapes will not carry a Bunnykins design. For example, the Stratford teacup will carry a design, while the Stratford saucer has a decoration of running rabbits around the edge. In our design/shape listing, we show only the item that carries the Bunnykins design. In this case, the Stratford teacup, which carries a design, will be listed but the saucer will not. It is understood that a saucer comes with the cup.

TABLE OF CONTENTS

PRICING OLD AND NEW

The Old

The first edition of Bunnykins, introduced in 1999, was priced in a manner similar to all the other catalogues we have published over the years.

We had developed four main streams of information upon which we relied for pricing.

(1) Auctions: Auction catalogues and their prices realized provide a wealth of information on what a collector or dealer is willing to pay for an item. We, of course, subscribe to and receive a variety of auction catalogues from all over the world.

(2) Dealers direct mail catalogues: There was always a number of active dealers in the direct mail field publishing and distributing detailed price lists. Incorporating these lists in to our analysis was another important factor in arriving at a market price.

(3) Request: Two or three months before a print date pricing requests were mailed to various dealers in different parts of the world requesting their opinion on market prices. These replies were tallied and incorporated into the above data.

(4) Newsletters: We subscribe to every and all newsletter that appears on the subject for which we are producing a price guide. Newsletters give a wealth of information on current happenings in various hobbies, but they also supply goodly quantities of pricing information.

The four streams were compiled into one, extreme high and lows removed, and the results averaged to arrive at a market value. After a while a trend would emerge indicating the direction of the market. We were then ready to build a pricing model that would allow us to arrive at a suggested evaluation.

Over the past three years dramatic changes have taken place in collecting, especially collectables produced in the 20th century which have continuity between similar items. Posters, art pottery, art glass, Bunnykins figurines and tableware, coins and stamps all belong to this category. They all fit the same mould, all have the same properties in common. They all have a high artistic design content, produced in small but reasonable quantities and widely distributed throughout the world. They started life as ornaments or decorations for the home.

The Evolution

The impact the internet would have on collectables was not fully anticipated. All the old avenues such as fairs, shows, dealer stores, retail outlets, direct mail and auction houses would come under severe pressure by the lowering of margins which the internet fostered. This would have a direct impact on pricing

When Royal Doulton Bunnykins, 1st edition, was up for revision in the winter of 2001, the process began of gathering prices to generate the 2nd. Our method of collecting pricing information had to change.

Why! Simply because of the tremendous growth of the internet, and looking deeper, the rapid growth of on-line auctions in which 20th century collectables fit so well. Our auction results multiplied more than a thousand fold.

Dealers' websites have all but replaced direct mail. The direct mail house of five years ago is now the virtual store of 2002. Items, prices can all be changed daily, with little effort or cost.

Land based auctions still contribute to pricing for they, through their historical connection with the collectors, gather in the scarce and rare pieces. The value of which is helpful in establishing an overall price trend. Seldom does the rare trend higher, without the basic items being carried along in unison.

Now, following this far, you are starting to wonder what has changed from the old model to the new, it is the internet component comprising two parts: on-line auctions and virtual stores, which were not available previously, but must now be inserted into the equation.

Category	Average items daily Jan. 2001	Jan. 2002	One Day in March 2002
Bunnykins	**350**	**475**	**650**
Coins	6,000	7,200	8,300
Disney	37,500	51,500	65,800
Harry Potter	2,300	12,000	9,600
Lalique	650	400	700
Moorcroft	250	300	290
Royal Doulton	3,500	3,700	4,600
Royal Worcester	600	800	1,000
Stamps	12,700	13,700	17,600
Star Wars	19,000	23,500	25,100

The above table produces what a few years ago would be considered mind-boggling numbers. Take for example **Bunnykins**, on a yearly basis nearly 130,000 items were offered for sale. By January 2002 the units offered were projected at over 170,000, by March 2002, the rate was running at almost 240,000. It is impossible to ignore such numbers.

The New

(1) Auctions:

   A. Land-based auctions. As before, we continually monitor auction results capturing the pricing data.

   B. Virtual auctions. With the new on-line auctions, both dealers and collectors participate. Prices become a true indication at that moment of the value of the item.

(2) Virtual stores: Dealers virtual stores have replaced our previous direct mail component.

The price gathering process has changed dramatically. The analizing of the data remains the same.

INTRODUCTION

COLLECTING BUNNYKINS TABLEWARE

Generations of children around the world have been weaned with Bunnykins nursery ware as it has been in continuous production since 1934. Few could have imagined that their favourite baby plate would one day become collectable but that is the fate of many of the Bunnykins designs, particularly the early pieces featuring Barbara Vernon's signature.

Barbara Vernon Designs

Barbara Vernon was a young nun in an English convent school when she first imagined the exploits of the Bunnykins family to entertain the children in her class. Her father was the Manager of the Royal Doulton Pottery in Stoke-on-Trent and he recognised the potential of her rabbit drawings for a range of nursery ware. Sister Mary Barbara, as she was known in the convent, began to send her sketches to the factory where they were adapted for the lithographic printing process by one of the resident designers, Hubert Light. He also created the backstamp from the *Tug of War* scene LF1 and designed the chain of running rabbits which has appeared around the rim of the Bunnykins pieces since their launch in 1934.

A surviving catalogue of 1937 shows that the range grew quickly to include two sizes of baby plate, a child's dinner plate, Don beakers and mugs, cereal and porridge bowls, a Jaffa fruit saucer, a jam pot, a Casino teapot, cup, saucer, sugar bowl and jugs in various sizes. These shapes were all made in a deep ivory glazed earthenware and decorated with colourful transfer prints. Barbara Vernon's bunnies were usually dressed in sky blue and cherry red and the background was coloured in subtle shades of brown and green.

More shapes had been added by 1940, notably an oval baby plate, a hot water plate with cover and a candle holder. Bunnykins collectors usually like to find an example of each shape featuring a Barbara Vernon design and the jam pot and candle holder, which were withdrawn in 1952, are amongst the hardest to find in the earthenware range.

Some of the early Bunnykins designs were also available in a white bone china body. This finer body was only produced until the Second World War and, as not many bone china pieces survived the rough and tumble of nursery life, they are very rare today. One collector was fortunate enough to find an original boxed bone china breakfast set, complete with silver spoons, whilst another boasts a tea set in pristine condition.

The condition of Bunnykins nursery ware, whether it is bone china or earthenware, is very important for serious collectors who seek out pieces with the minimum of scratches. Sometimes it is very hard to find early baby plates which have not been scraped by enthusiastic eaters scooping up their porridge to enjoy the scene underneath. Collectors also like to find scenes incorporating Barbara Vernon's facsimile signature although sometimes this was cut off the transfer.

Many of Barbara Vernon's scenes had been withdrawn by 1952 and these are amongst the most desirable today. Collectors appreciate her simple designs and the charming subjects which evoke her era, for example one of her bunnies in being dosed with castor oil at *Medicine Time* SF1 and others dance the *Lambeth Walk* HW16. Her quiet sense of humour can also be enjoyed in scenes like *Frightening Spider* SF4 and *Pressing Trousers* HW14 which shows the bunny struggling to remove the creases with a garden roller! Sadly, Barbara Vernon only produced Bunnykins drawings for a few years because of her commitments at the convent and so Walter Hayward, one of Royal Doultons Art Directors, took over the range after the Second World War.

Walter Hayward Designs

Initially Walter Hayward adapted the remaining Barbara Vernon drawings for production but he soon began to create his own scenes although her facsimile signature continued to appear on the ware until the mid 1950s. However, Walter Hayward's work can usually be identified by the presence of some lively little mice that became his trademark. Generally his scenes are much busier than their predecessors and some reflect new topical themes such as the advent of television and space travel. Over the years, he was encouraged to add more and more bunnies, particularly by Doulton's agent in Australia which was one of the strongest markets for Bunnykins. Some of his most ambitious designs, such as *Juggling* LF127 and *Hoopla* LF129, were only available for three years and so these are two of the hardest Hayward designs to find today.

The Bunnykins shapes remained much the same throughout the 1950s and 60s although some larger sizes of Casino teapots and jugs were added in 1952. They were all withdrawn in the late 1960s together with a wide range of scenes when the original earthenware body was replaced with new ivory bone china. By the late 1970s, new shapes had been developed for the china body including the Hug-a-mug which replaced the original Don mug and a range or egg-shaped boxes. Unfortunately, the egg boxes were not made for long and they are now very collectable. Savings books and money balls followed in the early 1980s and these were used occasionally to commemorate special events, such as royal births and weddings.

In the early 1980s, Walter Hayward was commissioned to design a range of scenes celebrating birthdays, christenings and Christmas. He also helped the Bunnykins family celebrate their own birthday with special commemorative pieces to mark their Golden Jubilee in 1984. In addition, all the nursery ware made during 1984 had the inscription Golden Jubilee Celebration added to the backstamp. Bunnykins birthday parties were held all over the world during 1984 and the resulting publicity attracted many new enthusiasts.

An anniversary weekend in Stoke-on-Trent was the catalyst for the largest Bunnykins collection in the U.K. which boasts examples of every scene and shape from 1934 to the present day. The first Bunnykins reference book was published at the end of 1984 and for the first time collectors could see the full extent of the range. Some scenes could only be illustrated from the pattern books and collectors all over the world began hunting for rarities like *Air Mail Delivery* LFa, *Carving the Chicken* LFc and *Dodgems* LF4.

No longer was Bunnykins intended exclusively for youngsters, Walter Hayward designed a set of Bunnykins for Grown Ups featuring bunnies with brief-cases dashing to work. These adult designs only remained in production from 1986 to 1988 so examples are very hard to find today. Walter Hayward's last Bunnykins design following his retirement was the plate to commemorate Australia's Bicentenary in 1988. Meanwhile, another artist was getting to know the Bunnykins family for a series of story books.

Colin Twinn Designs

In 1987, Colin Twinn was commissioned to produce a collection of Bunnykins books for the publishers, Frederick Warne, and many of his drawings were adapted for use on nursery ware. As a successful illustrator of children's books, Twinn had considerable experience with anthropomorphic characters, particularly rabbits, and he created a new look for the Bunnykins family. Pastel colours predominate in his detailed scenes and his bunnies seem softer and fluffier than the originals. Whilst this approach worked well in the little picture books, the new Bunnykins nursery ware designs did not have sufficient impact on the china shop shelves. Established collectors felt that the Bunnykins characters had lost their identity and it would appear that general gift buyers were not enthused either as production of Colin Twinn designs had ceased by the early 1990s.

Many of Colin Twinn's designs appeared on the new shapes which were developed in the late 1980s. An Albion style tea service was introduced in 1987 together with a Stratford tea cup and saucer which replaced the Casino shape. The traditional Don beaker was replaced by a straight sided Malvern beaker and a 10 ½ inch dinner plate was added to the range. Decorative accessories, such as a lamp and two picture plaques, were also available for a few years and these are now sought after by collectors.

Gradually, as Colin Twinn's designs began to disappear from the shops, new stocks of Barbara Vernon and Walter Hayward designs appeared. Around 50 patterns for hollow ware and flat ware had never been withdrawn and these were modified in line with new requirements for colour printing. A tuft of green grass on the left of the backstamp distinguishes the more recent Vernon/Hayward wares from earlier examples. A classic Barbara Vernon scene *Dancing in the Moonlight* was re-drawn for the 60th Anniversary of the Bunnykins range in 1994 and a set of commemorative ware was made for that year only. Royal Doulton's company in Australia commissioned their own exclusive anniversary scene featuring an Aussie picnic complete with kangaroos and koalas and this was one of the last designs by Colin Twinn as a new artist had been found to continue the Bunnykins tradition, Frank Endersby.

Frank Endersby Designs

Frank Endersby is a freelance illustrator who works from his own studio in the idyllic Cotswolds region. During his career, he has worked in a busy graphic design studio and also with a children's book publisher so he has a wide experience of all aspects of design and illustration. He quickly assimilated the essential qualities of the original Bunnykins style and his scenes feature the strong outlines used for the original characters as well as their bright blue and red clothes. To date he has worked on 20 new sets of Bunnykins designs and each set incorporates three scenes, the larger for decorating plates and two smaller ones to use on the front and reverse of cups and other hollow ware. These scenes began to appear in the shops in 1995 but it was a couple of years before dedicated collectors had located all his designs. Early indications are that the new Frank Endersby designs are being very well received by gift buyers and collectors alike, so much so that the original Vernon/Hayward scenes have now been phased out of production.

A few new Bunnykins shapes have been introduced in recent years, such as the divided children's dish and the photograph frame, but the most exciting new concept was the annual Bunnykins Christmas plate made exclusively for members of Royal Doulton International Collectors Club. These lively designs by Frank Endersby have a wealth of colourful detail, including some of Walter Hayward's cheeky mice and the running rabbits wearing Christmas hats! The limited distribution and short production period is guaranteed to make these very special Bunnykins pieces.

COLLECTING BUNNYKINS FIGURINES

Bunnykins figures made their debut in 1939 but the war soon halted production and the original six characters are extremely rare today. It is believed that they were modelled by Charles Noke, the Art Director who developed the HN range of Royal Doulton figures, as they resemble some of his early character animals. These large scale figures, which range in size from 3 to 7 inches, have little in common with Barbara Vernon's design which might explain why they were never revived after the war.

As well as these characters figures, Noke also introduced a Bunny shaped breakfast set, featuring a teapot, cream jug, sugar bowl, sugar sifter and egg cup, but this suffered a similar fate in the war years. The idea of Bunny shaped ware to accompany the successful nursery ware was not revived until 1967 when a Bunny money bank was added to the range and this remained in production until 1981.

The DB Range

When Royal Doulton took over the Beswick factory in 1969, they acquired the modelling skills of Albert Hallam who worked on the Beatrix Potter range figures. These little character animals were amongst Beswick's most successful product and it was decided to create a similar collection of Bunnykins figures. The first nine figures were launched in 1972 with DB pattern numbers and they averaged 4 inches in height. All were inspired by Walter Hayward's nursery ware patterns, for example *The Artist* DB13 is derived from *The Portrait Painter* SF20. This approach continued until 1974 when there was a total of 15 characters in the range but a new look developed in the 1980s.

Harry Sales Designs

Harry Sales, the Design Manager of the Beswick factory, took over responsibility for the Bunnykins range in 1980. He believed that the rabbit character should reflect the interests of contemporary children and his first figure of a guitar-playing rock star *Mr. Bunnybeat Strumming* DB16 was followed by a space traveller *Astro Bunnykins Rocket Man* DB20. After seeing his colleagues' response to these entertaining designs, it occurred to Harry that Bunnykins figures could also have an adult audience and he began to work on a collection of sporting subjects at the time of the Los Angeles Olympics in 1984. Adults began to purchase these figures as whimsical gifts, sharing Harry's sense of humour in subjects like *Freefall Bunnykins* DB41 whose pained expression suggested a not so perfect landing.

This new direction coincided with the Bunnykins Golden Jubilee when nursery ware first began to be taken seriously by collectors. Before long, the figures were also included in the hunt and early discontinued models, such as *Mr. Bunnykins Autumn Days* DB5 and *Daisy Bunnykins Spring Time* DB7 were sought at collectors fairs and markets. In 1987, the Royal Doulton International Collectors Club commissioned a figure exclusively for its members and *Collector Bunnykins* DB54 is now one of the most expensive figures on the secondary market.

Several special commissions were produced in the late 1980s and these now command premium prices. National subjects such as *Australian Bunnykins* DB58 were made to celebrate that country's bicentenary and new colourways of existing models were produced for sale at special events in the USA, notably *Mr. And Mrs. Bunnykins at the Easter Parade* DB51 and 52.

Graham Tongue Designs

When Harry Sales left Royal Doulton in 1986 to pursue a freelance career, Graham Tongue became the Beswick Studio Manager and he has been responsible for a number of Bunnykins figures, either as designer or modeller. His most popular figure is *Bedtime Bunnykins* DB55 which was made in four different colourways for special occasions. He also produced some figures inspired by Colin Twinn's nursery ware illustrations, for example *Lollipopman Bunnykins* DB65, but these were less

successful and were withdrawn after a few years. For a few years following his retirement in 1995, Graham has continued to model Bunnykins figures at his own studio and he created *Ballerina Bunnykins* DB176 and *Cavalier Bunnykins* DB179, a limited edition design.

Limited Edition Designs

The first limited edition Bunnykins figures were commissioned in 1990 for sale at a Doulton collectors fair in London. The *Oompah Band* was renamed the *Royal Doulton Collectors Band* for this occasion and the new blue colourway was so successful that other special editions swiftly followed. Denise Andrews, a freelance illustrator from Suffolk, was invited to produce special designs which were modelled by the team of resident artists at the Beswick studio. Her footballing and cricketing characters augmented the earlier sporting range and her colourful *Clown* and *Jester Bunnykins* have entertained collectors all over the world. Over the years, limited edition sizes have grown from 250 to 3,500 but many new Bunnykins figures are over-subscribed as soon as they are launched. Collectors were bewitched by *Trick or Treat Bunnykins* DB162, which was issued in 1995 and was soon changing hands for many times its issue price. In 1996, Royal Doulton introduced their first Bunnykins Figure of the Year and collectors responded enthusiastically to this new initiative.

Resin Bunnykins Figurines

In 1995, the Bunnykins characters became movie stars when an animated feature film was screened in North America and the UK. *Happy Birthday Bunnykins* was later distributed in video form and inspired a new collection of Bunnykins figures in a resin body. Resin is the name given to a cold cast sculptural material which retains intricate modelling detail more effectively than conventional fired clay bodies. The resin Bunnykins figures are smaller in scale than their ceramic cousins and are decorated primarily in pastel colours. During 1996 and 1997, twenty models were issued in the resin range, including two ambitious musical boxes and two photograph frames, but they did not appeal to collectors or gift buyers and were all withdrawn at the end of 1997. Fortunately the traditional ceramic figures continue to go from strength to strength.

The Success of the DB Range

After just 30 years in production, the DB figures are amongst the most collectable Royal Doulton products and Bunnykins fans are multiplying faster than rabbits. With this in mind, it is a good idea to buy the new Bunnykins figures as soon as they are issued. Royal Doulton have now allocated 280 DB numbers and, although a few intervening numbers have not been issued, committed collectors now have quite a challenge to find them all. Figures are now withdrawn regularly from the range, adding to the excitement of the chase so, in the words of the song, if you want to keep up you'll have to ..run rabbit…run rabbit…run..run..run!

ROYAL DOULTON

INTERNATIONAL COLLECTORS CLUB

Founded in 1980, the Royal Doulton International Collectors Club provides an information service on all aspects of the company's products, past and present. A club magazine, *Gallery*, is published four times a year with information on new products and current events that will keep the collector up-to-date on the happenings in the world of Royal Doulton. Upon joining the club, each new member will receive a free gift and invitations to special events and exclusive offers throughout the year.

To join the Royal Doulton Collectors Club, please contact your local stockist, or contact the club directly by writing to the address opposite or calling the appropriate number.

International Collectors Club
Sir Henry Doulton House
Forge Lane, Etruria
Stoke-on-Trent, Staffordshire
ST1 5NN, England

Telephone:
U.K.: 8702 412696
Overseas: +44 1782 404045
U.K. Fax: +44 (0) 1782 404000
On-line at www.doulton-direct.co.uk
E-mail: icc@royal-doulton.com

VISITOR CENTRE

Opened in the Summer of 1996, the Royal Doulton Visitor Centre houses the largest collection of Royal Doulton figurines in the world. Demonstration areas offer the collector a first hand insight on how figurines are assembled and decorated. Also at the Visitor Centre is a restaurant and a retail shop offering both best quality ware and slight seconds.

Factory tours may be booked, Monday to Friday.

Royal Doulton Visitor Centre
Nile Street, Burslem
Stoke-on-Trent, ST6 2AJ, England

Visitor Centre: Tel.: +44 (0) 1782 292434
                 Fax: +44 (0) 1782 292424
Factory Store: Tel.: +44 (0) 1782 292451

WEBSITE AND E-MAIL ADDRESS

Web Sites:
www.royal-doulton.com
www.doulton-direct.com.au
www.royal-doulton-brides.com

E-mail:
Visitor Centre: visitor@royal-doulton.com
Consumer Enquiries: enquiries@royal-doulton.com
Museum Curator: heritage@royal-doulton.com
Doulton-Direct: direct@royal-doulton.com

ROYAL DOULTON FACTORY SHOPS

Royal Doulton Group Factory Shop
Lawley Street, Longton,
Stoke-on-Trent ST3 2PH, England
Tel.: +44 (0) 1782 291237

Royal Doulton Factory Shop
Forge Lane, Etruria
Stoke-on-Trent ST1 5NN, England
Tel.: +44 (0) 1782 284056

Royal Doulton Factory Shop
Victoria Road, Fenton,
Stoke-on-Trent ST4 2PJ, England
Tel.: +44 (0) 1782 291869

Beswick Factory Shop
Barford Street, Longton,
Stoke-on-Trent ST3 2JP England
Tel.: +44 (0) 1782 291237

COLLECTOR CLUB CHAPTERS

Detroit Chapter
Frank Americk, President
1771 Brody, Allen Park, MI., 48101

Edmonton Chapter
Mildred's Collectibles
6813 104 Street, Edmonton, AB

New England Chapter
Robert Hicks, President
Lee Piper, Vice President
Michael Lynch, Secretary
Scott Reichenberg, Treasurer
E-mail doingantiq@aol.com

Northern California Chapter
Edward L. Khachadourian, President
P.O. Box 214, Moraga, Ca. 94556-0214
Tel.: (925) 376-2221 Fax: (925) 376-3581
E-mail: khack@pacbell.net

Northwest, Bob Haynes, Chapter
Alan Matthew, President
15202 93rd Place N.E., Bothell,
WA., 98011 Tel.: (425) 488-9604

Rochester Chapter
Judith L. Trost, President
103 Garfield Street, Rochester,
NY., 14611. Tel.: (716) 436-3321

Ohio Chapter
Reg Morris, President
5556 Whitehaven Avenue
North Olmstead, OH., 44070
Tel.: (216) 779-5554

Western Pennsylvania Chapter
John Re, President
9589 Parkedge Drive, Allison Park,
PA., 15101
Tel.: (412) 366-0201
Fax: (412) 366-2558

THE DOULTON MARKETS

LAND AUCTIONS

AUSTRALIA

Goodman's
7 Anderson Street,
Double Bay, Sydney, 2028, N.S.W. Australia
Tel.: +61 (0) 2 9327 7311; Fax: +61 (0) 2 9327 2917
Enquiries: Suzanne Brett
www.goodmans.com.au
E-mail: info@goodmans.com.au

Sotheby's
118-122 Queen Street, Woollahra,
Sydney, 2025, N.S.W., Australia
Tel.: +61 (0) 2 9362 1000; Fax: +61 (0) 2 9362 1100
www.sothebys.com E-mail:

CANADA

Empire Auctions

Montreal
5500 Paré Street, Montreal, Quebec H4P 2M1
Tel.: (514) 737-6586; Fax: (514) 342-1352
Enquiries: Isadoe Rubinfeld
E-mail: montreal@empireauctions.com

Ottawa
1380 Cyrville Road, Gloucester, On
Tel.: (613) 748-5343; Fax: (613) 748-0354
Enquiries: Elliot Melamed
E-mail: ottawa@empireauctions.com

Toronto
165 Tycos Drive
Toronto, On, M6B 1W6
Tel.: (416) 784-4261; Fax: (416) 784-4262
Enquiries: Micheal Rogozinsky
www.empireauctions.com
E-mail: toronto@empireauctions.com

Maynard's Industries Ltd.

Arts / Antiques
415 West 2nd Avenue, Vancouver, BC, V5Y 1E3
Tel.: (604) 876-1311; Fax: (604) 876-1323
www.maynards.com
E-mail: antiques@maynards.com

Ritchie's
288 King Street East, Toronto, On, M5A 1K4
Tel.: (416) 364-1864; Fax: (416) 364-0704
Enquiries: Caroline Kaiser
www.ritchies.com
E-mail: auction@ritchies.com

Waddington's
111 Bathurst Street, Toronto, On, M5V 2R1
Tel.: (416) 504-9100; Fax: (416) 504-0033
Enquiries: Bill Kime
www.waddingtonsauctions.com
E-mail: info@waddingtonsauctions.com

UNITED KINGDOM

BBR Auctions
Elsecar Heritage Centre, Nr. Barnsley,
South Yorkshire S74 8HJ, England
Tel.: +44 (0) 1226 745156; Fax: +44 (0) 1226 351561
Enquiries: Alan Blakeman
www.bbrauctions.co.uk
E-mail: sales@bbrauctions.com

Bonhams
Bond Street:
101 New Bond Street, London, WI5 1SR, England
Chelsea:
65-69 Lots Road, Chelsea, London, SW10 0RN, England
Knightsbridge:
Montpelier Street, Knightsbridge, London, SW7 1HH
Tel.: +44 (0) 20 7393 3900; Fax: +44 (0) 20 7393 3905
Enquiries:
    Decorative Arts: Joy McCall
    Tel.: +44 (0) 20 7393 3942
    Comtemporary Ceramics: Gareth Williams
    Tel.: +44 (0) 20 7393 3941
    Doulton Beswick Wares: Mark Oliver
    Tel.: +44 (0) 20 7468 8233
www.bonhams.com
E-mail: info@bonhams.com

Christie's
London
8 King Street, London, SW1 England
Tel.: +44 (0) ; Fax:+44 (0)
South Kensington
85 Old Brompton Road, London, SW7 3LD, England
Tel.: +44 (0) 20 7581 7611; Fax: +44 (0) 20 7321 3321
Enquires:
    Decorative Arts: Michael Jeffrey
    Tel.: +44 (0) 20 7321 3237
www.christies.com; E-mail: info@christies.com

Potteries Specialist Auctions
271 Waterloo Road, Cobridge, Stoke-on-Trent
Staffordshire, ST6 3HR, England
Tel.: +44 (0) 1782 286622; Fax: +44 (0) 1782 213777
Enquiries: Stella Ashbrooke
www.potteriesauctions.com
E-mail: enquiries@potteriesauctions.com

Sotheby's
London
34-35 New Bond Street, London, W1A 2AA, England
Tel.: +44 (0) 20 7293 5000; Fax: +44 (0) 20 7293 5989
Olympia
Hammersmith Road, London WI4 8UX, England
Tel.: +44 (0) 20 7293 5555; Fax: +44 (0) 20 7293 6939

Sotheby's

Sussex
Summers Place, Billingshurst, Sussex,
RH14 9AF, England
Tel.: +44 (0) 1403 833500; Fax: +44 (0) 1403 833699
www.sothebys.com:
E-mail: info@sothebys.com

Louis Taylor

Britannia House,
10 Town Road, Hanley
Stoke-on-Trent, Staffordshire, England
Tel.: +44 (0) 1782 214111; Fax:+44 (0) 1782 215283
Enquiries: Clive Hillier

Thomson Roddick & Medcalf

60 Whitesands
Dumfries, DG1 2RS
Scotland
Tel.: +44 (0) 1387 279879; Fax: +44 (0) 1387 266236
Enquiries: C. R. Graham-Campbell

Peter Wilson Auctioneers

Victoria Gallery, Market Street
Nantwich, Cheshire, CW5 5DG, England
Tel.: +44 (0) 1270 610508; Fax: +44 (0) 1270 610508
Enquiries: Peter Wilson

UNITED STATES

Christie's East

219 East 67th Street, New York, NY 10021
Tel.: +1 212 606 0400
Enquiries: Timothy Luke
www.christies.com

William Doyle Galleries

175 East 87th Street, New York, N.Y. 10128
Tel.: +1 212 427 2730
Fax: +1 212 369 0892

Sotheby's Arcade Auctions

1334 York Avenue, New York, N.Y. 10021
Tel.: +1 212 606 7000
Enquiries: Andrew Cheney
www.sothebys.com

VIRTUAL AUCTIONS

Amazon.com ® Auctions
Main site: www.amazon.com
Plus 4 International sites.

AOL.com Auctions ®
Main site: www.aol.com
Links to - E-bay.com
ubid.com.

E-BAY ® The World's On-line Market Place ™
Main site: www.ebay.com
Plus 20 International sites.

YAHOO! Auctions ®
Main site: www.yahoo.com
Plus 15 International auction sites.

FAIRS, MARKETS AND SHOWS

AUSTRALIA

Royal Doulton and Antique Collectable Fair
Marina Hall, Civic Centre,
Hurstville, Sydney

CANADA

Canadian Art & Collectables Show and Sale
Kitchener Memorial Auditorium, Kitchener, Ontario
Usually early May.
For information on times and location contact:
Trajan Publishing Corp.
103 Lakeshore Road, Suite 202,
St. Catherines, Ontario L2N 2T6
Tel.: (905) 646-7744; Fax: (905) 646-0995

UNITED KINGDOM

20th Century Fairs
266 Glossop Road, Sheffield S10 2HS, England
Usually in May or June.
For information on times and dates:
Tel.: +44 (0) 114 275-0333; Fax:+44 (0) 114 275 4443

Doulton And Beswick Collectors Fair
National Motorcycle Museum, Meriden, Birmingham,
Usually March and August.
For information on times and dates:
Doulton and Beswick Dealers Association
Tel.: +44 (0) 181 303-3316

DMG Antiques Fairs Ltd.
Newark, the largest in the UK with usually six fairs
annually. For information on times and dates for this
and many other fairs contact:
DMG
Newark, P.O.Box 100, Newark,
Nottinghamshire, NG2 1DJ
Tel.: +44 (0) 1636 702326; Fax: +44 (0) 1636 707923
www.dmgantiquefairs.com
www.antiquesdirectory.co.uk

U.K. Fairs
Doulton and Beswick Fair for collectors
River Park Leisure Centre, Winchester
Usually held in October for information on times
and dates contact:
Enquiries U.K. Fairs; Tel.; +44 (0) 20 8500 3505
www.portia.co.uk
E-mail: ukfairs@portia.co.uk

LONDON MARKETS

Alfies Antique Market
13-25 Church Street, London; Tuesday - Saturday

Camden Passage Market
London; Wednesday and Saturday

New Caledonia Market
Bermondsey Square, London; Friday morning

Portobello Road Market
Portobello Road, London; Saturday

UNITED STATES

Atlantique City

Atlantic City Convention Centre
Atlantic City, NJ

International Gift and Collectible Expo

Donald E. Stephens Convention Centre,
Rosemont, Illinois

For information on the above two shows contact:
Krause Publications
700 East State Street, Iola, WI, 54990-0001
Tel.: (877) 746-9757; Fax: (715) 445-4389
www.collectibleshow.com
E-mail: iceshow@krause.com

Doulton Convention and Sale International

Fort Lauderdale, Florida, U.S.A.
Usually February. For information on times and dates:
Pascoe & Company,
575 S.W. 22nd Ave., Miami, Florida 33135
Tel.: (305) 643-2550; Fax: (305) 643-2123
www.pascoeandcompany.com
E-mail: sales@pascoeandcompany.com

Royal Doulton Convention & Sale

John S. Knight Convention Centre
77 E. Mill Street, Akron, Ohio 44308
Usually August. For information on times and dates:
Colonial House Productions,
182 Front Street, Berea, Ohio 44017;
Tel.: (866) 885-9024; Fax: (905) 854-3117
www.Colonial-House-Collectibles.com
E-mail: yworry@aol.com

A rare Bunnykins gravy boat, *Feeding the Baby*, (HW13)

FURTHER READING

Storybook Figurines

The Charlton Standard Catalogue of Royal Doulton Beswick Storybook Figurines by Jean Dale
Cartoon Classics and other Character Figures by Louise Irvine
Royal Doulton Bunnykins Figures by Louise Irvine
Bunnykins Collectors Book by Louise Irvine
Beatrix Potter Figures and Giftware edited by Louise Irvine
The Beswick Price Guide by Harvey May

Animals, Figures and Character Jugs

Royal Doulton Figures by Desmond Eyles, Louise Irvine and Valerie Baynton
The Charlton Standard Catalogue of Beswick Animals, by Diane & John Callow
    and Marilyn & Peter Sweet
The Charlton Standard Catalogue of Royal Doulton Animals by Jean Dale
The Charlton Standard Catalogue of Royal Doulton Figurines by Jean Dale
The Charlton Standard Catalogue of Royal Doulton Jugs by Jean Dale
Collecting Character and Toby Jugs by Jocelyn Lukins
Collecting Doulton Animals by Jocelyn Lukins
Doulton Flambé Animals by Jocelyn Lukins
The Character Jug Collectors Handbook by Kevin Pearson
The Doulton Figure Collectors Handbook by Kevin Pearson

General

The Charlton Standard Catalogue of Beswick Pottery by Diane and John Callow
Discovering Royal Doulton by Michael Doulton
The Doulton Story by Paul Atterbury and Louise Irvine
Royal Doulton Series Ware by Louise Irvine (Vols. 1-5)
Limited Edition Loving Cups by Louise Irvine and Richard Dennis
Doulton for the Collector by Jocelyn Lukins
Doulton Kingsware Flasks by Jocelyn Lukins
Doulton Burslem Advertising Wares by Jocelyn Lukins
Doulton Lambeth Advertising Wares by Jocelyn Lukins
The Doulton Lambeth Wares by Desmond Eyles and Louise Irvine
The Doulton Burslem Wares by Desmond Eyles
Hannah Barlow by Peter Rose
George Tinwoth by Peter Rose
Sir Henry Doulton Biography by Edmund Gosse
Phillips Collectors Guide by Catherine Braithwaite
Royal Doulton by Jennifer Queree
John Beswick: A World of Imagination. Catalogue reprint (1950-1996)
Royal Doulton by Julie McKeown

Magazines and Newsletters

Rabbitting On (Bunnykins Newsletter) Contact Leah Selig: 2 Harper Street, Merrylands 2160
    New South Wales, Australia. Tel./Fax 61 2 9637 2410 (International), 02 637 2410 (Australia)
Collect It! Contact subscription departmen at: P.O. Box 3658, Bracknell, Berkshire RG12 7XZ
    Telephone: (1344)868280 or e-mail: collectit@dialpipex.com
Collecting Doulton Magazine, Contact Barry Hill, Collecting Doulton, P.O. Box 310, Richmond,
    Surrey TW10 7FU, England
Doulton News, published by Thorndon Antiques & Fine China Ltd., edited by David Harcourt
    P.O. Box 12-076 (109 Molesworth Street), Wellington, New Zealand
Beswick Quarterly (Beswick Newsletter) Contact Laura J. Rock-Smith: 10 Holmes Court, Sayville
    N.Y. 11782-2408, U.S.A. Tel./Fax (631) 589-9027
Cottontails (Bunnykins Newsletter) Contact Claire Green: 6 Beckett Way, Lewes, East Sussex,
    BN7 2EB, U.K. E-mail: claireg@2btinternet.com

PART ONE

BUNNYKINS TABLEWARE
Issues of 1934 to 2002

BUNNYKINS BREAKFAST SET
Issues of 1939 - 1945

BUNNYKINS TEAPOTS
Issues of 1994 - 1998

BUNNYKINS TEA SET
Issues of 1998 - 2001

BUNNYKINS TOBY JUGS
Issues of 1999 - 2001

Candle holder — Bedtime in Bunks (SF3)

BUNNYKINS TABLEWARE BACKSTAMPS

BKT-1. 1934 - 1937

1a   1b

1a. The crown and lion, MADE IN ENGLAND upon the ROYAL DOULTON logo, with or without date code.
1b. As 1a, but with "BUNNYKINS" added.

BKT-2. 1937 - c.1940

2a   2b

2a. First issue of the *Tug of War* group, crown, lion and Doulton logo supported by three bunnies from Barbara Vernon's *Tug of War* Scene, "BUNNYKINS" below.
2b. As 2a, but with date code (1927 + number = date of manufacture).

BKT-3. 1937 - 1953

3a   3c

3a. As 2a, but the lion is now coloured and "MADE In ENGLAND" is printed in green. The green print in found only on BKT-3.
3b. As 3a, but with additional "A" mark for kiln identification. (Not illustrated).
3c. As 3a, but an extra "A", crown, lion, Doulton logo added, with or without date code.
3d. As 3c but with BONE CHINA, in green added below England on the lion, crown and Doulton logo stamp (not illustrated).

BKT-4. 1940s

4

4. As 3a, but a completely monochrome logo.

BKT-5. 1954 - 1958

5

5. As 3a, but "MADE IN ENGLAND" is printed in black and under "BUNNYKINS" the registration symbol ® is added; all is encircled with registration and trade mark numbers.

BKT-6a. 1959 - 1975 Earthenware

BKT-6b. 1968 - 1975 Fine Bone China

6a   6b

6a. As 5a, but the cirle of registration and trade mark numbers is removed and replaced by "REGD TRADE MARK" below the registration symbol ®.
6b. As 6a, but now with " ENGLISH FINE BONE CHINA" added between the *Tug of War* group and "BUNNYKINS".

BKT-7. 1976 - 1984

7a   7b

7a. As 6a, but the "BUNNYKINS" and the registration symbol ® are now on one line with © ROYAL DOULTON / TABLEWARE LTD 1936, on two lines below.

7b As 7a but now with "ENGLISH FINE BONE CHINA" added between the *Tug of War* group and "BUNNYKINS" ®

BKT-8. 1976 - 1984

8a   8b

8a. As 7a, but with 19 — 84 on either side of the *Tug of War* logo, below is "GOLDEN JUBLIEE CELEBRATION"

8b As 8a but with "ENGLISH FINE BONE CHINA" added between the *Tug of War* group and "BUNNYKINS" ®

BKT-9. 1985 - 1987

9a   9b

9a. As 7a, but with (U.K.) added to the single copyright line © 1936 ROYAL DOULTON.

9b As 9a but with "ENGLISH FINE BONE CHINA" added between the *Tug of War* group and "BUNNYKINS"

BKT-10. 1988 - c.1993

10a   10b

10a. As 7a but with © 1936 ROYAL DOULTON (U.K.) replaced by © 1988 ROYAL DOULTON.

10b As 10a but with "ENGLISH FINE BONE CHINA" added between the *Tug of War* group and "BUNNYKINS" ®

BKT-11. c.1993 - 2002

11a   11b

11a. As 7a, but © 1988 is replaced by the original date © 1936.

11b As 11a but with "ENGLISH FINE BONE CHINA" added between the *Tug of War* group and "BUNNYKINS" ®

BKT-SPECIAL

Over the years special backstamps were created incorporating the *Tug of War* logo, and the various text changes with other special design elements such as the logo for the Australian Bicentenary or a wreath of holly leaves for the Christmas plate. We are classifying this group of backstamps under one heading "Special".

SHAPE GUIDE

This guide includes the standard Bunnykins shapes, their sizes and production dates. Originally Bunnykins was produced in either a deep ivory earthenware or a fine white bone china. The white china body was discontinued during the Second World War so examples are very hard to find today. A list of white china shapes from an early catalogue is included at the end of the guide.

In 1968, an ivory bone china body replaced the original earthenware and many early shapes were withdrawn. Those that remained were remodelled for the new body. Today, the majority of Bunnykins nurseryware is made in ivory bone china, the exceptions being the money ball and savings book which are made in a earthenware body.

Some shapes were remodelled specifically for the Bunnykins range, for example the candle holder. Others were adapted from existing tableware ranges. The Casino tea wares, for instance, were originally designed for a striking art deco pattern of that name and the Jaffa fruit saucer takes its name from a fruit set which was produced with various patterns in 1930s.

The early Casino teapots and jugs were sold in several different sizes that are described as 24s, 30s, 36s and 42s and usually this number is incised on the base. This method of sizing was an industry standard and referred to the number of pieces which could be fitted on to a potter's board as he took them from the wheel. Thus the largest size is 24 as only that number of pieces could be accommodated on the potters board compared to 42 smaller pieces. The capacity in pints is also given for reference. Collectors will find some slight differences in

capacity and sizes because of potting variations, such as clay thickness and kiln shrinkage. There were also slight modifications to handles and spouts in the early years.

The baby plates have also been altered over the years and the shape records indicate that the oval design was remodelled in 1947 and the round ones were reduced in weight by 5 ounces, also in 1947. Collectors will notice some variations in the profile and depth of baby plates.

From time to time, shapes have been developed for the Bunnykins range and then not produced. The model books record that a framed stand for Bunnykins subjects was modelled in 1940 but not approved. Stands featuring 'Going Shopping' SF10 and 'Dancing in the Moonlight' LFb have turned up in recent years. Other unusual shapes that have come to light include a vegetable tureen, a sauce boat, an oval plate and a small vase. In the early 1980s, a money box in the form of a post box was modelled but it did not go into production at that time and two examples were recorded, one in the Royal Doulton archives and another in a private collection. In 2001, a limited edition of this post box shape was produced for the Bunnykins Extravaganza Fair.

As with the original earthenware range, the Bunnykins fine white china shapes were also used for other patterns, for instance the Rex mug can be found with several different nurseryware designs. As yet, not all the fine white china shapes have appeared in the market-place so information is limited. It is believed that the majority of them were exported to the USA and Canada during the Second World War as this is where examples tend to be found.

Rare oval platter - "Dancing in the Moonlight"

PLATES AND SAUCERS

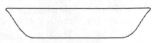

Oatmeal / cereal bowl
1937 to the present

Coupe / Porridge plate
1937 - 1960

Jaffa fruit saucer
wavy rim, 1937 - c.1950
plain rim, c.1950 - 2000

SUGAR BOWLS

STRATFORD BEAKER

Sugar bowl with handles
c.1950

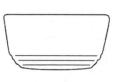

Casino sugar bowl
Large, 1½ pint, 30s,
1937 - 1968
Medium, 1 pint, 36s
1937 - 1968

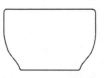

Albion sugar bowl
¼ pint
1987 - 1991

1983 - 1993

CANDLE HOLDER

TEACHING CLOCKS

PICTURE PLAQUES

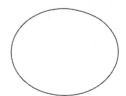

Small, 6½", 1991 - 1993
Large, 7¼", 1991 - 1993

1940 - 1952

NIGHT LIGHT
FINE CHINA

Small second hand   Long second hand
1983 to the present

1937 - c.1945

MONEY BALL   JAM POT   SAVINGS BOOK   CAKE STAND

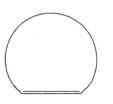

1982 to the present   1937 - 1952   1982 to the present   1987 - 1991

LAMP

1985 - 1991

BEAKER (PAD) COVER

   1940 - 1968

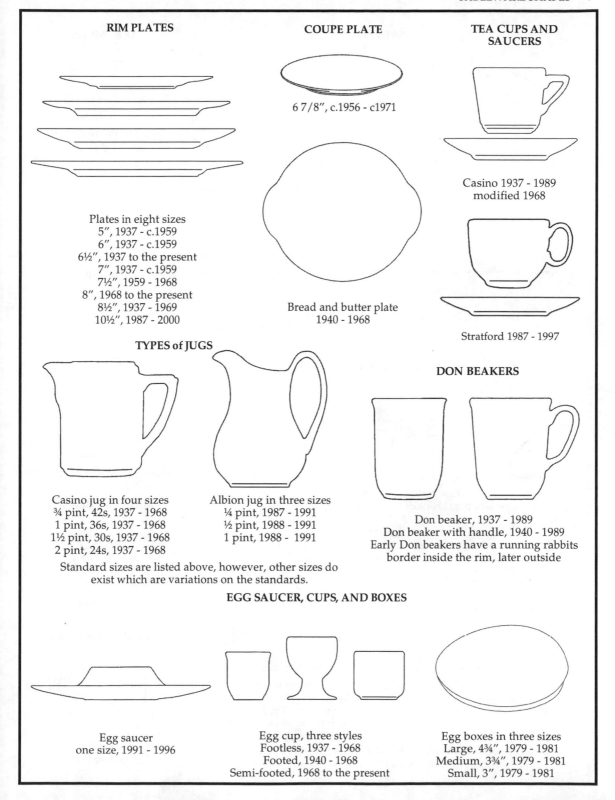

RIM PLATES

COUPE PLATE

TEA CUPS AND SAUCERS

6 7/8", c.1956 - c1971

Plates in eight sizes
5", 1937 - c.1959
6", 1937 - c.1959
6½", 1937 to the present
7", 1937 - c.1959
7½", 1959 - 1968
8", 1968 to the present
8½", 1937 - 1969
10½", 1987 - 2000

Casino 1937 - 1989
modified 1968

Stratford 1987 - 1997

Bread and butter plate
1940 - 1968

TYPES of JUGS

DON BEAKERS

Casino jug in four sizes
¾ pint, 42s, 1937 - 1968
1 pint, 36s, 1937 - 1968
1½ pint, 30s, 1937 - 1968
2 pint, 24s, 1937 - 1968

Albion jug in three sizes
¼ pint, 1987 - 1991
½ pint, 1988 - 1991
1 pint, 1988 - 1991

Don beaker, 1937 - 1989
Don beaker with handle, 1940 - 1989
Early Don beakers have a running rabbits
border inside the rim, later outside

Standard sizes are listed above, however, other sizes do
exist which are variations on the standards.

EGG SAUCER, CUPS, AND BOXES

Egg saucer
one size, 1991 - 1996

Egg cup, three styles
Footless, 1937 - 1968
Footed, 1940 - 1968
Semi-footed, 1968 to the present

Egg boxes in three sizes
Large, 4¾", 1979 - 1981
Medium, 3¾", 1979 - 1981
Small, 3", 1979 - 1981

BABY PLATES

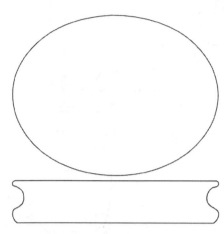

Round baby plate, small 6"
1937 to the present
modified in 1978 and 1988

Oval baby plate, two sizes
Small 8¼", 1940 - 1952
Large 8½", 1940 - 1968

Round baby plate, large
7½", 1937 - 1969

Slightly different shapes and
depths are found in baby plates

HOT WATER PLATES

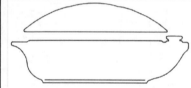

Hot Water Plate with Cover
One stopper, 1940 - 1959; Two stopper, 1959 - 1969

TEAPOTS

Albion teapot
1 pint size
1987 - 1991

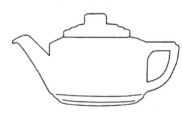

Casino teapot
1 pint size, 36s, 1937 - 1968
1½ pint size, 30s, 1937 - 1968
2 pint size, 24s, 1952 - 1968

Collectors will find teapots that differ slightly in capacity
from the standard sizes

DON MUGS

One handle, 1937 - 1983
modified in 1968

Two handles, 1940 - 1983

HUG-A-MUGS

One handle, 1979 to the present

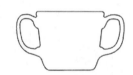

Two handles, 1979 to the present

MALVERN BEAKER

1989 - 1997

LARGE CUP / MUG

1937 - c.1945

THE COLLECTORS CHECKLIST OF SHAPES

The following provides the collector with a starting point to developing a checklist of designs vs. shapes. As the Barbara Vernon facsimile signature plays an important role in Bunnykins tableware we have also included that information in the listing. For continuity in the listing, we have noted where a signature was not included in the design.

On checking your collection you may find we have not included a particular design/shape with or without a signature. Why not bring this information to our attention? Please contact:

The Charlton Press at (416) 488-1418 or (800) 442-6042, you can fax us at (416) 488-4656 or (800) 442-1542, or you may e-mail us at chpress@charltonpress.com.

ALBION; 1987 - 1991

Cream jug
¼ pint, 1987 - 1991
without signature

Jug
¼ pint, 1987 - 1991
without signature
½ pint, 1988 - 1991
without signature
1 pint, 1988 - 1991
without signature

Sugar Bowl
¼ pint, 1987 - 1991
without signature

Teapot
1 pint, 1987 - 1991
without signature

BABY PLATES; 1937 to date

Small
oval, 8 ¼", 1940 - 1952
with signature
without signature
round, 6", first issue, 1937 - 1978
with signature
without signature
round, 6", second issue, 1978 - 1988
without signature
round, 6", third issue, 1988 to date
without signature

Large
oval, 8 ½", 1940 - 1968
with signature
without signature
round, 7 ½", 1937 - 1969
with signature
without signature

BEAKER PAD; 1940 - 1968
with signature
without signature

BREAD AND BUTTER PLATE; 1940 - 1968
with signature
without signature

CAKE STAND; 1987 - 1991
without signature

CANDLE HOLDER; 1940 - 1952
with signature
without signature

CASINO; 1937 - 1968

Jug
42s, ¾ pint, 1937 - 1968
with signature
without signature
36s, 1 pint, 1937 - 1968
with signature
without signature
30s, 1 ½ pint, 1937 - 1968
with signature
without signature
24s, 2 pint, 1937 - 1968
with signature
without signature

Saucer
1937 - 1989
with signature
without signature

Sugar
36s, 1 pint, 1937 - 1968
with signature
without signature
30s, 1 ½ pint, 1937 - 1968
with signature
without signature

Teacup
First issue, 1937 - 1968
with signature
without signature
Second issue, 1968 - 1989
without signature

Teapot
36s, 1 pint, 1937 - 1968
with signature
without signature
30s, 1 ½ pint, 1937 - 1968
with signature
without signature
24s, 2 pint, 1952 - 1968
with signature
without signature

CEREAL / OATMEAL BOWL; 1937 to date
with signature
without signature

CEREAL / PORRIDGE PLATE; 1937 - 1960
with signature
without signature

CLOCK; 1983 to date
without signature

COUPE; 1959 - 1971
> Plate, c.1959 - c.1971
>> without signature

CUP / MUG LARGE; 1937 - c.1945
> with signature

DIVIDER DISH; 1993 - 1997
> 8 ¾", 1993 - 1997
>> without signature

DON; 1937 - 1989
> Beaker, 1937 - 1989
>> with signature
>> without signature
> Beaker, one handle, 1940 - 1989
>> with signature
>> without signature
> Mug, one handle
>> First issue, 1937 - 1968
>>> with signature
>>> without signature
>> Second issue, 1968 - 1983
>>> without signature
> Mug, two handles, 1940 - 1983
>> with signature
>> without signature

EGG BOX; 1979 - 1981
> Small, 3", 1979 - 1981
>> without signature
> Medium, 3 ¾", 1979 - 1981
>> without signature
> Large, 4 ¾", 1979 - 1981
>> without signature

EGG CUPS; 1937 to date
> Style One, footless, 1937 - 1968
>> with signature
>> without signature
> Style Two, footed, 1940 - 1968
>> with signature
>> without signature
> Style Three, footless modified, 1968 to date
>> without signature

EGG SAUCER; 1991 - 1996
> without signature

HOT WATER PLATE WITH COVER; 1940 - 1969
> Plate
>> First issue, one stopper, 1940 - 1959
>>> with signature
>>> without signature
>> Second issue, two stoppers, 1959 - 1969
>>> without signature
> Cover, 1940 - 1969
>> with signature
>> without signature

HUG-A-MUG; 1979 to date
> One handle, 1979 to date
>> without signature
> Two handles, 1979 to date
>> without signature

JAFFA FRUIT SAUCER; 1937 - 2000
> Wavy rim, 1937 - c.1950
>> with signature
>> without signature
> Plain rim, c.1950 - 2000
>> with signature
>> without signature

JAM POT; 1937 - 1952
> with signature
> without signature

LAMP; 1985 - 1991
> without signature

MALVERN BEAKER; 1989 - 1997
> without signature

MONEY BALL; 1982 to date
> without signature

NIGHT LIGHT; 1937 - c.1945
> with signature

PICTURE PLAQUE; 1991 - 1993
> Small, 6 ½", 1991 - 1993
>> without signature
> Large, 7 ¼", 1991 - 1993
>> without signature

PLATES; 1937 to date
> 5", 1937 - c.1959
>> with signature
>> without signature
> 6", 1937 - c.1959
>> with signature
>> without signature
> 6 ½", 1937 to date
>> with signature
>> without signature
> 7", 1937 - c.1959
>> with signature
>> without signature
> 7 ½", 1937 - 1968
>> with signature
>> without signature
> 8", 1968 to date
>> without signature
> 8 ½", 1937 - 1969
>> with signature
>> without signature
> 10 ½", 1987 - 2000
>> without signature

SAVINGS BOOK; 1982 to date
> without signature

STRATFORD; 1983 - 1997
> Beaker, 1983 - 1993
>> without signature
> Saucer, 1987 - 1997
>> without signature
> Teacup, 1987 - 1997
>> without signature

SUGAR BOWL WITH HANDLES; c.1950
> with signature
> without signature

FINE WHITE CHINA

The following is a list of shapes that were included in a price list of 1937.

- Beaker
    - Large
    - Small
    - with one handle
- Beaker pad
- Bread and butter plate
- Carlton Jug
    - 24s (1 ¼ pint)
    - 30s (1 pint)
    - 36s (¾ pint)
    - 42s (½ pint)
- Cecil bowl UBC

- Egg cup
- Night light
- Oatmeal saucer
- Phillips bowl
    - 30s
    - 36s
    - 48s
- Plate
    - 4 inches
    - 5 inches
    - 6 inches
    - 7 inches

- Porridge plate
- Prince
    - Cream jug
        - 30s (½ pint)
    - Teapot
        - 30s (1 ½ pint)
        - 42s (1 pint)
- Rex Mug
    - large
    - small
- Teacup and saucer

Fine Bone China, Beaker with Handle, *Dunce* (HW1R)

'Sugar Bowl with Handles' Shape, *Feeding the Baby*, (HW13)

BUNNYKINS TABLEWARE
Issues of 1934 to the present

ABC THEME — Colin Twinn

ABCDEF SCENE

Design No.:	CT94 ABCDEF Scene
Designer:	Colin Twinn
Issued:	1994 - 1999

Shape	USD	CAD	GBP	AUD
Baby plate, round, small	30.00	45.00	20.00	65.00
Oatmeal / Cereal bowl	25.00	35.00	15.00	50.00
Plate, 8″	25.00	35.00	15.00	50.00

ABCDEF Scene (CT94)

ABC Scene (CT95)

ABC SCENE / A SCENE

Design No.:	Front — CT95 ABC Scene
	Reverse — CT96 A Scene
Designer:	Colin Twinn
Issued:	1994 - 1999

Shape	USD	CAD	GBP	AUD
Hug-a-mug, one handle	30.00	35.00	10.00	50.00
Money ball	35.00	40.00	15.00	60.00

A Scene (CT96)

Aerobics

Jogging

AEROBICS / JOGGING

A boxed Bunnykins for Grown Ups set containing a cereal bowl and hug-a-mug with one handle with the *Aerobics/Jogging* design, a 6" plate with the *Aeroplane* design, an 8" plate with the *Breakfast Time* design and a cereal bowl with *Tennis* design was distributed mainly in the U.S.A.

Design:	Front — Aerobics
	Reverse — Jogging
Designer:	Walter Hayward
Issued:	1986 - 1988
Series:	Bunnykins for Grown Ups

Shape	USD	CAD	GBP	AUD
Cereal / oatmeal bowl	40.00	60.00	25.00	60.00
Hug-a-mug, one handle	30.00	50.00	15.00	50.00
Complete set (M.I.B)	200.00	300.00	100.00	300.00

Note: See also *Aeroplane* below, *Breakfast Time* page 32 and *Tennis* page 160.

AEROPLANE

A boxed Bunnykins for Grown Ups set containing a cereal bowl and hug-a-mug with one handle with the *Aerobics/Jogging* design, a 6" plate with the *Aeroplane* design, an 8" plate with the *Breakfast Time* design and a cereal bowl with *Tennis* design was distributed mainly in the U.S.A.

Design:	Aeroplane
Designer:	Walter Hayward
Issued:	1986 - 1988
Series:	Bunnykins for Grown Ups

Shape	USD	CAD	GBP	AUD
Plate, 6"	40.00	65.00	25.00	65.00
Complete Set (M.I.B)	200.00	300.00	100.00	300.00

Aeroplane

Note: See Also *Aerobics above, Breakfast Time* page 32 and *Tennis* page 160.

AFTERNOON TEA / SERVING TEA

Design No.: Front — HW116 Afternoon Tea
Reverse — HW116R Serving Tea
Designer: Walter Hayward
Issued: 1959 - by 1998
Combined with: *Bugler with Toy Donkey*, HW26R
Dress Making, HW26
Hikers, EC124
Ice Cream on the Beach, HW136R
Playing with Dolls and Prams, HW115
Sheltering Under an Umbrella, EC3
Sledging, Style One, HW141
Trying on Hats, HW28R

Afternoon Tea (HW116)

Shape	USD	CAD	GBP	AUD
Albion cream jug	50.00	75.00	35.00	75.00
Albion jug, ½ pint	100.00	150.00	70.00	150.00
Albion jug, 1 pint	150.00	225.00	100.00	225.00
Albion sugar bowl	30.00	50.00	20.00	50.00
Albion teapot	50.00	85.00	35.00	95.00
Casino jug, 36s	125.00	200.00	85.00	200.00
Casino jug, 42s	100.00	150.00	70.00	150.00
Casino saucer	7.50	12.00	5.00	12.00
Casino sugar bowl, 30s	125.00	200.00	85.00	225.00
Casino sugar bowl, 36s	100.00	150.00	65.00	175.00
Casino teacup	7.50	12.00	5.00	12.00
Casino teapot, 30s	150.00	225.00	100.00	250.00
Divider dish	50.00	75.00	35.00	75.00
Don beaker	35.00	55.00	25.00	60.00
Don beaker, one handle	35.00	55.00	25.00	60.00
Don mug, one handle	15.00	25.00	10.00	25.00
Don mug, two handles	15.00	25.00	10.00	25.00
Egg box				
small	225.00	350.00	150.00	400.00
medium	300.00	450.00	200.00	500.00
large	375.00	550.00	250.00	600.00
Hug-a-mug, one handle	10.00	15.00	7.50	15.00
Hug-a-mug, two handles	10.00	15.00	7.50	15.00
Jaffa fruit saucer (plain)	15.00	25.00	10.00	25.00
Lamp	100.00	150.00	65.00	175.00
Lid of hot water plate	100.00	150.00	70.00	175.00
Malvern beaker	15.00	25.00	10.00	25.00
Money ball	10.00	15.00	7.50	15.00
Picture plaque, small	20.00	30.00	15.00	30.00
Plate, 6 ½"	12.50	20.00	8.00	25.00
Savings book	15.00	22.50	10.00	22.50
Stratford teacup	10.00	15.00	7.50	15.00

Serving Tea (HW116R)

Note: Retirement dates are all approximate. When a design is retired all remaining stocks of the retired litho prints are used until exhausted.

Airmail Delivery (LFa)

AIRMAIL DELIVERY

Design No.   LFa
Designer: Barbara Vernon
Issued: By 1937 - by 1952

Shape	USD	CAD	GBP	AUD
Baby plate, round, small	275.00	425.00	200.00	450.00
Baby plate, round, large	450.00	675.00	325.00	700.00
Bread and butter plate	800.00	1,250.00	500.00	1,600.00
Hot water plate	375.00	600.00	250.00	625.00
Plate, 8 ½"	300.00	475.00	200.00	500.00
Porridge plate	400.00	625.00	275.00	650.00

Note: This design should appear with the Barbara Vernon facsimile signature.

Casino Jugs — Three sizes
42s - *Family at Breakfast* (HW12), 36s - *Frightening Spider* (SF4), 24s - *Going Shopping* (SF10)

APPLE PICKING

Design No.:	SF25
Designer:	Walter Hayward
Issued:	1954 - by 1998
Combined with:	*Lunch Break*, HW29R
	Windy Day, HW27

Shape	USD	CAD	GBP	AUD
Baby plate, round, small				
with signature	60.00	75.00	30.00	90.00
without signature	20.00	30.00	15.00	30.00
Cake stand	150.00	250.00	100.00	300.00
Casino jug, 36s				
with signature	150.00	225.00	100.00	250.00
without signature	125.00	200.00	85.00	200.00
Casino saucer				
with signature	15.00	25.00	10.00	25.00
without signature	7.50	12.00	5.00	12.00
Casino sugar, 30s				
with signature	150.00	225.00	100.00	250.00
without signature	125.00	200.00	85.00	225.00
Cereal / oatmeal bowl				
with signature	25.00	40.00	15.00	45.00
without signature	10.00	15.00	7.50	15.00
Hot water plate				
with signature	150.00	250.00	135.00	275.00
without signature	125.00	200.00	85.00	225.00
Picture plaque, large	20.00	30.00	12.50	30.00
Plate, 6 ½"				
with signature	35.00	55.00	25.00	55.00
without signature	20.00	30.00	15.00	30.00
Plate, 7 ½"				
with signature	35.00	55.00	25.00	55.00
without signature	20.00	30.00	15.00	30.00
Plate, 8"	25.00	40.00	20.00	40.00
Plate, 8",' Special Events'	25.00	40.00	20.00	40.00

Apple Picking (SF25)

'Special Events Tour 1990'

Note: An 8" plate was issued for the 'U.S. Special Events Tour. 1990.' The year 1990 was incorporated under the design. The reverse is inscribed 'To' and 'From' to be completed by customer, and 'Special Events Tour 1990.'

Art Class (LF107)

ART CLASS

Design No.:	LF107
Designer:	Walter Hayward
Issued:	1959 - 1970

Shape	USD	CAD	GBP	AUD
Baby plate, oval, large	150.00	225.00	100.00	225.00
Baby plate, round, large	125.00	200.00	85.00	200.00
Plate, 8 ½"	75.00	125.00	50.00	135.00
Porridge plate	100.00	150.00	65.00	175.00

Artist (HW1)

ARTIST

Design No.:   HW1
Designer: Barbara Vernon
Issued: By 1937 - by 1952
Combined with: *Dunce*, HW1R
    Fishing in the Goldfish Bowl, HW3R
    Greetings, HW7
    Netting a Cricket, HW6
    Pulling on Trousers, HW2

Shape	USD	CAD	GBP	AUD
Baby plate, round, small				
with signature	125.00	200.00	90.00	225.00
without signature	100.00	150.00	70.00	175.00
Casino jug, 42s				
with signature	300.00	450.00	200.00	500.00
without signature	250.00	375.00	175.00	400.00
Casino saucer				
with signature	100.00	150.00	65.00	175.00
without signature	75.00	125.00	50.00	125.00
Casino sugar bowl, 30s				
with signature	250.00	375.00	175.00	400.00
without signature	175.00	275.00	125.00	325.00
Casino teacup				
with signature	100.00	150.00	65.00	175.00
without signature	75.00	125.00	50.00	125.00
Don beaker				
with signature	200.00	325.00	140.00	350.00
without signature	175.00	275.00	125.00	300.00
Don beaker, one handle				
with signature	200.00	325.00	140.00	350.00
without signature	175.00	275.00	125.00	300.00
Don mug, one handle				
with signature	150.00	250.00	100.00	275.00
without signature	125.00	200.00	90.00	225.00
Don mug, two handles				
with signature	150.00	250.00	100.00	275.00
without signature	125.00	200.00	90.00	225.00
Jam pot	1,500.00	2,500.00	1,000.00	3,000.00
Jaffa fruit saucer				
plain rim	150.00	250.00	95.00	275.00
wavy rim	100.00	150.00	75.00	175.00
Plate, 6 ½"				
with signature	90.00	150.00	60.00	175.00
without signature	60.00	100.00	40.00	100.00

FINE WHITE CHINA

Beaker, one handle	Very rare
Plate, 6"	Very rare
Plate, 7"	Very rare
Saucer	Very rare
Teacup	Very rare

ASLEEP IN THE OPEN AIR

Design No.:	HW10
Designer:	Barbara Vernon
Issued:	By 1937 - by 1967
Combined with:	*Bathtime*, Style One, SF18
	Convalescing, SF5
	Gardening, Style One, HW9
	Leapfrog, HW12R
	Washing in the Open Air, HW10R
	Wheelbarrow Race, Style One, HW22

Asleep in the Open Air (HW10)

Shape	USD	CAD	GBP	AUD
Casino jug, 30s				
with signature	500.00	800.00	350.00	950.00
without signature	400.00	700.00	300.00	850.00
Casino jug, 36s				
with signature	400.00	600.00	275.00	700.00
without signature	350.00	550.00	225.00	650.00
Casino jug, 42s				
with signature	300.00	450.00	200.00	500.00
without signature	250.00	375.00	175.00	325.00
Casino saucer				
with signature	100.00	150.00	65.00	175.00
without signature	75.00	125.00	50.00	125.00
Casino sugar bowl, 30s				
with signature	250.00	375.00	165.00	400.00
without signature	175.00	275.00	125.00	325.00
Casino sugar bowl 36s				
with signature	200.00	325.00	125.00	350.00
without signature	150.00	225.00	150.00	250.00
Casino teacup				
with signature	100.00	150.00	65.00	175.00
without signature	75.00	125.00	50.00	125.00
Casino teapot, 24s				
with signature	500.00	800.00	350.00	950.00
without signature	400.00	700.00	300.00	850.00

Shape	USD	CAD	GBP	AUD
Casino teapot, 30s				
with signature	400.00	600.00	275.00	700.00
without signature	300.00	450.00	200.00	500.00
Casino teapot, 36s				
with signature	350.00	550.00	225.00	650.00
without signature	275.00	400.00	175.00	450.00
Don beaker				
with signature	200.00	325.00	140.00	350.00
without signature	125.00	200.00	80.00	225.00
Don beaker, one handle				
with signature	200.00	325.00	140.00	350.00
without signature	125.00	200.00	80.00	225.00
Don mug, one handle				
with signature	150.00	250.00	100.00	275.00
without signature	65.00	100.00	45.00	100.00
Don mug, two handles				
with signature	150.00	250.00	100.00	275.00
without signature	65.00	100.00	45.00	100.00
Jaffa fruit saucer				
plain rim	95.00	150.00	65.00	165.00
wavy rim	95.00	150.00	65.00	165.00
Plate, 6 ½"				
with signature	90.00	150.00	60.00	175.00
without signature	50.00	80.00	35.00	80.00

AUSTRALIANA BUNNYKINS — Colin Twinn

PICNIC WITH KANGAROO AND KOALA
First Variation, Large Size

The 1994 plates have a leaf border with the inscription Bunnykins 60th Anniversary 1994.

Design No.:	Front — CT84 Picnic with Kangaroo and Koala
	Reverse — CT85 Commemorative Leaf Border
Designer:	Colin Twinn
Issued:	1994 - 1994
Backstamp:	'Bunnykins 60th Anniversary Australiana Bunnykins. Produced exclusively for Royal Doulton Australia.'

Shape	USD	CAD	GBP	AUD
Plate, 8"	35.00	50.00	20.00	50.00

Picnic with Kangaroo and Koala,
First Variation (CT84)

PICNIC WITH KANGAROO AND KOALA
Second Variation, Small Size

Design No.:	CT86 Picnic with Kangaroo and Koala
Designer:	Colin Twinn
Issued:	1994 - 1994
Backstamp:	'Australiana Bunnykins. Produced exclusively for Royal Doulton Australia.'

Shape	USD	CAD	GBP	AUD
Baby plate, round, small	35.00	50.00	20.00	50.00
Cereal / oatmeal bowl	25.00	40.00	15.00	40.00

Picnic with Kangaroo and Koala,
Second Variation (CT86)

Backstamp (CT86)

PICNIC SCENE / BUNNY WITH CAKE PLATE

The backstamp on this teacup and saucer does not refer to the 60th Anniversary celebrations.

Design No.:	Front — CT87 Picnic Scene
	Reverse — CT88 Bunny with Cake Plate
Designer:	Colin Twinn
Issued:	1994 - 1994

Shape	USD	CAD	GBP	AUD
Stratford teacup	40.00	60.00	25.00	60.00

Front — Picnic Scene (CT87)

Front — Picinic Scene with Hamper (CT89)

Reverse — Bunny with Cake Plate (CT88)

Reverse — Father Asleep (CT90)

PICNIC SCENE WITH HAMPER / FATHER ASLEEP

Design No.:	Front — CT89 Picnic Scene with Hamper
	Reverse — CT90 Father Asleep
Designer:	Colin Twinn
Issued:	1994 - 1994
Backstamp:	'Australiana Bunnykins. Produced exclusively for Royal Doulton Australia.'

Shape	USD	CAD	GBP	AUD
Hug-a-mug, one handle	25.00	40.00	15.00	40.00
Money ball	15.00	20.00	10.00	20.00

Baking (SF19)

BAKING

Design No.:	SF19
Designer:	Walter Hayward after Barbara Vernon
Issued:	By 1952 - by 1998
Combined with:	*Convalescing*, SF5
	Cricketer, HW22R
	Wheelbarrow Race, HW22

Shape	USD	CAD	GBP	AUD
Baby plate, round, large				
with signature	75.00	125.00	50.00	150.00
without signature	50.00	75.00	35.00	185.00
Baby plate, round, small				
with signature	45.00	75.00	30.00	90.00
without signature	15.00	25.00	10.00	30.00
Casino jug, 24s				
with signature	325.00	500.00	225.00	550.00
without signature	175.00	275.00	125.00	300.00
Casino jug, 30s				
with signature	250.00	400.00	175.00	425.00
without signature	150.00	250.00	100.00	250.00
Casino saucer				
with signature	15.00	25.00	10.00	25.00
without signature	7.50	12.00	5.00	12.00
Casino teapot, 24s				
with signature	275.00	400.00	175.00	450.00
without signature	175.00	275.00	125.00	325.00
Cereal / oatmeal bowl				
with signature	15.00	25.00	10.00	30.00
without signature	10.00	15.00	7.50	15.00
Hot water plate				
with signature	175.00	275.00	125.00	325.00
without signature	125.00	200.00	85.00	225.00
Jaffa fruit saucer				
plain rim	15.00	25.00	10.00	25.00
wavy rim	95.00	150.00	65.00	165.00
Picture plaque, large	20.00	30.00	12.50	30.00
Plate, 6 ½"				
with signature	35.00	55.00	25.00	55.00
without signature	20.00	30.00	15.00	30.00
Plate, 8"	25.00	40.00	18.00	40.00
Plate, 8 ½"				
with signature	35.00	55.00	25.00	60.00
without signature	25.00	40.00	18.00	40.00

BAKING THEME — *Frank Endersby*

BAKING CAKES WITH MOTHER

Design No.:	7 Baking Cakes with Mother			
Designer:	Frank Endersby			
Issued:	1995 to the present			

Shape	USD	CAD	GBP	AUD
Baby plate, round, small	N/I	**46.00**	**14.00**	**62.95**
Cereal / oatmeal bowl	N/I	**33.00**	**11.00**	**49.95**
Jaffa fruit saucer	15.00	25.00	10.00	25.00
Plate, 6 ½"	N/I	**25.00**	**8.00**	**34.95**
Plate, 8"	N/I	**35.00**	**11.00**	**49.95**

Baking Cakes with Mother (7)

Taking Cake from Oven (8)

TAKING CAKE FROM OVEN / DECORATING THE CAKE

Design No.:	Front — 8 Taking Cake from Oven			
	Reverse — 9 Decorating the Cake			
Designer:	Frank Endersby			
Issued:	1995 to the present			
Combined with:	*Carrying Letter*, (30)			

Shape	USD	CAD	GBP	AUD
Hug-a-mug, one handle	**30.00**	**33.00**	**11.00**	**49.95**
Hug-a-mug, two handles	**32.50**	**39.00**	**12.00**	**56.95**
Divider dish	50.00	75.00	35.00	75.00
Money ball	**33.75**	**40.00**	**15.00**	**62.95**
Stratford teacup	20.00	30.00	10.00	30.00

* Indicates scene on divider dish.

Decorating the Cake (9)

Note: 1. Bold type in the listing tables indicate a current design on a current shape.
2. N/I. Not issued individually. The item(s) will be found only in boxed sets in that market.

Bath Night (LF7)

BATH NIGHT

Design No.:	LF7
Designer:	Barbara Vernon
Issued:	By 1940 - by 1952

Shape	USD	CAD	GBP	AUD
Baby plate, oval, small				
with signature	400.00	625.00	275.00	625.00
without signature	300.00	475.00	200.00	475.00
Baby plate, round, large				
with silver rim		Rare		
with signature	300.00	450.00	150.00	500.00
without signature	250.00	375.00	125.00	375.00
Bread and butter plate				
with signature	500.00	800.00	350.00	900.00
without signature	400.00	625.00	275.00	650.00
Cereal / oatmeal bowl				
with signature	110.00	175.00	75.00	200.00
without signature	90.00	150.00	60.00	175.00
Plate, 8 ½"				
with signature	115.00	175.00	80.00	175.00
without signature	75.00	125.00	50.00	135.00
Porridge plate				
with signature	125.00	200.00	80.00	225.00
without signature	100.00	150.00	65.00	175.00

292‎‎‎‏‏‏

BATHTIME, Style One

Design No.: SF18
Designer: Walter Hayward after Barbara Vernon
Issued: By 1952 - 1994
Combined with: *Asleep in the Open Air*, HW10

Shape	USD	CAD	GBP	AUD
Baby plate, round, small				
with signature	45.00	75.00	30.00	90.00
without signature	20.00	30.00	15.00	30.00
Cake stand	150.00	250.00	100.00	300.00
Casino jug, 30s				
with signature	250.00	400.00	175.00	425.00
without signature	150.00	250.00	100.00	250.00
Casino saucer				
with signature	15.00	25.00	10.00	25.00
without signature	7.50	12.00	5.00	12.00
Cereal / oatmeal bowl				
with signature	25.00	40.00	15.00	45.00
without signature	10.00	15.00	7.50	15.00
Hot water plate				
with signature	175.00	275.00	125.00	325.00
without signature	125.00	200.00	85.00	225.00
Jaffa fruit saucer				
plain rim	15.00	25.00	10.00	25.00
wavy rim	95.00	150.00	65.00	165.00
Picture plaque, large	20.00	30.00	12.50	30.00
Plate, 6 ½"				
with signature	35.00	55.00	25.00	55.00
without signature	20.00	30.00	15.00	30.00
Plate, 7 ½"				
with signature	35.00	55.00	25.00	55.00
without signature	20.00	30.00	15.00	30.00
Plate, 8 ½"				
with signature	35.00	55.00	25.00	60.00
without signature	25.00	40.00	18.00	40.00

Bathtime, Style One (SF18)

BATHTIME THEME — Colin Twinn

Bathtime, Style Two (CT21)

BATHTIME
Style Two, First Variation

Design No.:   CT21 Bathtime
Designer: Colin Twinn
Issued: 1991 - 1993

Shape	USD	CAD	GBP	AUD
Albion jug, 1 pint	150.00	225.00	100.00	225.00
Albion teapot	50.00	85.00	35.00	95.00
Plate, 8"	25.00	40.00	18.00	40.00
Cereal / oatmeal bowl	10.00	15.00	7.50	15.00
Picture plaque, large	20.00	30.00	12.50	30.00

Bathtime Scene, Style Two (CT24)

BATHTIME SCENE
Style Two, Second Variation /
BUNNIES IN THE BATH, First Version

Design No.:   Front — CT24 Bathtime Scene
               Reverse — CT25 Bunnies in the Bath, First Version
Designer: Colin Twinn
Issued: 1991 - 1993
Combined with: *Bunnies in Bath*, Second Version, CT34
                Bunny on Trike, CT23
                School Gates, Second Variation, CT22

Shape	USD	CAD	GBP	AUD
Albion cream jug	50.00	75.00	35.00	75.00
Albion jug, ½ pint	100.00	150.00	70.00	150.00
Albion jug, 1 pint	150.00	225.00	100.00	225.00
Albion teapot	50.00	85.00	35.00	95.00
Hug-a-mug, one handle	10.00	15.00	7.50	15.00
Lamp	100.00	150.00	65.00	175.00
Malvern beaker	15.00	25.00	10.00	25.00
Money ball	10.00	15.00	7.50	15.00
Stratford straight beaker	15.00	25.00	10.00	25.00
Stratford teacup	7.50	12.00	5.00	12.00

Bunnies in the Bath, First Version (CT25)

Note: *Bunnies in the Bath* (CT34) is combined with *Bathtime Scene* (CT24) on a Stratford straight beaker.

BUNNIES IN THE BATH
Second Version

Design No.:   CT34
Designer: Colin Twinn
Issued: 1991 - 1993
Combined with: *Bathtime Scene*, Style Two,
                       Second Variation, (CT24)
                   Bunny with Mirror, CT35
                   Pushing the Wheelbarrow, CT3

Shape	USD	CAD	GBP	AUD
Albion sugar bowl	30.00	50.00	20.00	50.00
Albion teapot	50.00	85.00	35.00	95.00
Egg cup				
Style Three	7.50	12.50	5.00	12.50
Savings book	15.00	22.50	10.00	22.50
Stratford straight beaker	15.00	25.00	10.00	25.00

Bunnies in the Bath, Second Version (CT34)

Rex Mug, *Family at Breakfast* (HW12)

BATHTIME THEME — *Frank Endersby*

Bathtime, Style Three (22)

BATHTIME
Style Three

Design No.:   22 Bathtime
Designer: Frank Endersby
Issued: 1995 to the present

Shape	USD	CAD	GBP	AUD
Baby plate, round, small	N/I	46.00	14.00	62.95
Plate, 6½"	N/I	25.00	8.00	34.95
Plate, 8"	N/I	35.00	11.00	49.95

Blowing and Bursting Bubbles (23)

BLOWING AND BURSTING BUBBLES /
BLOWING BUBBLES AND SAILING BOATS

Design No.:   Front — 23 Blowing and Bursting Bubbles
              Reverse — 24 Blowing Bubbles and Sailing Boats
Designer: Frank Endersby
Issued: 1996 to the present

Shape	USD	CAD	GBP	AUD
Hug-a-mug, one handle	30.00	33.00	11.00	49.95
Hug-a-mug, two handles	32.50	39.00	12.00	56.95
Stratford teacup	7.50	12.00	5.00	12.00

Blowing Bubbles and Sailing Boats (24)

BEDTIME IN BUNKS, Style One

Design No.:	SF3
Designer:	Barbara Vernon
Issued:	By 1937 - by 1952
Combined with:	*Family at Breakfast*, HW12
	Feeding the Baby, HW13
	Pulling on Trousers, HW2

Shape	USD	CAD	GBP	AUD
Candle holder	2,000.00	3,000.00	1,250.00	4,000.00
Casino jug, 42s	300.00	450.00	200.00	500.00
Hot water plate	175.00	275.00	125.00	325.00
Plate, 7"	90.00	150.00	60.00	175.00
Plate, 7 ½"	90.00	150.00	60.00	175.00
Plate, 8 ½"	75.00	125.00	50.00	135.00

Note: This design should appear with the Barbara Vernon facsimile signature.

Bedtime in Bunks, Style One (SF3)

Bedtime Story (SF130)

BEDTIME STORY

Design No.:	SF130
Designer:	Walter Hayward
Issued:	1967 - 1994

Shape	USD	CAD	GBP	AUD
Baby plate round, small	20.00	30.00	15.00	30.00
Cake stand	150.00	250.00	100.00	300.00
Casino saucer	7.50	12.00	5.00	12.00
Casino teapot, 24s	175.00	275.00	125.00	325.00
Cereal / oatmeal bowl	10.00	15.00	7.50	15.00
Hot water plate	125.00	200.00	85.00	225.00
Jaffa fruit saucer (plain)	15.00	25.00	10.00	25.00
Picture plaque, large	20.00	30.00	12.50	30.00
Plate, 6"	20.00	30.00	15.00	30.00
Plate, 6 ½"	20.00	30.00	15.00	30.00
Plate, 8"	25.00	40.00	18.00	40.00

BEDTIME THEME — *Frank Endersby*

Bedtime in Bunks, Style Two (13)

BEDTIME IN BUNKS, *Style Two*

Design No.:   13 Bedtime in Bunks
Designer: Frank Endersby
Issued: 1995 to the present

Shape	USD	CAD	GBP	AUD
Baby plate, round, small	N/I	46.00	14.00	62.95
Cereal / oatmeal bowl	N/I	33.00	11.00	49.95
Plate, 6 ½"	N/I	25.00	8.00	34.95
Plate, 8"	N/I	35.00	11.00	49.95

Pillow Fight, Style Two (14)

PILLOW FIGHT, *Style Two* / PLAYING AND READING

Design No.:   Front — 14 Pillow Fight
                Reverse — 15 Playing and Reading
Designer: Frank Endersby
Issued: 1995 to the present
Combined with: *Playing with Ball*, (42)

Shape	USD	CAD	GBP	AUD
Hug-a-mug, one handle	**30.00**	**33.00**	**11.00**	**49.95**
Hug-a-mug, two handles	**32.50**	**39.00**	**12.00**	**56.95**
Divider dish	50.00	75.00	35.00	75.00
Stratford teacup	7.50	12.00	5.00	12.00

* Indicates scene on divider dish.

Playing and Reading (15)

Note: 1. Bold type in listing tables indicate a current design on a current shape.
2. N/I. Not issued individually. The item(s) will be found only in boxed sets in that market.

BEDTIME WITH DOLLIES

Design No.:	EC125
Designer:	Walter Hayward
Issued:	1959 - 1992
Combined with:	*Cricketer*, HW22R
	Drummer, EC2
	Drummer and Bugler, EC126
	Hikers, EC124
	Holding Hat and Coat, EC4
	Playing with Cup and Spoon, EC6
	Playing with Doll and Pram, EC123
	Raising Hat, Style Two, EC7
	Reading, EC122
	Sheltering Under an Umbrella, EC3
	Trumpeter, EC5
	Trying on Knitting, HW119R
	Unravelling the Knitting, HW119
	Wheelbarrow Race, Style One, HW22

Bedtime with Dollies (EC125)

Shape	USD	CAD	GBP	AUD
Albion sugar bowl	30.00	50.00	20.00	50.00
Beaker cover	125.00	175.00	75.00	175.00
Casino sugar bowl, 36s	100.00	150.00	65.00	175.00
Egg cup				
Style One	40.00	60.00	25.00	65.00
Style Two	80.00	125.00	50.00	135.00
Style Three	7.50	12.50	5.00	12.50
Lid of hot water plate	100.00	150.00	70.00	175.00

Beware of the Bull, (LF108)

BEWARE OF THE BULL

Design No.:	LF108
Designer:	Walter Hayward
Issued:	1959 - 1970

Shape	USD	CAD	GBP	AUD
Baby plate, oval, large	150.00	225.00	100.00	225.00
Baby plate, oval, small	150.00	225.00	100.00	225.00
Baby plate, round, large	125.00	200.00	85.00	225.00
Plate, 8"	45.00	70.00	30.00	75.00
Plate, 8 ½"	45.00	70.00	30.00	75.00
Porridge plate	85.00	125.00	55.00	150.00

BONFIRE

Design No.:	LF128
Designer:	Walter Hayward
Issued:	1967 - 1970

Shape	USD	CAD	GBP	AUD
Baby plate, round, large		Rare		
Plate, 8"		Rare		

Bonfire (LF128)

BREAKFAST TIME

A boxed Bunnykins for Grown Ups set containing a cereal bowl and hug-a-mug with one handle with the *Aerobics/Jogging* design, a 6" plate with the *Aeroplane* design, an 8" plate with the *Breakfast Time* design a cereal bowl in the *Tennis* design was distributed mainly in the U.S.A.

Design No.:	Breakfast Time
Designer:	Walter Hayward
Issued:	1986 - 1988
Series:	Bunnykins for Grown Ups

Shape	USD	CAD	GBP	AUD
Plate, 8"	45.00	70.00	30.00	75.00
Complete set (M.I.B.)	200.00	300.00	100.00	300.00

Breakfast Time

Note: See also *Aerobics/Jogging* and *Aeroplane* page 14 and *Tennis* page 160.

BUILDING SAND CASTLES / SAILING BOATS

Design No.:	Front — HW138 Building Sand Castles
	Reverse — HW138R Sailing Boats
Designer:	Walter Hayward
Issued:	1967 - by 1998
Combined with:	*Ice Cream on Beach*, HW136R
	Playing with Doll and Pram, EC123
	Roller Skating Arm in Arm, HW137R
	Roller Skating Race, HW137

Building Sand Castles (HW138)

Shape	USD	CAD	GBP	AUD
Albion cream jug	50.00	75.00	35.00	75.00
Albion jug, ½ pint	100.00	150.00	70.00	150.00
Albion teapot	50.00	85.00	35.00	95.00
Don beaker	35.00	55.00	25.00	60.00
Don beaker, one handle	35.00	55.00	25.00	60.00
Don mug, one handles	15.00	25.00	10.00	25.00
Don mug, two handles	15.00	25.00	10.00	25.00
Hug-a-mug, one handle	10.00	15.00	7.50	15.00
Hug-a-mug, two handles	10.00	15.00	7.50	15.00
Lamp	100.00	150.00	65.00	175.00
Lid of hot water plate	100.00	150.00	70.00	175.00
Malvern beaker	15.00	25.00	10.00	25.00
Money ball	10.00	15.00	7.50	15.00
Picture plaque, small	20.00	30.00	12.50	30.00
Stratford straight beaker	15.00	25.00	10.00	25.00
Stratford teacup	7.50	12.00	5.00	12.00
Savings book	15.00	22.50	10.00	22.50

Saling Boats (HW138R)

Bunnykins Build a Snowman (PN198)

BUNNYKINS BUILD A SNOWMAN

Design No.:   PN198
Designer: Frank Endersby
Issued: 1998 - 1998
Series: ICC Plate of the Year, Number 2

Shape	USD	CAD	GBP	AUD
Plate, 8"	30.00	45.00	20.00	50.00

Divider Dish decorated with Frank Endersby scenes;
Building Snowman (59), *Sleding,* Style Two (60)
and *Resting in Wheelbarrow* (57)

BUNNYKINS CELEBRATES YOUR CHRISTENING — *Walter Hayward*

BUNNYKINS CELEBRATE YOUR CHRISTENING
Style One, First Version

Design No.:	SF139 Bunnykins celebrate your Christening
Designer:	Walter Hayward
Issued:	1984 - 1989

Shape	USD	CAD	GBP	AUD
Plate, 8"	25.00	40.00	18.00	40.00

Bunnykins Celebrate Your Christening
First Version (SF139)

Bunnykins Celebrate Your Christening
Second Version (HW142)

Style One, Second Version

Design No.:	Front — HW142 Bunnykins celebrate your Christening
	Reverse — HW142R Christening inscription
Designer:	Walter Hayward
Issued:	1984 - 1990

Shape	USD	CAD	GBP	AUD
Hug-a-mug, one handle	10.00	15.00	7.50	15.00
Hug-a-mug, two handles	10.00	15.00	7.50	15.00
Money ball	10.00	15.00	7.50	15.00
Savings book	15.00	22.50	10.00	22.50

Christening Inscription (HW142R)

BUNNYKINS CELEBRATES YOUR CHRISTENING — Colin Twinn

Bunnykins Celebrate Your Christening
First Variation (CT38)

BUNNYKINS CELEBRATE YOUR CHRISTENING
Style Two, First Variation, Large Size

Design No.:	Front — CT38 Bunnykins Celebrate your Christening
	Reverse no. one — without rhyme
	Reverse no. two — CT65 with rhyme
Designer:	Colin Twinn
Issued:	1990 - 1993
Rhyme:	"Today, as your family welcomes you,
	To bless who you are and all you will do,
	The Bunnykins join in your bright celebration.
	And bring you a message of jubilation
	For, on this your day, we all wish for you
	A lifetime of love and much happiness too."

Shape	USD	CAD	GBP	AUD
Plate, 8"	25.00	40.00	18.00	40.00

Christening Rhyme (CT65)

Bunnykins Celebrate Your Christening
Second Variation (CT41)

Style Two, Second Variation, Small Size

Design No.:	Front — CT41 Bunnykins celebrate your Christening
	Reverse — CT42 Christening inscription
Designer:	Colin Twinn
Issued:	1991 - 1993

Shape	USD	CAD	GBP	AUD
Hug-a-mug, one handle	10.00	15.00	7.50	15.00
Hug-a-mug, two handles	10.00	15.00	7.50	15.00
Money ball	10.00	15.00	7.50	15.00

Christening Inscription (CT42)

BABY IN CRIB WITH FATHER LOOKING ON
Style Three, First Variation

Design No.:	Front — CT76 Baby in Crib with Father Looking On
	Reverse — CT77 Rhyme
Designer:	Colin Twinn
Issued:	1993 to the present
Rhyme:	"Today, as your family welcomes you,
	To bless who you are and all you will do,
	The Bunnykins join in your bright celebration.
	And bring you a message of jubilation
	For, on this your day, we all wish for you
	A lifetime of love and much happiness too."

Shape	USD	CAD	GBP	AUD
Plate, 8"	N/I	35.00	11.00	49.95

Baby in Crib with Father Looking On (CT76)

Baby in Crib (CT78)

BABY IN CRIB
Style Three, Second Variation

Design No.:	Front — CT78 Baby in Crib
	Reverse — CT79 Christening inscription
Designer:	Colin Twinn
Issued:	1993 to the present

Shape	USD	CAD	GBP	AUD
Hug-a-mug, one handle	30.00	33.00	11.00	49.95
Hug-a-mug, two handles	32.50	39.00	12.00	56.95
Money ball	33.75	40.00	15.00	62.95

Christening Inscription (CT79)

Note: 1. Bold type in the listing tables indicate a current design on a current shape.
2. N/I, Not issued individually. The item(s) will be found only in boxed sets in that market.

BUNNYKINS COLLECTORS CLUB, AUSTRALIA

Member of Bunnykins Club/Television Time
(SF112)

MEMBER OF BUNNYKINS CLUB
BUNNYKINS BUNNIES ARE CHILDREN
LIKE YOU

These plates, with the Member of Bunnykins Club inscription, were made exclusively for the Bunnykins club members in Australia. Other designs with this inscription may exist.

Design No.:   SF18 — Bathtime, Style One
             SF112 — Television Time
             SF113 — Camp Site
             SF130 — Bedtime Story
             SF131 — Home Decorating
             SF132 — Space Rocket Launch
             SF133 — Flying Kites
             SF134 — Toppling the Fruit Cart
             SF135 — Family in the Garden
Issued: 1979 - 1985

Shape	Design	USD	CAD	GBP	AUD
Plate, 6 ½"	Various	250.00	400.00	165.00	450.00

BUNNYKINS HELP SANTA

Design No.: PN175
Designer: Frank Endersby
Issued: 1997 - 1997
Series: ICC Plate of the Year, Number 1
Backstamp: ICC plus Bunnykins and Frank Endersby
             facsimile signature

Shape	USD	CAD	GBP	AUD
Plate, 8"	30.00	45.00	20.00	50.00

Bunnykins Help Santa (PN175)

BUNNYKINS TEACHING CLOCKS
Walter Hayward, Colin Twinn, Frank Endersby

BUNNYKINS TEACHING CLOCK
Classroom Scene, Style One

Design No.:	Front — SF138 Classroom Scene
	Reverse — Inscription
Designer:	Walter Hayward
Issued:	1983 - 2002
Rhyme:	"Learning can be hours of fun
	For Bunnykins and everyone
	To tell the time we learn today
	As we see the clock tick minutes away."

Shape	USD	CAD	GBP	AUD
Teaching clock	30.00	45.00	20.00	50.00

Bunnykins Teaching Clock
Classroom Scene, Style One (SF138)

Note: Two second hand varieties exist; long and short.

BUNNYKINS TEACHING CLOCK,
Classroom Scene, Style Two, First Version

Design No.:	Front — CT36 Classroom Scene
Designer:	Colin Twinn
Issued:	1991 - 1993
Rhyme:	"Learning can be hours of fun
	For Bunnykins and everyone
	To tell the time we learn today
	As we see the clock tick minutes away."

Shape	USD	CAD	GBP	AUD
Teaching clock	30.00	45.00	20.00	50.00

Bunnykins Teaching Clock
Classroom Scene, Style Two (CT36)

Note: 1. This clock has a short second hand.
2. For information on others shapes with this design
see page 46.

Bunnykins Teaching Clock
Four individual scenes

BUNNYKINS TEACHING CLOCK
Four Individual Scenes

Design No.:   None — Four individual scenes
Designer: Frank Endersby
Issued: 1996 to the present

Shape	USD	CAD	GBP	AUD
Teaching clock	95.00	100.00	31.00	165.00

Note: This clock has a short second hand.

CAMP SITE

Design No.:   SF113
Designer: Walter Hayward
Issued: 1959 - by 1998

Shape	USD	CAD	GBP	AUD
Baby plate, round, small	20.00	30.00	15.00	30.00
Cake stand	150.00	250.00	100.00	300.00
Casino saucer	7.50	12.00	5.00	12.00
Cereal / oatmeal bowl	10.00	15.00	7.50	15.00
Jaffa fruit saucer (plain)	15.00	25.00	10.00	25.00
Hot water plate	125.00	200.00	85.00	225.00
Picture plaque, large	20.00	30.00	12.50	30.00
Plate, 6 ½"	20.00	30.00	15.00	30.00
Plate, 7 ½"	20.00	30.00	15.00	30.00
Plate, 8"	25.00	40.00	18.00	40.00

Camp Site (SF113)

CAMPING THEME — *Frank Endersby*

CAMPING

Design No.:	34 Camping
Designer:	Frank Endersby
Issued:	1996 to the present

Shape	USD	CAD	GBP	AUD
Baby plate, round, small	N/I	46.00	14.00	62.95
Cereal / oatmeal bowl	N/I	33.00	11.00	49.95
Plate, 6 ½″	N/I	25.00	8.00	34.95
Plate, 8″	N/I	35.00	11.00	49.95

Camping (34)

Campfire (35)

CAMPFIRE / ASLEEP IN A SLEEPING BAG

Design No.:	Front — 35 Campfire
	Reverse — 36 Asleep in a Sleeping Bag
Designer:	Frank Endersby
Issued:	1996 to the present

Shape	USD	CAD	GBP	AUD
Hug-a-mug, one handle	30.00	33.00	11.00	49.95
Hug-a-mug, two handles	32.50	39.00	12.00	56.95
Stratford teacup	7.50	12.00	5.00	12.00

Note: 1. Bold type in the listing tables indicate a current design on a current shape.
2. N/I, Not issued individually. The item(s) will be found only in boxed sets in that market.

Asleep in a Sleeping Bag (36)

Carol Singer Bunnykins (CT70)

Christmas 1992 (CT71)

Carving the Chicken (LFc)

CAROL SINGER BUNNYKINS CHRISTMAS TREE ORNAMENT

Design No.:　Front — CT70
　　　　　　 Reverse — CT71
Designer:　 Colin Twinn
Issued:　　 1992 - 1992
Series:　　 Christmas Tree Ornaments

Shape	USD	CAD	GBP	AUD
Christmas tree ornament	40.00	65.00	25.00	70.00

Note: For other Christmas ornaments in this series see page 44, 80 143 and 165.

CARVING THE CHICKEN

Design No.:　LFc
Designer:　 Barbara Vernon
Issued:　　 By 1937 - by 1952

Shape	USD	CAD	GBP	AUD
Bread and butter plate	800.00	1,250.00	500.00	1,600.00
Casino teapot, 30s	650.00	1,200.00	425.00	1,250.00
Plate, 7 ½"	300.00	475.00	200.00	500.00
Plate, 8 ½"	300.00	475.00	200.00	500.00
Porridge plate	400.00	625.00	275.00	650.00

Note: This design should appear with the Barbara Vernon facsimile signature.

CHICKEN PULLING A CART

Chicken Pulling A Cart (SF8)

Design No.: SF8
Designer: Barbara Vernon
Issued: By 1940 - by 1952
Combined with: *Family at Breakfast*, HW12
                Family Going out on Washing Day, HW8

Fixing Braces, HW3
Gardener with Wheelbarrow, HW9R
Going Shopping, SF10
Leapfrog, HW12R
Pillow Fight, Style One, SF7

Shape	USD	CAD	GBP	AUD
Baby plate, round, small				
with signature	75.00	125.00	50.00	125.00
without signature	50.00	80.00	35.00	80.00
Casino jug, 24s				
with signature	400.00	625.00	275.00	650.00
without signature	350.00	550.00	250.00	550.00
Casino jug, 36s				
with signature	300.00	475.00	200.00	475.00
without signature	250.00	400.00	175.00	400.00
Casino jug, 42s				
with signature	250.00	400.00	175.00	400.00
without signature	200.00	325.00	150.00	325.00
Casino saucer				
with signature	75.00	125.00	50.00	125.00
without signature	50.00	75.00	35.00	75.00
Casino sugar bowl, 30s				
with signature	175.00	275.00	125.00	325.00
without signature	125.00	200.00	85.00	225.00
Casino teapot, 24s				
with signature	375.00	550.00	250.00	600.00
without signature	300.00	450.00	200.00	500.00
Casino teapot, 30s				
with signature	325.00	500.00	225.00	550.00
without signature	250.00	400.00	175.00	450.00

Shape	USD	CAD	GBP	AUD
Cereal / oatmeal bowl				
with signature	50.00	80.00	35.00	80.00
without signature	35.00	55.00	25.00	55.00
Don beaker				
with signature	150.00	250.00	110.00	275.00
without signature	125.00	200.00	90.00	225.00
Don Beaker, one handle				
with signature	150.00	250.00	110.00	275.00
without signature	125.00	200.00	90.00	225.00
Jaffa fruit saucer				
plain rim	95.00	150.00	65.00	175.00
wavy rim	60.00	95.00	40.00	100.00
Hot water plate				
with signature	175.00	275.00	125.00	325.00
without signature	125.00	200.00	85.00	225.00
Plate, 6 ½"				
with signature	60.00	95.00	40.00	100.00
without signature	40.00	65.00	25.00	70.00
Plate, 7 ½"				
with signature	60.00	95.00	40.00	100.00
without signature	40.00	65.00	25.00	70.00
Plate, 8 ½"				
with signature	70.00	115.00	45.00	125.00
without signature	45.00	70.00	30.00	75.00

FINE WHITE CHINA
Saucer   Very rare
Teacup   Very rare

Note: This scene was re-issued on an 8" plate in 1984 with the Bunnykins Golden Jubilee backstamp (see page 191).

Christmas Morn

Christmas Morn backstamp

Christmas Party (LF9)

CHRISTMAS MORN
CHRISTMAS TREE ORNAMENT

This Christmas tree ornament has a rabbit-shaped rim. It was commissioned by Royal Doulton U.S.A. and made in the U.S.A.

Design No.: None
Designer: Frank Endersby
Issued: 1996 - 1996
Backstamp: "Christmas Morn" Christmas 1996 Royal Doulton "Bunnykins" ® © 1996 Royal Doulton made in U.S.A.
Series: Christmas Tree Ornaments

Shape	USD	CAD	GBP	AUD
Christmas tree ornament	40.00	65.00	25.00	70.00

Note: For other Christmas ornaments in this series see pages 42, 80, 143 and 165.

CHRISTMAS PARTY

Design No.: LF9
Designer: Barbara Vernon
Issued: By 1940 - 1967

Shape	USD	CAD	GBP	AUD
Baby plate, oval, large				
with signature	400.00	625.00	275.00	650.00
without signature	300.00	475.00	200.00	500.00
Baby plate, round, large				
with silver rim		Rare		
with signature	300.00	450.00	200.00	500.00
without signature	250.00	375.00	175.00	375.00
Bread and butter plate				
with signature	500.00	800.00	350.00	900.00
without signature	400.00	625.00	275.00	650.00
Plate, 8 ½"				
with signature	115.00	175.00	80.00	175.00
without signature	75.00	125.00	50.00	135.00
Porridge plate				
with signature	125.00	200.00	80.00	225.00
without signature	100.00	150.00	65.00	175.00

CHRISTMAS TREE

Design No.: LF16
Designer: Walter Hayward
Issued: 1954 - 1967

Shape	USD	CAD	GBP	AUD
Baby plate, oval, large				
with signature	200.00	325.00	150.00	325.00
without signature	150.00	225.00	100.00	225.00
Baby plate, round, large				
with signature	150.00	250.00	100.00	275.00
without signature	125.00	200.00	85.00	225.00
Bread and butter plate				
with signature	250.00	400.00	175.00	400.00
without signature	200.00	325.00	150.00	325.00
Plate, 8 ½"				
with signature	70.00	115.00	45.00	125.00
without signature	45.00	70.00	30.00	75.00
Porridge plate				
with signature	110.00	175.00	70.00	200.00
without signature	85.00	125.00	55.00	150.00

Christmas Tree (LF16)

Christmas Morn Christmas ornament, 1996

CLASSROOM SCENE
Style Two, First Version

Design No.:   CT36 Classroom Scene
Designer: Colin Twinn
Issued: 1991 - 1993
Combined with: *Bunny with Mirror*, CT35

Shape	USD	CAD	GBP	AUD
Albion jug, 1 pint	150.00	225.00	100.00	225.00
Plate, 6"	20.00	30.00	15.00	30.00
Plate, 8"	25.00	40.00	18.00	40.00

For illustration of this design see Bunnykins Teaching Clock page 39.

Note: For information on the Bunnykins Teaching Clock with this design see page 39.

CLASSROOM SCENE
Style Two, Second Version

Design No.:   CT16 Classroom
Designer: Colin Twinn
Issued: 1990 - 1993
Combined with: *Bunny on Trike*, CT23
                  Bunny with Mirror, CT35
                  Picking Daisies, CT4

Shape	USD	CAD	GBP	AUD
Albion cream jug	50.00	75.00	35.00	75.00
Albion jug, ½ pint	100.00	150.00	70.00	150.00
Albion jug, 1 pint	150.00	225.00	100.00	225.00
Albion teapot	50.00	85.00	35.00	95.00
Baby plate, round small	15.00	25.00	10.00	30.00
Cake stand	150.00	250.00	100.00	300.00
Jaffa fruit saucer (plain)	30.00	45.00	20.00	50.00
Stratford straight beaker	15.00	25.00	10.00	25.00

Classroom Scene, Style Two (CT16)

CONDUCTING THE ORCHESTRA

Design No.: LF5
Designer: Barbara Vernon
Issued: By 1940 - by 1952
Combined with: *Frightening Spider, SF4*

Shape	USD	CAD	GBP	AUD
Baby plate, oval, large				
with signature	200.00	325.00	150.00	325.00
without signature	150.00	225.00	100.00	225.00
Baby plate, round, large				
with silver rim		Rare		
with signature	150.00	250.00	100.00	275.00
without signature	125.00	200.00	85.00	225.00
Bread and butter plate				
with signature	250.00	400.00	175.00	400.00
without signature	200.00	325.00	150.00	325.00
Casino jug, 24s				
with signature	400.00	625.00	275.00	650.00
without signature	350.00	550.00	250.00	550.00
Hot water plate				
with signature	175.00	275.00	125.00	325.00
without signature	125.00	200.00	85.00	225.00
Plate, 8 ½"				
with signature	70.00	115.00	45.00	125.00
without signature	45.00	70.00	30.00	75.00
Porridge plate				
with signature	110.00	175.00	70.00	200.00
without signature	85.00	125.00	50.00	150.00

Conducting the Orchestra (LF5)

Convalescing (SF5)

CONVALESCING

Design No.: SF5
Designer: Barbara Vernon
Issued: By 1940 - by 1952
Combined with: *Asleep in the Open Air, HW10*
Baking, SF19
Leapfrog, HW12R
Soldiers Marching to the Music, HW18
Washing in the Open Air, HW10R

Shape	USD	CAD	GBP	AUD
Baby plate, round, small	75.00	125.00	50.00	125.00
Bread and butter plate	250.00	400.00	175.00	400.00
Casino jug, 42s	250.00	400.00	175.00	400.00
Casino saucer	75.00	125.00	50.00	125.00
Casino teapot, 24s	375.00	550.00	250.00	600.00
Cereal / oatmeal bowl	50.00	80.00	35.00	80.00
Jaffa fruit saucer				
plain rim	95.00	150.00	65.00	175.00
wavy rim	60.00	95.00	40.00	100.00
Hot water plate	175.00	275.00	125.00	325.00
Plate, 6 ½"	60.00	95.00	40.00	100.00
Plate, 7 ½"	60.00	95.00	40.00	100.00

Note: This design should appear with the Barbara Vernon facsimile signature

Cowboys and Indians (HW140)

Cowboy on Rocking Horse (HW140R)

COWBOYS AND INDIANS / COWBOY ON ROCKING HORSE

Design No.:   Front — HW140 Cowboys and Indians
                Reverse — HW140R Cowboy on Rocking Horse
Designer: Walter Hayward
Issued: 1967 - by 1998
Combined with: *Hobby Horse*, Style Two, EC121

Shape	USD	CAD	GBP	AUD
Albion cream jug	50.00	75.00	35.00	75.00
Albion teapot	50.00	85.00	35.00	95.00
Casino teacup	7.50	12.00	5.00	12.00
Divider dish	50.00	75.00	35.00	75.00
Don beaker	25.00	40.00	20.00	45.00
Don beaker, one handle	25.00	40.00	20.00	45.00
Don mug, one handle	15.00	25.00	10.00	25.00
Don mug, two handles	15.00	25.00	10.00	25.00
Egg box				
small	225.00	350.00	150.00	400.00
medium	300.00	450.00	200.00	500.00
large	375.00	550.00	250.00	600.00
Hug-a-mug, one handle	10.00	15.00	7.50	15.00
Hug-a-mug, two handles	10.00	15.00	7.50	15.00
Lamp	100.00	150.00	65.00	175.00
Lid of hot water plate	100.00	150.00	70.00	175.00
Malvern beaker	15.00	25.00	10.00	25.00
Money ball	10.00	15.00	7.50	15.00
Picture plaque, small	20.00	30.00	12.50	30.00
Savings book	15.00	22.50	10.00	22.50
Stratford teacup	7.50	12.00	5.00	12.00

CRICKET GAME

Design No.:　　　LF12
Designer:　　　Walter Hayward after Barbara Vernon
Issued:　　　　1952 - 1967

Shape	USD	CAD	GBP	AUD
Baby plate, oval, large				
with signature	200.00	325.00	150.00	325.00
without signature	150.00	275.00	100.00	225.00
Baby plate, oval, small				
with signature	200.00	325.00	150.00	325.00
without signature	150.00	275.00	100.00	225.00
Baby plate, round large				
with signature	150.00	250.00	100.00	275.00
without signature	125.00	200.00	85.00	225.00
Bread and butter plate				
with signature	250.00	400.00	175.00	400.00
without signature	200.00	325.00	150.00	325.00
Plate, 8 ½"				
with signature	70.00	115.00	45.00	125.00
without signature	45.00	70.00	30.00	75.00
Porridge plate				
with signature	110.00	175.00	70.00	200.00
without signature	85.00	125.00	55.00	150.00

Cricket Game (LF12)

Cuddling under a Mushroom (HW4)

CUDDLING UNDER A MUSHROOM

Design No.:　　　　HW4
Designer:　　　　Barbara Vernon
Issued:　　　　　By 1937 - by 1952
Combined with:　*Footballer*, HW13R
　　　　　　　　Golfer, HW4R
　　　　　　　　Netting a Cricket, HW6

Shape	USD	CAD	GBP	AUD
Casino sugar bowl, 30s				
with signature	250.00	375.00	175.00	400.00
without signature	175.00	275.00	125.00	325.00
Casino teacup				
with signature	100.00	150.00	65.00	175.00
without signature	75.00	125.00	50.00	125.00
Don beaker				
with signature	200.00	325.00	140.00	350.00
without signature	175.00	275.00	125.00	300.00
Don beaker, one handle				
with signature	200.00	325.00	140.00	350.00
without signature	175.00	275.00	125.00	300.00
Don mug, one handle				
with signature	150.00	250.00	100.00	275.00
without signature	125.00	200.00	90.00	225.00
Don mug, two handles				
with signature	150.00	250.00	100.00	275.00
without signature	125.00	200.00	90.00	225.00
Lid of hot water plate				
with signature	150.00	225.00	100.00	250.00
without signature	125.00	200.00	85.00	225.00

FINE WHITE CHINA
Saucer			Very Rare	
Teacup			Very Rare	

Cycling (HW15R)

CYCLING

Design No.:	HW15R
Designer:	Barbara Vernon
Issued:	By 1937 - by 1967
Combined with:	*Family at Breakfast*, HW12
	Family Going Out on Washing Day, HW8
	Family with Pram, Style One, HW15
	Feeding the Baby, HW13
	Fixing Braces, HW3
	Golfer, HW4R
	Kissing Under Mistletoe, HW11R
	Pressing Trousers, HW14
	Proposal, HW11
	Reading the Times, HW2R

Shape	USD	CAD	GBP	AUD
Casino jug, 42s				
with signature	300.00	450.00	200.00	500.00
without signature	250.00	375.00	175.00	400.00
Casino sugar bowl, 36s				
with signature	200.00	325.00	125.00	350.00
without signature	150.00	225.00	100.00	250.00
Casino teacup				
with signature	100.00	150.00	65.00	175.00
without signature	75.00	125.00	50.00	125.00
Casino teapot, 30s				
with signature	400.00	600.00	275.00	700.00
without signature	300.00	450.00	200.00	500.00
Don beaker, one handle				
with signature	200.00	325.00	140.00	350.00
without signature	125.00	200.00	80.00	225.00
Don mug, one handle				
with signature	150.00	250.00	100.00	275.00
without signature	65.00	100.00	45.00	100.00
Don mug, two handles				
with signature	150.00	250.00	100.00	275.00
without signature	65.00	100.00	45.00	100.00
Jam pot	1,500.00	2,500.00	1,000.00	3,000.00
Lid of hot water plate				
with signature	150.00	225.00	100.00	250.00
without signature	125.00	200.00	85.00	225.00

FINE WHITE CHINA

Rex mug, small, 2 ½"	Very Rare
Rex mug, large, 3"	Very Rare
Teacup	Very Rare

Note: The Rex mugs are found combining *Cycling* (HW15R) with *Proposal* (HW11) and *Cycling* (HW15R) with *Pressing Trousers* (HW14).

CYCLING THEME — Frank Endersby

CYCLE RIDE

Design No.: 46 Cycle Ride
Designer: Frank Endersby
Issued: 1995 to the present

Shape	USD	CAD	GBP	AUD
Baby plate, round, small	N/I	**46.00**	**14.00**	**62.95**
Jaffa fruit saucer	10.00	15.00	7.50	15.00
Plate, 6 ½"	N/I	**25.00**	**8.00**	**34.95**
Plate, 8"	N/I	**35.00**	**11.00**	**49.95**

Cycle Ride (46)

Resting (47)

RESTING / CLEANING BIKE

Design No.: Front — 47 Resting, Style Three
Reverse — 48 Cleaning Bike
Designer: Frank Endersby
Issued: 1995 to the present

Shape	USD	CAD	GBP	AUD
Hug-a-mug, one handle	**30.00**	**33.00**	**11.00**	**49.95**
Hug-a-mug, two handles	**32.50**	**39.00**	**12.00**	**56.95**

Cleaning Bike (48)

Note: 1. Bold type in the listing tables indicate a current design on a current shape.
2. N/I, Not issued individually. The item(s) will be found only in boxed sets in that market.

DAISY CHAINS / SMELLING FLOWERS

Daisy Chains (HW25)

Smelling Flowers (HW25R)

Design No.: Front — HW25 Daisy Chains
　　　　　　Reverse — HW25R Smelling Flowers
Designer:　　Walter Hayward

Issued:　　　　　1954 - by 1998
Combined with:　*Hikers*, EC124
　　　　　　　　　Ice Cream Vendor, HW23
　　　　　　　　　Playing with Cup and Spoon, EC6

Shape	USD	CAD	GBP	AUD
Albion cream jug	50.00	75.00	35.00	75.00
Albion jug, ½ pint	100.00	150.00	70.00	150.00
Albion jug, 1 pint	150.00	225.00	100.00	225.00
Albion teapot	50.00	85.00	35.00	95.00
Casino jug, 36s				
with signature	175.00	275.00	125.00	275.00
without signature	125.00	200.00	85.00	200.00
Casino jug, 42s				
with signature	150.00	225.00	100.00	225.00
without signature	100.00	150.00	70.00	150.00
Casino saucer				
with signature	15.00	25.00	10.00	25.00
without signature	7.50	12.00	5.00	12.00
Casino teacup				
with signature	15.00	25.00	10.00	25.00
without signature	7.50	12.00	5.00	12.00
Casino teapot, 30s				
with signature	200.00	325.00	125.00	350.00
without signature	150.00	225.00	100.00	250.00
Don beaker				
with signature	75.00	125.00	50.00	150.00
without signature	35.00	55.00	25.00	60.00
Don beaker, one handle				
with signature	75.00	125.00	50.00	150.00
without signature	35.00	55.00	25.00	60.00
Don mug, one handle				
with signature	65.00	100.00	45.00	75.00
without signature	15.00	25.00	10.00	25.00

Shape	USD	CAD	GBP	AUD
Don mug, two handles				
with signature	65.00	100.00	45.00	75.00
without signature	15.00	25.00	10.00	25.00
Egg box				
small	225.00	350.00	150.00	400.00
medium	300.00	450.00	200.00	500.00
large	375.00	550.00	250.00	600.00
Hug-a-mug, one handle	10.00	15.00	7.50	15.00
Hug-a-mug, two handles				
Regular issue	10.00	15.00	7.50	15.00
Special Events	10.00	15.00	7.50	15.00
Jaffa fruit saucer (plain)	15.00	25.00	10.00	25.00
Lamp	100.00	150.00	65.00	175.00
Lid of hot water plate				
with signature	125.00	200.00	85.00	225.00
without signature	100.00	150.00	70.00	175.00
Malvern beaker	15.00	25.00	10.00	25.00
Money ball	10.00	15.00	7.50	15.00
Picture plaque, small	20.00	30.00	12.50	30.00
Plate, 6 ½"				
with signature	35.00	55.00	25.00	55.00
without signature	20.00	30.00	15.00	30.00
Savings book	15.00	22.50	10.00	22.50
Stratford straight beaker	15.00	22.50	10.00	22.50
Stratford teacup	7.50	12.00	5.00	12.00

Note: 1. A Hug-a-mug (two handles) was issued for the U.S. Special Event Tour in 1993. The front illustrates *Daisy Chains* (HW25), and the back *Hikers* (EC124) with the words *'US Special Events Tour 1993'*.
　　　2. A Casino jug combines *Daisy Chains*, (HW25) with *Ice Cream Vendor*, (HW23).

DANCING IN THE MOONLIGHT
First Version

Design No.: LFb
Designer: Barbara Vernon
Issued: 1937 - by 1952

Shape	USD	CAD	GBP	AUD
Baby plate, round, large				
with signature	450.00	675.00	325.00	700.00
without signature	400.00	600.00	275.00	625.00
Bread and butter plate				
with signature	800.00	1,250.00	500.00	1,600.00
without signature	600.00	1,000.00	400.00	1,100.00
Plate, 8 ½"				
with signature	300.00	475.00	200.00	500.00
without signature	250.00	400.00	175.00	425.00
Porridge plate				
with signature	400.00	625.00	275.00	650.00
without signature	375.00	575.00	250.00	600.00

Dancing in the Moonlight, First Version (LFb)

Note: See also Bunnykins 60th Anniversary page 193.

A rare Bunnykins stand, *Dancing in the Moonlight* (LFb)

Dancing Round the Barrel Organ (HW139)

Skipping Game (HW139R)

DANCING ROUND THE BARREL ORGAN / SKIPPING GAME

Design No.:	Front — HW139 Dancing Round the Barrel Organ
	Reverse — HW139R Skipping Game
Designer:	Walter Hayward
Issued:	1967 - by 1998
Combined with:	*Sailing Boats, HW138R

Shape	USD	CAD	GBP	AUD
Albion cream jug	50.00	75.00	35.00	75.00
Albion jug, ½ pint	100.00	150.00	70.00	150.00
Albion jug, 1 pint	150.00	225.00	100.00	225.00
Albion teapot	50.00	85.00	35.00	95.00
Casino jug, 36s	125.00	200.00	85.00	200.00
Casino saucer	7.50	12.00	5.00	12.00
Casino teacup	7.50	12.00	5.00	12.00
Divider dish	50.00	75.00	35.00	75.00
Don beaker	35.00	55.00	25.00	60.00
Don beaker, one handle	35.00	55.00	25.00	60.00
Don mug, one handle	15.00	25.00	10.00	25.00
Don mug, two handles	15.00	25.00	10.00	25.00
Egg box				
small	225.00	350.00	150.00	400.00
medium	300.00	450.00	200.00	500.00
large	375.00	550.00	250.00	600.00
Hug-a-mug, one handle	10.00	15.00	7.50	15.00
Hug-a-mug, two handles	10.00	15.00	7.50	15.00
Jaffa fruit saucer (plain)	15.00	25.00	10.00	25.00
Lamp	100.00	150.00	65.00	175.00
Malvern beaker	15.00	25.00	10.00	25.00
Money ball	10.00	15.00	7.50	15.00
Picture plaque, small	20.00	30.00	12.50	30.00
Plate, 6 ½"	20.00	30.00	15.00	30.00
Savings book				
regular issue	15.00	22.50	10.00	22.50
Special Events 1994	15.00	22.50	10.00	22.50
Stratford straight beaker	15.00	22.50	10.00	22.50
Stratford teacup	7.50	12.00	5.00	12.00

* Indicates scene on divider dish.

Note: A savings book was issued for the U.S. Special Events Tour 1994. The front features *Skipping Game* (HW139R) and the reverse is inscribed 'To' and 'From' for the customer to complete and 'US Special Events Tour 1994.'

DINNER THEME — *Frank Endersby*

PREPARING DINNER

Design No.:	43 — Preparing Dinner	
Designer:	Frank Endersby	
Issued:	1995 to the present	

Shape	USD	CAD	GBP	AUD
Baby plate, round, small	N/I	46.00	14.00	62.95
Jaffa fruit saucer	15.00	25.00	10.00	25.00
Plate, 6 ½"	N/I	25.00	8.00	34.95
Plate, 8"	N/I	35.00	11.00	49.95

Preparing Dinner (43)

Serving Dinner (44)

SERVING DINNER / CARRYING PLATES

Design No.:	Front — 44 Serving Dinner	
	Reverse — 45 Carrying Plates	
Designer:	Frank Endersby	
Issued:	1995 to the present	
Combined with:	*Sitting on Suitcase*, (51)	

Shape	USD	CAD	GBP	AUD
Hug-a-mug, one handle	30.00	33.00	11.00	49.95
Hug-a-mug, two handles	32.50	39.00	12.00	56.95
Divider dish	50.00	75.00	35.00	75.00
Stratford teacup	7.50	12.00	5.00	12.00

* Indicates scenes on divider dish.

Carrying Plates (45)

Disturbing Sleeping Father (HW118)

Pea Shooter (HW118R)

DISTURBING SLEEPING FATHER / PEA SHOOTER

Design No.:	Front — HW118 Disturbing Sleeping Father
	Reverse — HW118R Pea Shooter
Designer:	Walter Hayward
Issued:	1959 - by 1998
Combined with:	*Dancing with Doll*, HW115R
	Nipped by a Crab, HW21R
	Wheelbarrow Race, Style One, (HW22)

Shape	USD	CAD	GBP	AUD
Albion cream jug	50.00	75.00	35.00	75.00
Albion jug, ½ pint	100.00	150.00	70.00	150.00
Albion jug, 1 pint	150.00	225.00	100.00	225.00
Albion teapot	50.00	85.00	35.00	95.00
Casino jug, 36s	125.00	200.00	85.00	200.00
Casino jug, 42s	100.00	150.00	70.00	150.00
Casino saucer	7.50	12.00	5.00	12.00
Casino teacup	7.50	12.00	5.00	12.00
Divider dish	50.00	75.00	35.00	75.00
Don beaker, one handle	35.00	55.00	25.00	60.00
Don mug, one handle	15.00	25.00	10.00	25.00
Don mug, two handles	15.00	25.00	10.00	25.00
Egg box				
small	225.00	350.00	150.00	400.00
medium	300.00	450.00	200.00	500.00
large	375.00	550.00	250.00	600.00
Hug-a-mug, one handle	10.00	15.00	7.50	15.00
Hug-a-mug, two handles	10.00	15.00	7.50	15.00
Jaffa fruit saucer (plain)	15.00	25.00	10.00	25.00
Lamp	100.00	150.00	65.00	175.00
Lid of hot water plate	100.00	150.00	70.00	175.00
Malvern beaker	15.00	25.00	10.00	25.00
Money ball	10.00	15.00	7.50	15.00
Picture plaque, small	20.00	30.00	12.50	30.00
Plate, 6 ½"	20.00	30.00	15.00	30.00
Stratford straight beaker	15.00	22.50	10.00	22.50
Stratford teacup	7.50	12.00	5.00	12.00

* Indicates scene on divider dish.

Note: An Albion teapot combines *Pea Shooter* (HW118R) with *Wheelbarrow Race*, Style One (HW22).

DODGEM CARS

Design No.: LF4
Designer: Barbara Vernon
Issued: By 1940 - by 1952

Shape	USD	CAD	GBP	AUD
Baby plate, oval, large				
with signature	200.00	325.00	150.00	325.00
without signature	150.00	225.00	100.00	225.00
Baby plate, round large				
with signature	150.00	250.00	100.00	275.00
without signature	125.00	200.00	85.00	225.00
Bread and butter plate				
with signature	250.00	400.00	175.00	400.00
without signature	200.00	325.00	150.00	325.00
Cereal / oatmeal bowl				
with signature	50.00	80.00	35.00	80.00
without signature	35.00	55.00	25.00	55.00
Plate 8 ½"				
with signature	70.00	115.00	45.00	125.00
without signature	45.00	70.00	30.00	75.00
Porridge bowl				
with signature	110.00	175.00	70.00	200.00
without signature	85.00	125.00	55.00	150.00

Dodgem Cars (LF4)

Dog Carriage (LFe)

DOG CARRIAGE

Design No.: LFe
Designer: Barbara Vernon
Issued: By 1937 - by 1952

Shape	USD	CAD	GBP	AUD
Baby plate, oval, large				
with signature	600.00	1,000.00	400.00	1,100.00
without signature	500.00	800.00	350.00	950.00
Baby plate, round large				
with signature	450.00	675.00	325.00	700.00
without signature	400.00	600.00	275.00	625.00
Bread / butter plate, handles				
with signature	800.00	1,250.00	500.00	1,600.00
without signature	600.00	1,000.00	400.00	1,100.00
Cereal / oatmeal bowl				
with signature		Rare		
without signature		Rare		
Plate 8 ½"				
with signature	300.00	475.00	200.00	500.00
without signature	250.00	400.00	175.00	425.00
Porridge bowl				
with signature	400.00	625.00	275.00	650.00
without signature	375.00	575.00	250.00	600.00

The Doll's House (HW120)

Playing with Doll and Teddy (HW120R)

THE DOLL'S HOUSE / PLAYING WITH DOLL AND TEDDY

Design No.:   Front — HW120 The Doll's House
                 Reverse — HW120R Playing with Doll and Teddy
Designer: Walter Hayward
Issued: 1959 - by 1998
Combined with: *Dancing with Doll, HW115R
                 Hikers, EC124
                 *Nipped by a Crab, HW21R
                 Reading, EC122
                 *Serving Tea, HW116R

Shape	USD	CAD	GBP	AUD
Albion cream jug	50.00	75.00	35.00	75.00
Albion jug, ½ pint	100.00	150.00	70.00	150.00
Albion teapot	50.00	85.00	35.00	95.00
Cake stand	150.00	250.00	100.00	300.00
Casino saucer	7.50	12.00	5.00	12.00
Casino teacup	7.50	12.00	5.00	12.00
Divider dish	50.00	75.00	35.00	75.00
Don beaker	35.00	55.00	25.00	60.00
Don beaker, one handle	35.00	55.00	25.00	60.00
Don mug, one handle	15.00	25.00	10.00	25.00
Don mug, two handles	15.00	25.00	10.00	25.00
Egg box				
small	225.00	350.00	150.00	400.00
medium	300.00	450.00	200.00	500.00
large	375.00	550.00	250.00	600.00
Hug-a-mug, one handle	10.00	15.00	7.50	15.00
Hug-a-mug, two handles	10.00	15.00	7.50	15.00
Jaffa fruit saucer (plain)	15.00	25.00	10.00	25.00
Lamp	100.00	150.00	65.00	175.00
Lid of hot water plate	100.00	150.00	70.00	175.00
Malvern beaker	15.00	25.00	10.00	25.00
Money ball	10.00	15.00	7.50	15.00
Picture plaque, small	20.00	30.00	12.50	30.00
Plate, 6 ½"	20.00	30.00	15.00	30.00
Savings book	15.00	22.50	10.00	22.50
Stratford straight beaker	15.00	22.50	10.00	22.50
Stratford teacup	7.50	12.00	5.00	12.00

* Indicates scene on divider dish.

DRESS MAKING /
BUGLER WITH TOY DONKEY

Dress Making (HW26)

Bugler with Toy Donkey (HW26R)

Design No.: Front — HW26 Dress Making
Reverse — HW26R Bugler with Toy Donkey
Designer: Walter Hayward
Issued: 1954 - by 1998

Combined with: *Proposal*, HW11
Serving Tea, HW116R
Sleeping in a Rocking Chair, EC1
Toast for Tea Today, SF23
Windy Day, HW27

Shape	USD	CAD	GBP	AUD
Albion cream jug	50.00	75.00	35.00	75.00
Albion jug, ½ pint	100.00	150.00	70.00	150.00
Albion jug, 1 pint	150.00	225.00	100.00	225.00
Albion teapot	50.00	85.00	35.00	95.00
Casino jug, 30s				
with signature	200.00	300.00	150.00	300.00
without signature	150.00	250.00	100.00	250.00
Casino jug, 36s				
with signature	150.00	225.00	100.00	225.00
without signature	125.00	200.00	85.00	200.00
Casino jug, 42s				
with signature	125.00	200.00	90.00	200.00
without signature	100.00	150.00	70.00	150.00
Casino saucer				
with signature	15.00	25.00	10.00	25.00
without signature	7.50	12.00	5.00	12.00
Casino teacup				
with signature	15.00	25.00	10.00	25.00
without signature	7.50	12.00	5.00	12.00
Casino teapot, 24s				
with signature	225.00	350.00	150.00	400.00
without signature	175.00	275.00	125.00	325.00
Casino teapot, 30s				
with signature	200.00	325.00	125.00	350.00
without signature	150.00	225.00	100.00	250.00
Don beaker				
with signature	75.00	125.00	50.00	150.00
without signature	35.00	55.00	25.00	60.00

Shape	USD	CAD	GBP	AUD
Don beaker, one handle				
with signature	75.00	125.00	50.00	150.00
without signature	35.00	55.00	25.00	60.00
Don mug, one handle				
with signature	65.00	100.00	45.00	75.00
without signature	15.00	25.00	10.00	25.00
Don mug, two handles				
with signature	65.00	100.00	45.00	75.00
without signature	15.00	25.00	10.00	25.00
Egg box				
small	225.00	350.00	150.00	400.00
medium	300.00	450.00	200.00	500.00
large	375.00	550.00	250.00	600.00
Hug-a-mug, one handle	10.00	15.00	7.50	15.00
Hug-a-mug, two handles	10.00	15.00	7.50	15.00
Jaffa fruit saucer (plain)				
with signature	70.00	110.00	45.00	125.00
without signature	15.00	25.00	10.00	25.00
Lamp	100.00	150.00	65.00	175.00
Lid of hot water plate				
with signature	125.00	200.00	85.00	225.00
without signature	100.00	150.00	70.00	175.00
Malvern beaker	15.00	25.00	10.00	25.00
Money ball	10.00	15.00	7.50	15.00
Picture plaque, small	20.00	30.00	12.50	30.00
Savings book	15.00	22.50	10.00	22.50
Stratford straight beaker	15.00	22.50	10.00	22.50
Stratford teacup	7.50	12.00	5.00	12.00

Dressing Up, First Version (SF22)

DRESSING UP
First Version

Design No.:   SF22
Designer: Walter Hayward
Issued: 1954 - by 1998
Combined with: *Toast for Tea Today*, SF23

Shape	USD	CAD	GBP	AUD
Albion jug, 1 pint	150.00	225.00	100.00	225.00
Baby plate, round, small				
with signature	30.00	50.00	20.00	60.00
without signature	15.00	25.00	10.00	30.00
Cake stand	150.00	250.00	100.00	300.00
Casino jug, 30s				
with signature	200.00	300.00	150.00	300.00
without signature	150.00	250.00	100.00	250.00
Casino saucer				
with signature	15.00	25.00	10.00	25.00
without signature	7.50	12.00	5.00	12.00
Casino teapot, 30s				
with signature	175.00	275.00	125.00	300.00
without signature	125.00	200.00	85.00	200.00
Cereal / oatmeal bowl				
with signature	25.00	40.00	15.00	45.00
without signature	10.00	15.00	7.50	15.00
Jaffa fruit saucer (plain)	15.00	25.00	10.00	25.00
Hot water plate				
with signature	150.00	225.00	100.00	250.00
without signature	125.00	200.00	85.00	225.00
Picture plaque, large	20.00	30.00	12.50	30.00
Plate, 6 ½"				
with signature	35.00	55.00	25.00	55.00
without signature	20.00	30.00	15.00	30.00
Plate, 8"	25.00	40.00	18.00	40.00

DRESSING UP
Second Version

This design incorporates scenes from SF22 and EC4.

Design No.: None
Designer: Monica Ford based on designs by Walter Hayward
Issued: 1987 - 1993

Shape	USD	CAD	GBP	AUD
Plate, 10 ½"	35.00	55.00	25.00	60.00

Dressing Up, Second Version

DRUMMER

Design No.: EC2
Designer: Barbara Vernon
Issued: 1937 to the present
Combined with:

Bedtime with Dollies, EC125	*Raising Hat*, Style Two, EC7
Cricketer, HW22R	*Reading*, EC122
Drummer and Bugler, EC126	*Sheltering Under an Umbrella*, EC3
Hikers, EC124	*Sleeping in a Rocking Chair*, EC1
Hobby Horse, Style Two, EC121	*Trumpeter*, EC5
Holding Hat and Coat, EC4	*Wheelbarrow Race*, Style One, HW22
Playing with Cup and Spoon, EC6	*Windy Day*, HW27
Playing with Doll and Pram, EC123	

Shape	USD	CAD	GBP	AUD
Albion sugar bowl	30.00	50.00	20.00	50.00
Beaker cover				
with signature	125.00	175.00	75.00	175.00
without signature	85.00	135.00	50.00	150.00
Casino sugar bowl				
with signature	125.00	200.00	85.00	225.00
without signature	100.00	150.00	65.00	175.00
Egg cup				
Style One	40.00	60.00	25.00	65.00
Style Two	80.00	125.00	50.00	135.00
Style Three	**N/I**	**15.00**	**5.00**	**19.95**
Money Ball	**33.75**	**40.00**	**15.00**	**62.95**

Drummer (EC2)

DRUMMER AND BUGLER

Drummer and Bugler (EC126)

Design No.: EC126
Designer: Walter Hayward
Issued: 1959 to the present
Combined with: *Bedtime with Dollies*, EC125
Drummer, EC2
Hat Shop, HW28
Hikers, EC124
Hobby Horse, Style Two, EC121
Holding Hat and Coat, EC4
Playing with Cup and Spoon, EC6
Playing with Doll and Pram, EC123
Raising Hat, Style Two, EC7
Reading, EC122
Sleeping in a Rocking Chair, EC1
Trumpeter, EC5
Trying on Hats, HW28R

Shape	USD	CAD	GBP	AUD
Albion sugar bowl	30.00	50.00	20.00	50.00
Beaker cover	125.00	175.00	75.00	175.00
Egg cup				
Style One	40.00	60.00	25.00	65.00
Style Two	80.00	125.00	50.00	135.00
Style Three	**N/I**	**15.00**	**5.00**	**19.95**
Lid of hot water plate	100.00	150.00	75.00	175.00

The Duet (LF13)

DUET, THE

Design No.:   LF13
Designer: Walter Hayward after Barbara Vernon
Issued: By 1952 - 1970

Shape	USD	CAD	GBP	AUD
Baby plate, oval, large				
with signature	200.00	325.00	150.00	325.00
without signature	150.00	225.00	100.00	225.00
Baby plate, round large				
with signature	150.00	250.00	100.00	275.00
without signature	125.00	200.00	85.00	225.00
Bread and butter plate				
with signature	250.00	400.00	175.00	400.00
without signature	200.00	325.00	150.00	325.00
Cereal / oatmeal bowl				
with signature	50.00	80.00	35.00	80.00
without signature	35.00	55.00	25.00	55.00
Hot water plate				
with signature	150.00	225.00	100.00	250.00
without signature	125.00	200.00	85.00	225.00
Plate, 8"	45.00	70.00	30.00	75.00
Plate, 8 ½"				
with signature	70.00	115.00	45.00	125.00
without signature	45.00	70.00	30.00	75.00
Porridge bowl				
with signature	110.00	175.00	70.00	200.00
without signature	85.00	125.00	55.00	150.00

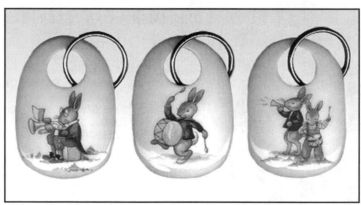

Key fobs commemorating the 2000 Australian Tour
Trumpeter (EC5), *Drummer* (EC2), *Drummer and Bugler* (EC126)

DUNCE

Design No.:	HW1R
Designer:	Barbara Vernon
Issued:	By 1937 - by 1952
Combined with:	*Artist*, HW1
	Embracing at a Window, HW5
	Greetings, HW7
	Netting a Cricket, HW6
	Pressing Trousers, HW14
	Proposal, HW11

Dunce (HW1R)

Shape	USD	CAD	GBP	AUD
Casino jug, 42s				
with signature	300.00	450.00	200.00	500.00
without signature	250.00	375.00	175.00	400.00
Casino sugar bowl, 30s				
with signature	250.00	375.00	175.00	400.00
without signature	175.00	275.00	125.00	325.00
Casino sugar bowl, 36s				
with signature	200.00	325.00	125.00	350.00
without signature	150.00	225.00	100.00	250.00
Casino teacup				
with signature	100.00	150.00	65.00	175.00
without signature	75.00	125.00	50.00	125.00
Casino teapot, 36s				
with signature	350.00	550.00	225.00	650.00
without signature	275.00	400.00	175.00	450.00
Don beaker				
with signature	200.00	325.00	140.00	350.00
without signature	175.00	275.00	125.00	300.00
Don beaker, one handle				
with signature	200.00	325.00	140.00	350.00
without signature	175.00	275.00	125.00	300.00
Don mug, one handle				
with signature	150.00	250.00	100.00	275.00
without signature	125.00	200.00	90.00	225.00
Don mug, two handles				
with signature	150.00	250.00	100.00	275.00
without signature	125.00	200.00	90.00	225.00
Lid of hot water plate				
with signature	150.00	225.00	100.00	250.00
without signature	125.00	200.00	85.00	225.00

FINE WHITE CHINA

Beaker, one handle	Very rare
Rex mug	Very rare

Note: *Dunce* (HW1R) is combined with *Proposal* (HW11) on the Rex mug.

Embracing at a Window (HW5)

EMBRACING AT A WINDOW

Design No.: HW5
Designer: Barbara Vernon
Issued: By 1937 - by 1952
Combined with: *Dunce*, HW1R
Fixing Braces, HW3
Leapfrog, HW12R
Top Hat, HW14R

Shape	USD	CAD	GBP	AUD
Casino saucer	150.00	225.00	100.00	225.00
Casino teacup	150.00	225.00	100.00	225.00
Casino teapot, 30s	650.00	1,200.00	425.00	1,250.00
Don beaker	325.00	475.00	225.00	500.00
Don beaker, one handle	325.00	475.00	225.00	500.00
Don mug, one handle	250.00	400.00	175.00	425.00
Don mug, two handles	250.00	400.00	175.00	425.00
Jaffa fruit saucer	175.00	275.00	125.00	300.00
Plate, 6 ½"	150.00	250.00	100.00	275.00

Note: This design should appear with the Barbara Vernon facsimile signature.

Jam Pot combining *Proposal* (HW11), and *Netting a Cricket* (HW6).

ENGINE PULLING A CARRIAGE / TO THE STATION

Engine Pulling a Carriage (HW17)

To the Station (HW17R)

Design No.: Front — HW17 Engine Pulling a Carriage
Reverse — HW17R To the Station
Designer: Walter Hayward after Barbara Vernon
Issued: By 1952 - by 1998

Combined with: *Family with Pram*, Style One, HW15
Ice Cream on the Beach, HW136R
Ice Cream Vendor, HW23
Raising Hat, Style Two, EC7
See-saw, Style One, SF14
Snowball Fight, HW141R

Shape	USD	CAD	GBP	AUD
Albion cream jug	50.00	75.00	35.00	75.00
Albion jug, ½ pint	100.00	150.00	70.00	150.00
Albion teapot	50.00	85.00	35.00	95.00
Casino jug, 36s				
with signature	175.00	275.00	125.00	275.00
without signature	125.00	200.00	85.00	200.00
Casino jug, 42s				
with signature	150.00	225.00	100.00	225.00
without signature	100.00	150.00	70.00	150.00
Casino saucer				
with signature	22.50	36.00	15.00	36.00
without signature	7.50	12.00	5.00	12.00
Casino sugar bowl, 36s				
with signature	125.00	200.00	85.00	225.00
without signature	100.00	150.00	65.00	175.00
Casino teacup				
with signature	22.50	36.00	15.00	36.00
without signature	7.50	12.00	5.00	12.00
Casino teapot, 24s				
with signature	275.00	400.00	175.00	450.00
without signature	175.00	275.00	125.00	325.00
Casino teapot, 30s				
with signature	250.00	375.00	165.00	400.00
without signature	150.00	225.00	100.00	250.00
Don beaker				
with signature	75.00	125.00	50.00	150.00
without signature	35.00	55.00	25.00	60.00
Don beaker, one handle				
with signature	75.00	125.00	50.00	150.00

Shape	USD	CAD	GBP	AUD
Don beaker, one handle				
without signature	35.00	55.00	25.00	60.00
Don mug, one handle				
with signature	65.00	100.00	45.00	75.00
without signature	15.00	25.00	10.00	25.00
Don mug, two handles				
with signature	65.00	100.00	45.00	75.00
without signature	15.00	25.00	10.00	25.00
Egg box				
small	225.00	350.00	150.00	400.00
medium	300.00	450.00	200.00	500.00
large	375.00	550.00	250.00	600.00
Jaffa fruit saucer (plain)	15.00	25.00	10.00	25.00
Lamp	100.00	150.00	65.00	175.00
Lid of hot water plate				
with signature	150.00	225.00	100.00	225.00
without signature	100.00	150.00	70.00	175.00
Malvern beaker	15.00	25.00	10.00	25.00
Money ball	10.00	15.00	7.50	15.00
Picture plaque, small	20.00	30.00	12.50	30.00
Plate, 6 ½"				
with signature	35.00	55.00	25.00	55.00
without signature	20.00	30.00	15.00	30.00
Plate, 7 ½"				
with signature	35.00	55.00	25.00	55.00
without signature	20.00	30.00	15.00	30.00
Savings book	15.00	22.50	10.00	22.50
Stratford straight beaker	15.00	22.50	10.00	22.50
Stratford teacup	7.50	12.00	5.00	12.00

FAIRGROUND THEME — *Frank Endersby*

Swinging Boats (31)

SWINGING BOATS

Design No.:	31 Swinging Boats
Designer:	Frank Endersby
Issued:	1995 to the present

Shape	USD	CAD	GBP	AUD
Baby plate, round, small	N/I	46.00	14.00	62.95
Cereal / oatmeal bowl	N/I	33.00	11.00	49.95
Plate, 6 ½″	N/I	25.00	8.00	34.95
Plate, 8″	N/I	35.00	11.00	49.95

Coconut Shy (32)

COCONUT SHY / PLAYING WITH BALLOONS

Design No.:	Front — 32 Coconut Shy
	Reverse — 33 Playing with Balloons
Designer:	Frank Endersby
Issued:	1995 to the present
Combined with:	*Butterfly Net, (6)

Shape	USD	CAD	GBP	AUD
Hug-a-mug, one handle	30.00	33.00	11.00	49.95
Hug-a-mug, two handles	32.50	39.00	12.00	56.95
Divider dish	50.00	75.00	35.00	75.00
Malvern beaker	15.00	25.00	10.00	25.00
Money ball	33.75	40.00	15.00	62.95
Stratford teacup	7.50	12.00	5.00	12.00

* Indicates scene on divider dish.

Note: 1. Bold type in the listing tables indicate a current design on a current shape.
  2. N/I, Not issued individually. The item(s) will be found only in boxed sets in that market.

Playing with Balloons (33)

FAMILY AT BREAKFAST

Design No.:	HW12
Designer:	Barbara Vernon
Issued:	By 1937 - by 1952
Combined with:	*Bedtime in Bunks*, SF3
	Chicken Pulling a Cart, SF8
	Cycling, HW15R
	Feeding the Baby, HW13
	Fixing Braces, HW3
	Footballer, HW13R
	Golfer, HW4R
	Kissing Under the Mistletoe, HW11R
	Lambeth Walk, HW16
	Leapfrog, HW12R
	Proposal, HW11
	Pulling On Trousers, HW2
	Raising Hat, Style One, HW16R
	Smoking in the Doorway, SF2
	Washing Day, HW8R
	Wedding, LFd

Family at Breakfast (HW12)

Shape	USD	CAD	GBP	AUD
Baby plate, round, small				
with signature	125.00	200.00	90.00	200.00
without signature	100.00	150.00	70.00	175.00
Candle holder	2,000.00	3,000.00	1,250.00	4,000.00
Casino jug, 42s				
with signature	250.00	400.00	175.00	400.00
without signature	200.00	325.00	150.00	325.00
Casino saucer				
with signature	75.00	125.00	50.00	125.00
without signature	50.00	75.00	35.00	75.00
Casino sugar bowl, 30s				
with signature	200.00	325.00	125.00	350.00
without signature	150.00	225.00	100.00	250.00
Casino sugar bowl, 36s				
with signature	175.00	275.00	125.00	325.00
without signature	125.00	200.00	85.00	225.00
Casino teacup				
with signature	75.00	125.00	50.00	125.00
without signature	50.00	75.00	35.00	75.00
Casino teapot, 30s				
with signature	325.00	500.00	225.00	550.00
without signature	250.00	400.00	175.00	450.00
Casino teapot, 36s				
with signature	250.00	375.00	165.00	400.00
without signature	225.00	350.00	150.00	375.00
Cup / mug, large			Rare	
Don beaker				
with signature	150.00	250.00	110.00	275.00
without signature	125.00	200.00	90.00	225.00

Shape	USD	CAD	GBP	AUD
Don beaker, one handle				
with signature	150.00	250.00	110.00	275.00
without signature	125.00	200.00	90.00	225.00
Don mug, one handle				
with signature	100.00	150.00	70.00	150.00
without signature	75.00	125.00	50.00	125.00
Don mug, two handles				
with signature	100.00	150.00	70.00	150.00
without signature	75.00	125.00	50.00	125.00
Hot water plate				
with signature	175.00	275.00	125.00	325.00
without signature	125.00	200.00	85.00	225.00
Jaffa fruit saucer (wavy)				
with signature	70.00	110.00	45.00	125.00
without signature	60.00	95.00	40.00	110.00
Jam pot	1,500.00	2,500.00	1,000.00	3,000.00
Lid of hot water plate				
with signature	125.00	200.00	85.00	225.00
without signature	100.00	150.00	70.00	175.00
Plate, 6 ½"				
with signature	90.00	150.00	60.00	175.00
without signature	60.00	100.00	40.00	100.00
Plate, 7 ½"				
with signature	90.00	150.00	60.00	175.00
without signature	60.00	100.00	40.00	100.00

FINE WHITE CHINA

Shape			
Beaker, one handle		Very Rare	
Rex mug		Very Rare	
Saucer		Very Rare	
Teacup		Very Rare	

Note: *Family at Breakfast* (HW12) is combined with *Gardener with Wheelbarrow* (HW9R) on the fine white china beaker.

Family Cycling (LF11)

FAMILY CYCLING

Design No.: LF11
Designer: Walter Hayward
Issued: By 1952 - 1970

Shape	USD	CAD	GBP	AUD
Baby plate, oval, large				
with signature	200.00	325.00	150.00	325.00
without signature	150.00	225.00	100.00	225.00
Baby plate, round large				
with signature	150.00	250.00	100.00	275.00
without signature	125.00	200.00	85.00	225.00
Bread and butter plate				
with signature	250.00	400.00	175.00	400.00
without signature	200.00	325.00	150.00	325.00
Cereal / oatmeal bowl				
with signature	50.00	80.00	35.00	80.00
without signature	35.00	55.00	25.00	55.00
Hot water plate				
with signature	150.00	225.00	100.00	250.00
without signature	125.00	200.00	85.00	225.00
Plate, 8 ½"				
with signature	70.00	115.00	45.00	125.00
without signature	45.00	70.00	30.00	75.00
Porridge bowl				
with signature	110.00	175.00	70.00	200.00
without signature	85.00	125.00	55.00	150.00

Note: Retirement dates are all approximate. When a design is retired all remaining stocks of the retired litho prints are used until exhausted.

FAMILY GOING OUT ON WASHING DAY

Design No.: HW8
Designer: Barbara Vernon
Issued: By 1937 - by 1967
Combined with: *Chicken Pulling a Cart*, SF8
Cycling, HW15R
Leapfrog, HW12R
Netting a Cricket, HW6
Sheltering Under Umbrella, EC3
Trumpeter, EC5
Washing Day, HW8R

Family Going out on Washing Day (HW8)

Shape	USD	CAD	GBP	AUD
Casino jug, 24s				
with signature	600.00	950.00	425.00	975.00
without signature	500.00	800.00	350.00	825.00
Casino saucer				
with signature	100.00	150.00	65.00	175.00
without signature	75.00	125.00	50.00	125.00
Casino sugar bowl, 36s				
with signature	200.00	325.00	125.00	350.00
without signature	150.00	225.00	100.00	250.00
Casino teacup				
with signature	100.00	150.00	65.00	175.00
without signature	75.00	125.00	50.00	125.00
Casino teapot, 30s				
with signature	400.00	600.00	275.00	700.00
without signature	300.00	450.00	200.00	500.00
Don beaker				
with signature	200.00	325.00	140.00	350.00
without signature	125.00	200.00	80.00	225.00
Don beaker, one handle				
with signature	200.00	325.00	140.00	350.00
without signature	125.00	200.00	80.00	225.00
Don mug, one handle				
with signature	150.00	250.00	100.00	275.00
without signature	65.00	100.00	45.00	100.00
Don mug, two handles				
with signature	150.00	250.00	100.00	275.00
without signature	65.00	100.00	45.00	100.00
Jaffa fruit saucer				
plain rim	95.00	150.00	65.00	165.00
wavy rim	95.00	150.00	65.00	165.00
Plate, 6 ½"				
with signature	90.00	150.00	60.00	175.00
without signature	60.00	100.00	40.00	100.00

Note: Four standard sizes of Casino jugs exist; ¾, 1, 1½ and
2 pint capacity. Only these sizes are listed in the shape
book. However in between sizes are found in 1¼, 1¾
and 2¼ pint capacity which may have been standard
sizes modified for numerous reasons.

Family in the Garden (SF135)

FAMILY IN THE GARDEN

Design No.:   SF135
Designer: Walter Hayward
Issued: 1967 - by 1998

Shape	USD	CAD	GBP	AUD
Albion jug, 1 pint	150.00	225.00	100.00	225.00
Baby plate, round, large	50.00	75.00	35.00	85.00
Baby plate, round, small	20.00	30.00	15.00	30.00
Cake stand	150.00	250.00	100.00	300.00
Cereal / oatmeal bowl	10.00	15.00	7.50	15.00
Hot water plate	125.00	200.00	85.00	225.00
Jaffa fruit saucer (plain)	15.00	25.00	10.00	25.00
Picture plaque, large	20.00	30.00	12.50	30.00
Plate, 8"	25.00	40.00	18.00	40.00

FAMILY PHOTOGRAPH

Design No.:   LF15
Designer: Walter Hayward
Issued: By 1954 - 1970

Shape	USD	CAD	GBP	AUD
Baby plate, oval, large				
with signature	200.00	325.00	150.00	325.00
without signature	150.00	225.00	100.00	225.00
Baby plate, round large				
with signature	150.00	250.00	100.00	275.00
without signature	125.00	200.00	85.00	225.00
Bread and butter plate				
with signature	300.00	450.00	200.00	500.00
without signature	150.00	225.00	100.00	250.00
Cereal / oatmeal bowl				
with signature	50.00	80.00	35.00	80.00
without signature	35.00	55.00	25.00	55.00
Plate, 8"	45.00	70.00	30.00	75.00
Plate, 8 ½"	45.00	70.00	30.00	75.00
Porridge bowl				
with signature	110.00	175.00	70.00	200.00
without signature	85.00	125.00	55.00	150.00

Family Photograph (LF15)

FAMILY WITH PRAM
Style One

Design No.:   HW15
Designer: Barbara Vernon
Issued: By 1937 - by 1952
Combined with: *Cycling*, HW15R
               Engine Pulling a Carriage, HW17
               Footballer, HW13R
               Leapfrog, HW12R
               Proposal, HW11
               Pulling on Trousers, HW2
               Raising Hat, Style One, HW16R
               Raising Hat, Style Two, EC7
               Rowboat, HW21
               Washing in the Open Air, HW10R

Family with Pram, Style One (HW15)

Shape	USD	CAD	GBP	AUD	Shape	USD	CAD	GBP	AUD
Baby plate, oval, large	200.00	325.00	150.00	325.00	Don beaker	150.00	250.00	110.00	275.00
Baby plate, round, large	150.00	250.00	100.00	275.00	Don beaker, one handle	150.00	250.00	110.00	275.00
Casino jug, 30s	300.00	475.00	200.00	475.00	Don mug, one handle	100.00	150.00	70.00	150.00
Casino saucer	75.00	125.00	50.00	125.00	Don mug, two handles	100.00	150.00	70.00	150.00
Casino sugar bowl, 30s	200.00	325.00	125.00	350.00	Jaffa fruit saucer	60.00	95.00	40.00	100.00
Casino teacup	75.00	125.00	50.00	125.00	Jam pot	1,500.00	2,500.00	1,000.00	3,000.00
Casino teapot, 24s	375.00	550.00	250.00	600.00	Lid of hot water plate	150.00	225.00	100.00	250.00
Casino teapot, 30s	325.00	500.00	225.00	550.00	Plate, 6 ½"	60.00	95.00	40.00	100.00

Note: 1. This design should appear with the Barbara Vernon facsimile signature.
       2. This design is found on in-between sizes of Casino jugs.

Family with Pram (HW15) / Raising Hat (HW16R)

FAMILY WITH PRAM / RAISING HAT

The unusual combination of *Family with Pram*, Style One (HW15) and *Raising Hat*, Style One (HW16R), has been found on large round and oval baby plates, a casino teapot and a 7½" plate.

Design No.:   HW15 / HW16R
Designer: Barbara Vernon
Issued: By 1937 - by 1952

Shape	USD	CAD	GBP	AUD
Baby plate, oval, large		Rare		
Baby plate, round, large		Rare		
Casino teapot, 30s		Rare		
Plate, 7 ½"		Rare		

Family with Pram, Style Two (CT14)

Standing by Pram (CT6)

FAMILY WITH PRAM
Style Two

Design No.:   Front — CT14 Family with Pram
                 Reverse — CT6 Standing by Pram
Designer: Colin Twinn
Issued: 1989 - 1993
Combined with: *Bunny on Rocking Horse*, CT29
                 Father Bunnykins with Fishing Rod, CT27
                 Home from Fishing, CT26
                 Nursery, First Version, CT19
                 Picking Daisies, CT4

Shape	USD	CAD	GBP	AUD
Albion cream jug	50.00	75.00	35.00	75.00
Albion jug, ½ pint	100.00	150.00	70.00	150.00
Albion jug, 1 pint	150.00	225.00	100.00	225.00
Cake stand	150.00	250.00	100.00	300.00
Divider dish	75.00	125.00	50.00	125.00
Hug-a-mug, one handle	10.00	15.00	7.50	15.00
Hug-a-mug, two handles	10.00	15.00	7.50	15.00
Lamp	100.00	150.00	65.00	175.00
Malvern beaker	15.00	25.00	10.00	25.00
Money ball	10.00	15.00	7.50	15.00
Stratford teacup	7.50	12.00	5.00	12.00

Note: *Standing by Pram*, CT6 is combined with *Picking Daisies*, CT4 on Albion 1 pint and ½ pint jugs.

FEEDING THE BABY

Feeding the Baby (HW13)

Design No.: HW13
Designer: Barbara Vernon
Issued: By 1937 - by 1967
Combined with: *Bedtime in Bunks*, 3F3
Cycling, HW15R
Family at Breakfast, HW12
Footballer, HW13R
Golfer, HW4R
Kissing under the Mistletoe, HW11R

Leapfrog, HW12R
Pressing Trousers, HW14
Pulling on Trousers, HW2
Raising Hat, Style One, HW16R
Santa Claus, SF9
Sleeping in a Rocking Chair, EC1
Top Hat, HW14R
Trumpeter, EC5
Washing in the Open Air, HW10R

Shape	USD	CAD	GBP	AUD
Baby plate, round, small				
with signature	75.00	125.00	50.00	125.00
without signature	50.00	80.00	35.00	80.00
Candle holder	2,000.00	3,000.00	1,250.00	4,000.00
Casino jug, 36s				
with signature	300.00	475.00	200.00	475.00
without signature	250.00	400.00	175.00	400.00
Casino jug, 42s				
with signature	250.00	400.00	175.00	400.00
without signature	200.00	325.00	150.00	325.00
Casino saucer				
with signature	75.00	125.00	50.00	125.00
without signature	50.00	75.00	35.00	75.00
Casino sugar bowl, 30s				
with signature	200.00	325.00	125.00	350.00
without signature	150.00	225.00	100.00	250.00
Casino teacup				
with signature	75.00	125.00	50.00	125.00
without signature	50.00	75.00	35.00	75.00
Casino teapot, 36s				
with signature	250.00	375.00	165.00	400.00
without signature	225.00	350.00	150.00	400.00
Don beaker				
with signature	150.00	250.00	110.00	275.00
without signature	85.00	135.00	60.00	150.00
Don beaker, one handle				
with signature	150.00	250.00	110.00	275.00

Shape	USD	CAD	GBP	AUD
Don beaker, one handle				
without signature	85.00	135.00	60.00	150.00
Don mug, one handle				
with silver rim		Very rare		
with signature	100.00	150.00	70.00	150.00
without signature	35.00	55.00	25.00	60.00
Don mug, two handles				
with signature	100.00	150.00	70.00	150.00
without signature	35.00	55.00	25.00	60.00
Jaffa fruit saucer				
plain rim	60.00	95.00	40.00	100.00
wavy rim	60.00	95.00	40.00	100.00
Jam pot	1,500.00	2,500.00	1,000.00	3,000.00
Lid of hot water plate				
with signature	150.00	225.00	100.00	250.00
without signature	125.00	200.00	85.00	225.00
Plate, 6 ½"				
with signature	60.00	95.00	40.00	100.00
without signature	40.00	65.00	25.00	70.00
Sugar bowl with handles	3,500.00	6,000.00	2,500.00	7,000.00

FINE WHITE CHINA

Shape				
Saucer		Very Rare		
Teacup		Very Rare		

FIRE STATION THEME — Frank Endersby

Washing the Fire Engine (10)

WASHING THE FIRE ENGINE

Design No.:	10 Washing the Fire Engine
Designer:	Frank Endersby
Issued:	1995 to the present

Shape	USD	CAD	GBP	AUD
Cereal / oatmeal bowl	N/I	**33.00**	**11.00**	**49.95**
Jaffa fruit saucer	15.00	25.00	10.00	25.00
Plate, 6 ½"	N/I	**25.00**	**8.00**	**34.95**
Plate, 8"	N/I	**35.00**	**11.00**	**49.95**

Pumping Water (11)

PUMPING WATER / TRYING ON HAT

Design No.:	Front — 11 Pumping Water
	Reverse — 12 Trying on Hat
Designer:	Frank Endersby
Issued:	1995 to the present
Combined with:	*Carrying Net, (6)

Shape	USD	CAD	GBP	AUD
Hug-a-mug, one handle	**30.00**	**33.00**	**11.00**	**49.95**
Hug-a-mug, two handles	**32.50**	**39.00**	**12.00**	**56.95**
Divider dish	50.00	75.00	35.00	75.00
Malvern beaker	15.00	25.00	10.00	25.00
Money ball	**33.75**	**40.00**	**15.00**	**62.95**
Stratford teacup	7.50	12.00	5.00	12.00

* Indicates scenes on divider dish.

Trying on Hat (12)

Note:
1. Bold type in the listing tables indicate a current design on a current shape.
2. N/I, Not issued individually. The item(s) will be found only in boxed sets in that market.

FISHING THEME — Frank Endersby

FISHING AT THE POND

Design No.: 4 Fishing at the Pond
Designer: Frank Endersby
Issued: 1995 to the present

Shape	USD	CAD	GBP	AUD
Baby plate, round, small	N/I	33.00	11.00	49.95
Jaffa fruit saucer	15.00	25.00	10.00	25.00
Plate, 6 ½"	N/I	25.00	8.00	34.95
Plate, 8"	N/I	35.00	11.00	49.95

Fishing at the Pond (4)

Resting by Pond (5)

RESTING BY POND / CARRYING NET

Design No.: Front — 5 Resting by Pond
Reverse — 6 Carrying Net
Designer: Frank Endersby
Issued: 1995 to the present
Combined with: *Playing with Balloons*, (33)

Shape	USD	CAD	GBP	AUD
Hug-a-mug, one handle	30.00	33.00	11.00	49.95
Hug-a-mug, two handles	32.50	39.00	12.00	56.95
Divider dish	50.00	75.00	35.00	75.00
Money ball	33.75	40.00	15.00	62.95
Stratford teacup	7.50	12.00	5.00	12.00

* Indicates scene on divider dish.

Carrying Net (6)

Fishing in the Goldfish Bowl (HW3R)

FISHING IN THE GOLDFISH BOWL

Design No.:	HW3R
Designer:	Barbara Vernon
Issued:	By 1937 - by 1952
Combined with:	*Artist*, HW1
	Fixing Braces, HW3
	Mr. Piggly's Stores, SF14
	Netting a Cricket, HW6
	Playing with Cup and Spoon, EC6
	Pressing Trousers, HW14
	Pulling on Trousers, HW2
	Sheltering Under an Umbrella, EC3

Shape	USD	CAD	GBP	AUD
Casino jug, 24s	600.00	950.00	425.00	975.00
Casino jug, 36s	400.00	600.00	275.00	700.00
Casino teacup	100.00	150.00	65.00	175.00
Don beaker	200.00	325.00	140.00	350.00
Don mug, one handle	150.00	250.00	100.00	275.00

FINE WHITE CHINA

Teacup	Very Rare

Note: This design should appear with the Barbara Vernon facsimile signature.

FISHING ON THE PIER

Design No.:	LF3
Designer:	Barbara Vernon
Issued:	By 1940 - by 1952

Shape	USD	CAD	GBP	AUD
Baby plate, round, large				
with silver rim			Rare	
with signature	450.00	675.00	325.00	700.00
without signature	400.00	600.00	275.00	625.00
Bread and butter plate				
with signature	800.00	1,250.00	500.00	1,600.00
without signature	600.00	1,000.00	400.00	1,100.00
Cereal / oatmeal bowl				
with signature	225.00	350.00	150.00	375.00
without signature	200.00	325.00	125.00	350.00
Plate, 8 ½"				
with signature	300.00	475.00	200.00	500.00
without signature	250.00	400.00	175.00	425.00
Porridge plate				
with signature	400.00	625.00	275.00	650.00
without signature	375.00	575.00	250.00	600.00

Fishing on the Pier (LF3)

FIXING BRACES

Design No.:   HW3
Designer: Barbara Vernon
Issued: By 1937 - by 1952
Combined with: *Chicken Pulling a Cart*, SF8
                Cycling, HW15R
                Embracing at a Window, HW5
                Family at Breakfast, HW12
                Fishing in the Goldfish Bowl, HW3R
                Going Shopping, SF10
                Leapfrog, HW12R
                Smoking in the Doorway, SF2

Fixing Braces (HW3)

Shape	USD	CAD	GBP	AUD
Candle holder	2,000.00	3,000.00	1,250.00	4,000.00
Casino jug, 24s	400.00	625.00	275.00	650.00
Casino jug, 36s	300.00	475.00	200.00	475.00
Casino saucer	75.00	125.00	50.00	125.00
Casino teacup	75.00	125.00	50.00	125.00
Cup / mug, large			Rare	
Don beaker	150.00	250.00	110.00	275.00
Don beaker, one handle	150.00	250.00	110.00	275.00
Don mug, one handle	100.00	150.00	70.00	150.00
Don mug, two handles	100.00	150.00	70.00	150.00
Jaffa fruit saucer				
plain rim	95.00	150.00	65.00	175.00
wavy rim	60.00	95.00	40.00	100.00
Plate, 6 ½"	60.00	95.00	40.00	100.00

FINE WHITE CHINA
Night light   Very Rare
Rex mug   Very Rare

Note: This design should appear with the Barbara Vernon
facsimile signature.

Flying Kites (SF133)

FLYING KITES

Design No.:   SF133
Designer: Walter Hayward
Issued: 1967 - by 1998

Shape	USD	CAD	GBP	AUD
Baby plate, round, small	20.00	30.00	15.00	30.00
Cake stand	150.00	250.00	100.00	300.00
Casino saucer	7.50	12.00	5.00	12.00
Cereal / oatmeal bowl	10.00	15.00	7.50	15.00
Jaffa fruit saucer (plain)	15.00	25.00	10.00	25.00
Hot water plate	125.00	200.00	85.00	225.00
Picture plaque, large	20.00	30.00	12.50	30.00
Plate, 6 ½"	20.00	30.00	15.00	30.00
Plate, 8"	25.00	40.00	18.00	40.00

Footballer (HW13R)

FOOTBALLER

Design No.:	HW13R	
Designer:	Barbara Vernon	
Issued:	By 1937 - by 1967	
Combined with:	*Cuddling under a Mushroom*, HW4	
	Family at Breakfast, HW12	
	Family with Pram, Style One, HW15	
	Feeding the Baby, HW13	
	Gardening, Style One (HW9)	
	Lambeth Walk, HW16	
	Pressing Trousers, HW14	
	Proposal, HW11	
	Reading the Times, HW2R	
	Sleeping in a Rocking Chair, EC1	

Shape	USD	CAD	GBP	AUD
Casino jug, 42s				
with signature	250.00	400.00	175.00	400.00
without signature	200.00	325.00	150.00	325.00
Casino sugar bowl, 36s				
with signature	175.00	275.00	125.00	325.00
without signature	125.00	200.00	85.00	225.00
Casino teacup				
with signature	75.00	125.00	50.00	125.00
without signature	50.00	75.00	35.00	75.00
Don beaker				
with signature	150.00	250.00	110.00	275.00
without signature	85.00	135.00	60.00	150.00
Don beaker, one handle				
with signature	150.00	250.00	110.00	275.00
without signature	85.00	135.00	60.00	150.00
Don mug, one handle				
with silver rim			Rare	
with signature	100.00	150.00	70.00	150.00
without signature	35.00	55.00	25.00	55.00
Don mug, two handles				
with signature	100.00	150.00	70.00	150.00
without signature	35.00	55.00	25.00	55.00
Lid of hot water plate				
with signature	150.00	225.00	100.00	250.00
without signature	125.00	200.00	85.00	225.00
Sugar bowl with handles		Very rare		

FINE WHITE CHINA

Rex mug	Very Rare
Teacup	Very Rare

Note: On the fine white china Rex mug *Lambeth Walk*, First Version (HW16) is combined with the *Footballer* (HW13R).

FRIGHTENING SPIDER

Design No.:	SF4
Designer:	Barbara Vernon
Issued:	By 1937 - by 1952
Combined with:	*Conducting the Orchestra*, LF5
	Greetings, HW7
	Medicine Time, SF1
	Pressing Trousers, HW14

Shape	USD	CAD	GBP	AUD
Baby plate, round, large	150.00	250.00	100.00	275.00
Baby plate, round, small	75.00	125.00	50.00	125.00
Casino jug, 24s	400.00	625.00	275.00	650.00
Casino jug, 36s	300.00	475.00	200.00	475.00
Casino saucer	75.00	125.00	50.00	125.00
Casino teapot, 24s	375.00	550.00	250.00	600.00
Cereal / oatmeal bowl	50.00	80.00	35.00	80.00
Jaffa fruit saucer				
plain rim	95.00	150.00	65.00	175.00
wavy rim	60.00	95.00	40.00	100.00
Hot water plate	175.00	275.00	125.00	325.00
Plate, 6 ½"	60.00	95.00	40.00	100.00
Plate, 7"	60.00	95.00	40.00	100.00
Plate, 7 ½"	60.00	95.00	40.00	100.00
Plate, 8"	70.00	115.00	45.00	125.00

FINE WHITE CHINA

Saucer	Very Rare
Teacup	Very Rare

Frightening Spider (SF4)

Note: This design should appear with the Barbara Vernon facsimile signature. A round baby plate has been recorded featuring the facsimile name of Dorothy Vernon instead of Barbara Vernon.

Frightening Spider with
"Dorothy Vernon" facsimile name

Fun in the Snow

FUN IN THE SNOW
CHRISTMAS TREE ORNAMENT

This Christmas tree ornament, which has a rabbit-shaped rim, was commissioned by Royal Doulton U.S.A. and produced in the U.S.A. The words *Fun in the Snow* appear on the reverse.

Design No.:	None
Designer:	Frank Endersby
Issued:	1995 - 1995
Series:	Christmas Tree Ornaments

Shape	USD	CAD	GBP	AUD
Christmas tree ornament	40.00	65.00	25.00	70.00

Note: For other Christmas ornaments in this series see page 42, 44, 143 and 165.

GAME OF GOLF

Game of Golf (SF11)

Design No.:	SF11
Designer:	Barbara Vernon
Issued:	By 1940 - by 1952
Combined with:	*Gardening*, Style One, HW9
	Picnic, Second Version, LF10
	Pulling on Trousers, HW2

Shape	USD	CAD	GBP	AUD
Baby plate, round, small				
with signature	75.00	125.00	150.00	125.00
without signature	50.00	80.00	35.00	80.00
Baby plate, round, large				
with signature	150.00	250.00	100.00	275.00
without signature	125.00	200.00	85.00	225.00
Casino jug, 36s				
with signature	300.00	475.00	200.00	475.00
without signature	250.00	400.00	175.00	400.00
Casino saucer				
with signature	75.00	125.00	50.00	125.00
without signature	50.00	75.00	35.00	75.00
Casino teapot, 24s				
with signature	375.00	550.00	250.00	600.00
without signature	300.00	450.00	200.00	500.00
Casino teapot, 30s				
with signature	400.00	600.00	275.00	700.00
without signature	300.00	450.00	200.00	500.00
Cereal / oatmeal bowl				
with signature	50.00	80.00	35.00	80.00
without signature	35.00	55.00	25.00	55.00
Jaffa fruit saucer				
plain rim	95.00	150.00	65.00	175.00
wavy rim	60.00	95.00	40.00	100.00
Plate, 6 ½"				
with signature	60.00	95.00	40.00	100.00
without signature	40.00	65.00	25.00	70.00
Plate, 7 ½"				
with signature	60.00	95.00	40.00	100.00
without signature	40.00	65.00	25.00	70.00

Note: See also *Golfer* (HW4R) page 87.

GARAGE THEME — *Frank Endersby*

PETROL IN THE SPORTS CAR

Design No.:	37 Petrol in the Sports Car
Designer:	Frank Endersby
Issued:	1995 to the present

Shape	USD	CAD	GBP	AUD
Baby plate, round, small	N/I	33.00	11.00	49.95
Plate, 6 ½"	N/I	25.00	8.00	34.95
Plate, 8"	N/I	35.00	11.00	49.95

Petrol in the Sports Car (37)

Pumping Tyre (38)

PUMPING TYRE / SITTING ON OIL DRUM

Design No.:	Front — 38 Pumping Tyre
	Reverse — 39 Sitting on Oil Drum
Designer:	Frank Endersby
Issued:	1995 to the present
Combined with:	*Pillar Money Box*

Shape	USD	CAD	GBP	AUD
Hug-a-mug, one handle	30.00	33.00	11.00	49.95
Hug-a-mug, two handles	32.50	39.00	12.00	56.95
Malvern beaker	15.00	25.00	10.00	25.00

Sitting on Oil Drum (39)

Gardener with Wheelbarrow (HW9R)

GARDENER WITH WHEELBARROW

Design No.:	HW9R
Designer:	Barbara Vernon
Issued:	By 1937 - by 1967
Combined with:	*Chicken Pulling a Cart*, SF8
	Gardening, Style One, HW9
	Leapfrog, HW12R
	Netting a Cricket, HW6

Shape	USD	CAD	GBP	AUD
Casino jug, 42s				
with signature	250.00	400.00	175.00	400.00
without signature	200.00	325.00	150.00	325.00
Casino sugar bowl, 30s				
with signature	200.00	325.00	125.00	350.00
without signature	150.00	225.00	100.00	250.00
Casino sugar bowl, 36s				
with signature	175.00	275.00	125.00	325.00
without signature	125.00	200.00	85.00	225.00
Casino teacup				
with signature	75.00	125.00	50.00	125.00
without signature	50.00	75.00	35.00	75.00
Cup / mug, large		Rare		
Don beaker				
with signature	150.00	250.00	100.00	275.00
without signature	85.00	135.00	60.00	150.00
Don mug, one handle				
with silver rim		Rare		
with signature	100.00	150.00	70.00	150.00
without signature	35.00	55.00	25.00	60.00
Don mug, two handles				
with signature	100.00	150.00	70.00	150.00
without signature	35.00	55.00	25.00	60.00
Lid of hot water plate				
with signature	150.00	225.00	100.00	250.00
without signature	125.00	200.00	85.00	225.00

Note: Retirement dates are all approximate. When a design is retired all remaining stocks of the retired litho prints are used until exhausted.

GARDENING
Style One

Gardening, Style One (HW9)

Design No.: HW9
Designer: Barbara Vernon
Issued: By 1937 - by 1967

Combined with: *Asleep in the Open Air*, HW10
Footballer, HW13R
Game of Golf, SF11
Gardener with Wheelbarrow, HW9R
Greetings, HW7
Leapfrog, HW12R
Washing in the Open Air, HW10R

Shape	USD	CAD	GBP	AUD
Baby plate, round, small				
with signature	125.00	200.00	90.00	200.00
without signature	100.00	150.00	70.00	175.00
Casino jug, 36s				
with signature	400.00	600.00	275.00	700.00
without signature	350.00	550.00	225.00	650.00
Casino jug, 42s				
with signature	300.00	450.00	200.00	500.00
without signature	250.00	375.00	175.00	400.00
Casino saucer				
with signature	100.00	150.00	65.00	175.00
without signature	75.00	125.00	50.00	125.00
Casino sugar bowl, 36s				
with signature	200.00	325.00	125.00	350.00
without signature	150.00	225.00	100.00	250.00
Casino teacup				
with signature	100.00	150.00	65.00	175.00
without signature	75.00	125.00	50.00	125.00
Casino teapot, 24s				
with signature	500.00	800.00	350.00	950.00
without signature	400.00	700.00	300.00	850.00
Cereal / oatmeal bowl				
with signature	110.00	175.00	75.00	200.00
without signature	90.00	150.00	60.00	175.00

Shape	USD	CAD	GBP	AUD
Don beaker				
with signature	200.00	325.00	140.00	350.00
without signature	125.00	200.00	80.00	225.00
Don beaker, one handle				
with signature	200.00	325.00	140.00	350.00
without signature	125.00	200.00	80.00	225.00
Don mug, one handle				
with silver rim			Rare	
with signature	150.00	250.00	100.00	275.00
without signature	65.00	100.00	45.00	100.00
Don mug, two handles				
with signature	150.00	250.00	100.00	275.00
without signature	65.00	100.00	45.00	100.00
Jaffa fruit saucer				
plain rim	95.00	150.00	65.00	165.00
wavy rim	95.00	150.00	65.00	165.00
Jam pot	1,500.00	2,500.00	1,000.00	3,000.00
Lid of hot water plate				
with signature	150.00	225.00	100.00	250.00
without signature	125.00	200.00	85.00	225.00
Plate, 6 ½"				
with signature	90.00	150.00	60.00	175.00
without signature	60.00	100.00	40.00	100.00

GARDENING THEME — *Frank Endersby*

Gardening, Style Two (55)

GARDENING
Style Two

Design No.:   55 Gardening
Designer: Frank Endersby
Issued: 1995 to the present

Shape	USD	CAD	GBP	AUD
Baby plate, round, small	**N/I**	**33.00**	**11.00**	**49.95**
Cake stand	150.00	250.00	100.00	300.00
Plate, 6 ½″	**N/I**	**25.00**	**8.00**	**34.95**
Plate, 8″	**N/I**	**35.00**	**11.00**	**49.95**
Plate, 10 ½″	35.00	55.00	25.00	60.00

Playing in Tree House (56)

PLAYING IN TREE HOUSE / RESTING IN WHEELBARROW

Design No.:   Front — 56 Playing in Tree House
                 Reverse — 57 Resting in Wheelbarrow
Designer: Frank Endersby
Issued: 1995 to the present
Combined with: *Butterfly Net,* (6)

Shape	USD	CAD	GBP	AUD
Hug-a-mug, one handle	**30.00**	**33.00**	**11.00**	**49.95**
Hug-a-mug, two handles	**32.50**	**39.00**	**12.00**	**56.95**
Divider Dish	50.00	75.00	35.00	75.00
Money Ball	**33.75**	**40.00**	**15.00**	**62.95**

* Indicates scene on divider dish.

Resting in Wheelbarrow (57)

GEOGRAPHY LESSON

Design No.:	LF17
Designer:	Walter Hayward
Issued:	1954 - 1970

Shape	USD	CAD	GBP	AUD
Baby plate, oval, large				
with signature	200.00	325.00	150.00	325.00
without signature	150.00	225.00	100.00	225.00
Baby plate, round, large				
with signature	150.00	250.00	100.00	275.00
without signature	125.00	200.00	85.00	225.00
Bread and butter plate				
with signature	250.00	400.00	175.00	400.00
without signature	200.00	325.00	150.00	325.00
Cereal / oatmeal bowl				
with signature	50.00	80.00	35.00	80.00
without signature	35.00	55.00	25.00	55.00
Plate, 8"	45.00	70.00	30.00	75.00
Plate, 8 ½"				
with signature	70.00	115.00	45.00	125.00
without signature	45.00	70.00	30.00	75.00
Porridge plate				
with signature	110.00	175.00	70.00	200.00
without signature	85.00	125.00	55.00	150.00

Geography Lesson (LF17)

Getting Dressed (LF2)

GETTING DRESSED

Design No.:	LF2
Designer:	Barbara Vernon
Issued:	By 1940 - by 1952

Shape	USD	CAD	GBP	AUD
Baby plate, round, large				
with signature	450.00	675.00	325.00	700.00
without signature	400.00	600.00	275.00	625.00
Bread / butter plate, handles				
with signature	800.00	1,250.00	500.00	1,600.00
without signature	600.00	1,000.00	400.00	1,100.00
Hot water plate				
with signature	375.00	600.00	250.00	625.00
without signature	325.00	500.00	225.00	525.00
Plate, 8 ½"				
with signature	300.00	475.00	200.00	500.00
without signature	250.00	400.00	175.00	425.00
Porridge plate				
with signature	400.00	625.00	275.00	650.00
without signature	375.00	575.00	250.00	600.00

Going Shopping (SF10)

GOING SHOPPING

Design No.:	SF10
Designer:	Barbara Vernon
Issued:	By 1940 - by 1952
Combined with:	*Chicken Pulling a Cart*, SF8
	Fixing Braces, HW3
	Lambeth Walk, second version, HW16

Shape	USD	CAD	GBP	AUD
Baby plate, round, small				
with signature	75.00	125.00	50.00	125.00
without signature	50.00	80.00	35.00	80.00
Casino jug, 30s				
with signature	300.00	475.00	200.00	475.00
without signature	225.00	325.00	150.00	325.00
Casino saucer				
with signature	75.00	125.00	50.00	125.00
without signature	50.00	75.00	35.00	75.00
Casino teapot, 24s				
with signature	375.00	550.00	250.00	600.00
without signature	300.00	450.00	200.00	500.00
Cereal / oatmeal bowl				
with signature	50.00	80.00	35.00	80.00
without signature	35.00	55.00	25.00	55.00
Don beaker				
with signature	150.00	250.00	110.00	275.00
without signature	125.00	200.00	90.00	225.00
Don beaker, one handle				
with signature	150.00	250.00	110.00	275.00
without signature	125.00	200.00	90.00	225.00
Jaffa fruit saucer (wavy)				
with signature	95.00	150.00	65.00	175.00
without signature	60.00	95.00	40.00	100.00
Hot water plate				
with signature	175.00	275.00	125.00	325.00
without signature	125.00	200.00	85.00	225.00
Plate, 6 ½"				
with signature	60.00	95.00	40.00	100.00
without signature	40.00	65.00	25.00	70.00
Plate, 7 ½"				
with signature	60.00	95.00	40.00	100.00
without signature	40.00	65.00	25.00	70.00

FINE WHITE CHINA

Cereal bowl	Very Rare
Cereal / oatmeal bowl	Very Rare

Note: Early Don beakers may come with a border of running rabbits inside the beaker, a little down from the rim.

GOLFER

Design No.:   HW4R
Designer: Barbara Vernon
Issued: By 1937 - by 1952
Combined with:
Cuddling under a Mushroom, HW4   *Pressing Trousers*, HW14
Cycling, HW15R   *Proposal*, HW11
Family at Breakfast, HW12   *Pulling on Trousers*, HW2
Feeding the Baby, HW13   *Reading the Times*, HW2R

Shape	USD	CAD	GBP	AUD
Casino jug, 36s	300.00	475.00	200.00	475.00
Casino teacup	75.00	125.00	50.00	125.00
Don beaker	150.00	250.00	110.00	275.00
Don beaker, one handle	150.00	250.00	110.00	275.00
Don mug, one handle	100.00	150.00	70.00	150.00
Don mug, two handles	75.00	125.00	50.00	125.00

FINE WHITE CHINA
Rex mug   Very Rare

Golfer (HW4R)

Note: 1. This design should appear with the Barbara Vernon facsimile signature. See also *Game of Golf* (SF11) page 80.
    2. *Golfer* (HW4R) is combined with *Proposal* (HW11) on the Rex mug.

GREETINGS

Design No.:   HW7
Designer: Barbara Vernon
Issued: By 1937 - by 1952
Combined with: *Artist*, HW1
                Dunce, HW1R
                Frightening Spider, SF4
                Gardening, Style One, HW9

Greetings (HW7)

Shape	USD	CAD	GBP	AUD
Baby plate, round, small	75.00	125.00	50.00	125.00
Casino jug, 36s	300.00	475.00	200.00	475.00
Casino jug, 42s	250.00	400.00	175.00	400.00
Casino saucer	75.00	125.00	50.00	125.00
Casino teacup	75.00	125.00	50.00	125.00
Casino teapot, 24s	375.00	550.00	250.00	600.00
Casino teapot, 30s	325.00	500.00	225.00	550.00
Cereal / oatmeal bowl	50.00	80.00	35.00	80.00
Don beaker	150.00	250.00	110.00	275.00
Don beaker, one handle	150.00	250.00	110.00	275.00

Shape	USD	CAD	GBP	AUD
Don mug, one handle	100.00	150.00	70.00	150.00
Don mug, two handles	100.00	150.00	70.00	150.00
Jaffa fruit saucer				
plain rim	95.00	150.00	65.00	175.00
wavy rim	60.00	95.00	40.00	100.00
Lid of hot water plate	125.00	200.00	85.00	225.00
Plate, 6 ½″	60.00	95.00	40.00	100.00
Plate, 7 ½″	60.00	95.00	40.00	100.00
FINE CHINA				
Plate, 7″			Very Rare	
Rex mug			Very Rare	

Note: This design should appear with the Barbara Vernon facsimile signature.

HAPPY BIRTHDAY FROM BUNNYKINS — *Walter Hayward*

Happy Birthday From Bunnykins,
Style One, (SF136)

Reverse Birthday Inscription

Style One

Design No.:	Front — SF136 Happy Birthday from Bunnykins
	Reverse — Birthday Inscription
Designer:	Walter Hayward
Issued:	1982 - 1989
Inscription:	"Birthdays are lots and lots of fun,
	With cards and gifts for everyone
	There are cakes and jellies and lots to eat,
	Parties and games and your favourite treat.
	So on this your very special day
	The Bunnykins wish you a Happy Birthday"

Shape	USD	CAD	GBP	AUD
Plate, 8"	25.00	40.00	18.00	40.00

HAPPY BIRTHDAY FROM BUNNYKINS — *Colin Twinn*

Style Two, First Version

The rhyme used on the reverse of this plate is the same as that used on style one, however a new border and copyright date are shown.

Design No.:   Front — CT37 Happy Birthday from Bunnykins
                Reverse — CT64 Birthday Inscription
Designer: Colin Twinn
Issued: 1990 - 1992
Inscription: Birthdays are lots and lots of fun,
             With cards and gifts for everyone
             There are cakes and jellies and lots to eat
             Parties and games and your favourite treat.
             So on this your very special day
             The Bunnykins wish you a Happy Birthday

Shape	USD	CAD	GBP	AUD
Plate, 8″	20.00	40.00	18.00	40.00

Happy Birthday from Bunnykins
Style Two, First Version (CT37)

Birthday Inscription (CT64)

Happy Birthday from Bunnykins
Style Two, Second Version (CT60)

Style Two, Second Version

Design No.:   Front — CT60 Happy Birthday from Bunnykins
                Reverse — CT61 Inscription
Designer: Colin Twinn
Issued: 1992 - 1992

Shape	USD	CAD	GBP	AUD
Hug-a-mug, one handle	10.00	15.00	7.50	15.00
Money ball				
with 1992	10.00	15.00	7.50	15.00
without 1992	10.00	15.00	7.50	15.00

Note: Two money balls were issued for the U.S. Special Events Tour in 1992. The ball sold on the Spring tour depicted *Queen of the May* (CT7) page 135, and the Fall tour ball was listed as below.
The Special Events Tour money was incribed U.S. Special Event Tour 1992 and To….. From….. to be completed by the customer.

Happy Birthday Bunnykins
Inscription (CT61)

HAPPY EASTER FROM BUNNYKINS — *Colin Twinn*

Happy Easter from Bunnykins
First Version (CT40)

First Version, Large Design

Design No.:	Front — CT40 Happy Easter from Bunnykins
	Reverse no. one - without inscription
	Reverse no. two — CT67 with inscription
Designer:	Colin Twinn
Issued:	1990 - 1992
Rhyme:	The Easter Bunnykins romp and play,
	Loving the joy of this Easter Day.
	Gone is the frost, the long winter lost,
	The sunshine brings light and new blossoms bright,
	So Bunnykins send you this warm invitation
	To Easter party, a grand celebration.

Shape	USD	CAD	GBP	AUD
Plate, 8"	20.00	40.00	18.00	40.00

Happy Easter from Bunnykins
Second Version (CT62)

Second Version, Small Design

Design No.:	Front — CT62 Happy Easter from Bunnykins
	Reverse — CT63 Happy Easter Inscription
Designer:	Colin Twinn
Issued:	1992 - 1992

Shape	USD	CAD	GBP	AUD
Hug-a-mug, one handle	10.00	15.00	7.50	15.00

Happy Easter Inscription (CT63)

HAT SHOP / TRYING ON HATS

Hat Shop (HW28)

Trying on Hats (HW28R)

Design No.: Front — HW28 Hat Shop
Reverse — HW28R Trying on Hats
Designer: Walter Hayward
Issued: Hat Shop - 1954 - by 1998
Trying on Hats - 1954 to the present

Combined with: *Afternoon Tea*, HW116
Dancing with Doll, HW115R
Drummer and Bugler, EC126
Serving Tea, HW116R
Trumpeter, EC5

Shape	USD	CAD	GBP	AUD
Albion cream jug	50.00	75.00	35.00	75.00
Albion jug, ½ pint	100.00	150.00	70.00	150.00
Albion jug, 1 pint	150.00	225.00	100.00	125.00
Albion teapot	50.00	85.00	35.00	95.00
Casino jug, 36s				
with signature	175.00	275.00	125.00	275.00
without signature	125.00	200.00	85.00	300.00
Casino jug, 42s				
with signature	150.00	225.00	100.00	225.00
without signature	100.00	150.00	70.00	150.00
Casino saucer				
with signature	15.00	25.00	10.00	25.00
without signature	7.50	12.00	5.00	12.00
Casino teacup				
with signature	15.00	25.00	10.00	25.00
without signature	7.50	12.00	5.00	12.00
Divider dish	50.00	75.00	35.00	75.00
Don beaker				
with signature	75.00	125.00	50.00	150.00
without signature	35.00	55.00	25.00	60.00
Don beaker, one handle				
with signature	75.00	125.00	50.00	150.00
without signature	35.00	55.00	25.00	60.00
Don mug, one handle				
with signature	65.00	100.00	45.00	75.00
without signature	15.00	25.00	10.00	25.00

Shape	USD	CAD	GBP	AUD
Don mug, two handles				
with signature	65.00	100.00	45.00	75.00
without signature	15.00	25.00	10.00	25.00
Egg box				
small	225.00	350.00	150.00	400.00
medium	300.00	450.00	200.00	500.00
large	375.00	550.00	250.00	600.00
Hug-a-mug, one handle	10.00	15.00	7.50	15.00
Hug-a-mug, two handles	10.00	15.00	7.50	15.00
Jaffa fruit saucer (plain)	15.00	25.00	10.00	25.00
Lamp	100.00	150.00	65.00	175.00
Lid of hot water plate				
with signature	125.00	200.00	85.00	225.00
without signature	100.00	150.00	75.00	175.00
Malvern beaker	15.00	25.00	10.00	25.00
Money ball	10.00	15.00	7.50	15.00
Picture plaque, small	20.00	30.00	12.50	30.00
Plate, 6 ½"				
with signature	35.00	55.00	25.00	55.00
without signature	20.00	30.00	15.00	30.00
Savings book	15.00	22.50	10.00	22.50
Stratford straight beaker	15.00	25.00	10.00	25.00
Stratford teacup	7.50	12.00	5.00	12.00

Note: *Trying on Hats* (HW28R) was paired with *Dancing with Doll* (HW115R) on the Savings book. The divider dish combines *Afternoon Tea* (HW116), *Serving Tea* (HW116R) and *Trying on Hats* (HW28R) and the lid of the hot water plate combines *Hat Shop* (HW28), *Trying on Hats* (HW28R) and *Drummer and Bugler* (EC126).

HAYMAKING / LUNCH BREAK

Haymaking (HW29)

Lunch Break (HW29R)

Design No.: Front — HW29 Haymaking
Reverse — HW29R Lunch Break
Designer: Walter Hayward
Issued: 1954 - by 1998

Combined with: *Apple Picking*, SF25
Dancing with Doll, HW115R
Holding Hat and Coat, EC4
Sleeping in a Rocking Chair, EC1
Toast for Tea Today, SF3

Shape	USD	CAD	GBP	AUD
Albion cream jug	50.00	75.00	35.00	75.00
Albion jug, ½ pint	100.00	150.00	70.00	150.00
Albion jug, 1 pint	150.00	225.00	100.00	225.00
Albion teapot	50.00	85.00	35.00	95.00
Casino jug, 36s				
with signature	175.00	275.00	125.00	275.00
without signature	125.00	200.00	85.00	200.00
Casino jug, 42s				
with signature	150.00	225.00	100.00	225.00
without signature	100.00	150.00	70.00	150.00
Casino saucer				
with signature	15.00	25.00	10.00	25.00
without signature	7.50	12.00	5.00	12.00
Casino sugar, 30s				
with signature	175.00	275.00	125.00	300.00
without signature	125.00	200.00	85.00	225.00
Casino teacup				
with signature	15.00	25.00	10.00	25.00
without signature	7.50	12.00	5.00	12.00
Casino teapot, 30s				
with signature	250.00	375.00	165.00	400.00
without signature	150.00	225.00	100.00	250.00
Don beaker				
with signature	75.00	125.00	50.00	150.00
without signature	35.00	55.00	25.00	60.00
Don beaker, one handle				
with signature	75.00	125.00	50.00	150.00
without signature	35.00	55.00	25.00	60.00

Shape	USD	CAD	GBP	AUD
Don mug, one handle				
with signature	65.00	100.00	45.00	75.00
without signature	15.00	25.00	10.00	25.00
Don mug, two handles				
with signature	65.00	100.00	45.00	75.00
without signature	15.00	25.00	10.00	25.00
Egg box				
small	225.00	350.00	150.00	400.00
medium	300.00	450.00	200.00	500.00
large	375.00	550.00	250.00	600.00
Hug-a-mug, one handle	10.00	15.00	7.50	15.00
Hug-a-mug, two handles	10.00	15.00	7.50	15.00
Jaffa fruit saucer (plain)	15.00	25.00	10.00	25.00
Lamp	100.00	150.00	65.00	175.00
Lid of hot water plate				
with signature	125.00	200.00	85.00	225.00
without signature	100.00	150.00	75.00	175.00
Malvern beaker	15.00	25.00	10.00	25.00
Money ball	10.00	15.00	7.50	15.00
Picture plaque, small	20.00	30.00	12.50	30.00
Plate, 6 ½"				
with signature	35.00	55.00	25.00	55.00
without signature	20.00	30.00	15.00	30.00
Savings book	15.00	22.50	10.00	22.50
Stratford straight beaker	15.00	25.00	10.00	25.00
Stratford teacup	7.50	12.00	5.00	12.00

HIKERS

Design No.:   EC124
Designer: Walter Hayward
Issued: 1959 to the present
Combined with: *Afternoon Tea,* HW116
    Bedtime with Dollies, EC125
    Daisy Chains, HW25
    The Doll's House, HW120
    Drummer, EC2
    Drummer and Bugler, EC126
    Hobby Horse, Style Two, EC121
    Holding Hat and Coat, EC4
    Nipped by a Crab, HW21R
    Playing with Cup and Spoon, EC6
    Playing with Doll and Pram, EC123
    Playing with Doll and Teddy, HW120R
    Playing with Dolls and Prams, HW115
    Raising Hat, Style Two, EC7
    Reading, EC122
    Row Boat, HW21
    Sheltering Under an Umbrella, EC3
    Sleeping in a Rocking Chair, EC1
    Trumpeter, EC5

Hikers (EC124)

Shape	USD	CAD	GBP	AUD
Albion sugar bowl	30.00	50.00	20.00	50.00
Beaker cover	125.00	175.00	75.00	175.00
Egg cup				
Style One	40.00	60.00	25.00	65.00
Style Two	80.00	125.00	50.00	135.00
Style Three	**N/I**	**15.00**	**5.00**	**19.95**
Hug-a-mug, 1993	10.00	15.00	7.50	15.00
Lid of hot water plate	100.00	150.00	70.00	175.00
Money Ball	**33.75**	**40.00**	**15.00**	**62.95**

Note: This scene was combined with *Daisy Chains,* (HW25) on a
Hug-a-mug for the U.S. Special Events Tour in 1993.

Hobby Horse, Style Two (EC121)

HOBBY HORSE
Style Two

Design No.:	EC121
Designer:	Walter Hayward
Issued:	1959 to the present
Combined with:	*Cowboy on Rocking Horse*, HW140R
	Cowboys and Indians, HW140
	Drummer, EC2
	Drummer and Bugler, EC126
	Hikers, EC124
	Holding Hat and Coat, EC4
	Lasso Games, HW117
	Lassoing, HW117R
	Playing with Cup and Spoon, EC6
	Playing with Doll and Pram, EC123
	Raising Hat, Style Two, EC7
	Reading, EC122
	Sheltering Under an Umbrella, EC3
	Sleeping in a Rocking Chair, EC1
	Trumpeter, EC5

Shape	USD	CAD	GBP	AUD
Albion sugar bowl	30.00	50.00	20.00	50.00
Beaker cover	125.00	175.00	75.00	175.00
Egg cup				
Style One	40.00	60.00	25.00	65.00
Style Two	80.00	125.00	50.00	135.00
Style Three	**N/I**	**15.00**	**5.00**	**19.95**
Lid of hot water plate	100.00	150.00	75.00	175.00

China teacup combining. *Pulling on Trousers* (HW2) and *Proposal* (HW11)

HOLDING HAT AND COAT

Design No.:	EC4
Designer:	Barbara Vernon
Issued:	1937 to the present
Combined with:	*Bedtime with Dollies*, EC125
	Drummer, EC2
	Drummer and Bugler, EC126
	Haymaking, HW29
	Hikers, EC124
	Hobby Horse, Style Two, EC121
	Lunch Break, HW29R
	Playing with Cup and Spoon, EC6
	Playing with Doll and Pram, EC123
	Proposal, HW11
	Pulling on Trousers, HW2
	Raising Hat, Style Two, EC7
	Sheltering Under an Umbrella, EC3
	Skipping, HW20R
	Swinging, HW20
	Trumpeter, EC5
	Wheelbarrow Race, Style One, HW22

Holding Hat and Coat (EC4)

Shape	USD	CAD	GBP	AUD
Albion sugar bowl	30.00	50.00	20.00	50.00
Beaker cover				
with signature	125.00	175.00	75.00	175.00
without signature	85.00	135.00	50.00	150.00
Casino sugar bowl, 36s				
with signature	125.00	200.00	85.00	225.00
without signature	100.00	150.00	65.00	175.00
Egg cup				
Style One	40.00	60.00	25.00	65.00
Style Two				
with signature	150.00	225.00	100.00	250.00
without signature	80.00	125.00	50.00	135.00
Style Three	**N/I**	**15.00**	**5.00**	**19.95**
Lid of hot water plate				
with signature	125.00	200.00	85.00	225.00
without signature	100.00	150.00	75.00	175.00
Money ball	**33.75**	**40.00**	**15.00**	**62.95**

Home Decorating (SF131)

HOME DECORATING

Design No.: SF131
Designer: Walter Hayward
Issued: 1967 -by 1998

Shape	USD	CAD	GBP	AUD
Baby plate, round, small	20.00	30.00	15.00	30.00
Cake stand	150.00	250.00	100.00	300.00
Casino saucer	7.50	12.00	5.00	12.00
Cereal / oatmeal bowl	10.00	15.00	7.50	15.00
Coupe plate, 6 ¾"	Very Rare			
Hot water plate	125.00	200.00	85.00	225.00
Jaffa fruit saucer (plain)	15.00	25.00	10.00	25.00
Picture plaque, large	20.00	30.00	12.50	30.00
Plate, 6 ½"	20.00	30.00	15.00	30.00
Plate, 8"	25.00	40.00	18.00	40.00
Plate, 10 ½"	35.00	55.00	25.00	60.00

HOME FROM FISHING
First Variation, Large Size

Design No.: CT18 Home from Fishing
Designer: Colin Twinn
Issued: 1990 - 1993

Shape	USD	CAD	GBP	AUD
Albion cream jug	50.00	75.00	35.00	75.00
Albion jug, 1 pint	150.00	225.00	100.00	225.00
Baby plate, round, small	20.00	30.00	15.00	30.00
Divider dish	75.00	125.00	50.00	125.00
Jaffa fruit saucer	30.00	45.00	20.00	50.00
Picture plaque, large	20.00	30.00	12.50	30.00
Picture plaque, small	20.00	30.00	12.50	30.00
Plate, 8"	25.00	40.00	18.00	40.00

Home from Fishing, First Variation (CT18)

HOME FROM FISHING
Second Variation, Small Size /
FATHER BUNNYKINS WITH FISHING ROD

Design No.:	Front — CT26 Home from Fishing
	Reverse — CT27 Father Bunnykins with
	Fishing Rod
Designer:	Colin Twinn
Issued:	1990 - 1993
Combined with:	*Bunny on Rocking Horse*, CT29
	Family with Pram, Style Two, CT14
	Standing by Pram, CT6

Shape	USD	CAD	GBP	AUD
Albion cream jug	50.00	75.00	35.00	75.00
Albion jug, ½ pint	100.00	150.00	70.00	150.00
Albion jug, 1 pint	150.00	225.00	100.00	225.00
Albion teapot	50.00	85.00	35.00	95.00
Hug-a-mug, two handles	10.00	15.00	7.50	15.00
Lamp	100.00	150.00	65.00	175.00
Malvern beaker	15.00	25.00	10.00	25.00
Money ball	10.00	15.00	7.50	15.00
Picture plaque, small	20.00	30.00	12.50	30.00
Savings book	15.00	22.50	10.00	22.50
Stratford straight beaker	15.00	25.00	10.00	25.00
Stratford teacup	7.50	12.00	5.00	12.00

Note: Bunny on Rocking Horse (CT29) is combined with Home from Fishing (CT26) on a savings book.

Home from Fishing, Second Variation (CT26)

Father Bunnykins with Fishing Rod (CT27)

Hoopla (LF129)

HOOPLA

Design No.:	LF129
Designer:	Walter Hayward
Issued:	1967 - 1970

Shape	USD	CAD	GBP	AUD
Baby plate, oval, large		Rare		
Baby plate, round, large		Rare		
Plate, 8 ½"		Rare		

ICE CREAM THEME — Colin Twinn

Ice Cream Seller, First Variation (CT5)

ICE CREAM SELLER
First Variation, Large Size

Design No.:   CT5 Ice Cream Seller
Designer: Colin Twinn
Issued: 1989 - 1993
Combined with: *Pushing the Wheelbarrow*, CT3
                 Splashing at Sink, CT33
                 Washing Up, CT32

Shape	USD	CAD	GBP	AUD
Hug-a-mug, one handle	10.00	15.00	7.50	10.00
Hug-a-mug, two handles	10.00	15.00	7.50	10.00
Lamp	100.00	150.00	65.00	175.00
Malvern beaker	15.00	25.00	10.00	25.00
Money ball	10.00	15.00	7.50	15.00
Picture plaque, small	20.00	30.00	12.50	30.00
Stratford straight beaker	15.00	25.00	10.00	25.00
Stratford teacup	7.50	12.00	5.00	12.00

ICE CREAM SELLER
Second Variation, Small Size

Design No.:   CT11 Ice Cream Seller
Designer: Colin Twinn
Issued: 1989 - 1993
Combined with: *Bunny on Trike*, CT23
                 Picking Daisies, CT4

Shape	USD	CAD	GBP	AUD
Albion cream jug	50.00	75.00	35.00	75.00
Albion jug, ½ pint	100.00	150.00	70.00	150.00
Albion jug, 1 pint	150.00	225.00	100.00	225.00
Albion teapot	50.00	85.00	35.00	95.00
Baby plate, round, small	20.00	30.00	15.00	30.00
Cake stand	150.00	250.00	100.00	300.00
Cereal / oatmeal bowl	15.00	25.00	10.00	25.00
Plate, 6"	20.00	30.00	15.00	30.00

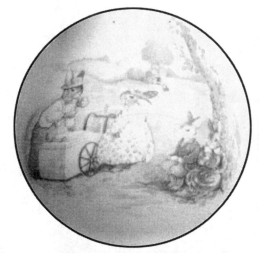

Ice Cream Seller, Second Variation (CT11)

ICE CREAM VENDOR / HIKER RESTING WITH ICE CREAM

Ice Cream Vendor (HW23)   Hiker Resting with Ice Cream (HW23R)

Design No.:   Front — HW23 Ice Cream Vendor
              Reverse — HW23R Hiker Resting with Ice Cream
Designer: Walter Hayward
Issued: By 1952 - by 1998

Combined with: *Daisy Chains*, HW25
                 *Skipping Game, HW139R
                 *Snowball Fight, HW141R

Shape	USD	CAD	GBP	AUD	Shape	USD	CAD	GBP	AUD
Albion cream jug	50.00	75.00	35.00	75.00	Don beaker				
Albion jug, ½ pint	100.00	150.00	70.00	150.00	without signature	35.00	55.00	25.00	60.00
Albion jug, 1 pint	150.00	225.00	100.00	225.00	Don beaker, one handle				
Albion teapot	50.00	85.00	35.00	95.00	with signature	75.00	125.00	50.00	150.00
Baby plate, round, small					without signature	35.00	55.00	25.00	60.00
with signature	60.00	75.00	30.00	90.00	Don mug, one handle				
without signature	20.00	30.00	15.00	30.00	with signature	65.00	100.00	45.00	75.00
Casino jug, 30s					without signature	15.00	25.00	10.00	25.00
with signature	250.00	400.00	175.00	425.00	Don mug, two handles				
without signature	150.00	250.00	100.00	250.00	with signature	65.00	100.00	45.00	75.00
Casino jug, 36s					without signature	15.00	25.00	10.00	25.00
with signature	175.00	275.00	125.00	275.00	Egg box				
without signature	125.00	200.00	85.00	200.00	small	225.00	350.00	150.00	400.00
Casino jug, 42s					medium	300.00	450.00	200.00	500.00
with signature	150.00	225.00	100.00	225.00	large	375.00	550.00	250.00	600.00
without signature	100.00	150.00	70.00	150.00	Hug-a-mug, one handle	10.00	15.00	7.50	15.00
Casino saucer					Hug-a-mug, two handles	10.00	15.00	7.50	15.00
with signature	15.00	25.00	10.00	25.00	Jaffa fruit saucer				
without signature	7.50	12.00	5.00	12.00	plain rim	15.00	25.00	10.00	25.00
Casino sugar bowl, 30s					wavy rim	30.00	45.00	20.00	50.00
with signature	175.00	275.00	125.00	300.00	Lamp	100.00	150.00	65.00	175.00
without signature	125.00	200.00	85.00	225.00	Lid of hot water plate				
Casino sugar bowl, 36s					with signature	150.00	225.00	100.00	250.00
with signature	150.00	225.00	100.00	250.00	without signature	125.00	200.00	85.00	225.00
without signature	100.00	150.00	65.00	175.00	Malvern Beaker	15.00	25.00	10.00	25.00
Casino teacup					Money ball	10.00	15.00	7.50	15.00
with signature	15.00	25.00	10.00	25.00	Picture plaque, small	20.00	30.00	12.50	20.00
without signature	7.50	12.00	5.00	12.00	Plate, 6 ½"				
Casino teapot, 30s					with signature	35.00	55.00	25.00	55.00
with signature	250.00	375.00	165.00	400.00	without signature	20.00	30.00	18.00	30.00
without signature	150.00	225.00	100.00	250.00	Savings book	15.00	22.50	10.00	22.50
Divider dish	50.00	75.00	35.00	75.00	Stratford straight beaker	15.00	25.00	10.00	25.00
Don beaker					Stratford teacup	7.50	12.00	5.00	12.00
with signature	75.00	125.00	50.00	150.00					

* Indicates scene on divider dish

Ice Skating (SF24)

ICE SKATING

Design No.:	SF24
Designer:	Walter Hayward
Issued:	1954 - 1967

Shape	USD	CAD	GBP	AUD
Baby plate, round, small				
with signature	75.00	125.00	50.00	125.00
without signature	50.00	80.00	35.00	80.00
Baby plate, round, large				
with signature	150.00	250.00	100.00	275.00
without signature	125.00	200.00	85.00	225.00
Casino jug, 24s				
with signature	400.00	625.00	275.00	650.00
without signature	350.00	550.00	250.00	550.00
Casino saucer				
with signature	75.00	125.00	50.00	125.00
without signature	50.00	75.00	35.00	75.00
Cereal / oatmeal bowl				
with signature	50.00	80.00	35.00	80.00
without signature	35.00	55.00	25.00	55.00
Hot water plate				
with signature	175.00	275.00	125.00	325.00
without signature	125.00	200.00	85.00	225.00
Plate, 6 ½"				
with signature	60.00	95.00	40.00	100.00
without signature	40.00	65.00	25.00	70.00
Plate, 7 ½"				
with signature	60.00	95.00	40.00	100.00
without signature	40.00	65.00	25.00	70.00
Plate, 8 ½"				
with signature	70.00	115.00	45.00	125.00
without signature	45.00	70.00	30.00	75.00

Note: Retirement dates are all approximate. When a design is retired all remaining stocks of the retired litho prints are used until exhausted.

JACK AND JILL

Design No.:	Front — CT9 Jack and Jill
	Reverse — CT10 Jack and Jill Nursery Rhyme
Designer:	Colin Twinn
Issued:	1989 - 1993

Shape	USD	CAD	GBP	AUD
Hug-a-mug, one handle	10.00	15.00	12.50	15.00

Jack and Jill (CT9)

Jack and Jill Nursery Rhyme (CT10)

Juggling (LF127)

JUGGLING

Design No.:	LF127
Designer:	Walter Hayward
Issued:	1967 - 1970

Shape	USD	CAD	GBP	AUD
Baby plate, round, large			Rare	
Plate, 8 ½"			Rare	
Porridge bowl			Rare	

Kissing Under the Mistletoe
(with mistletoe)

KISSING UNDER THE MISTLETOE
First Version, With Mistletoe

Design No.:   HW11R
Designer: Barbara Vernon
Issued: By 1937 - by 1947
Combined with: *Cycling*, HW15R
                  Family at Breakfast, HW12
                  Feeding the Baby, HW13
                  Medicine Time, SF1
                  Proposal, HW11
                  Reading the Times, HW2R

Shape	USD	CAD	GBP	AUD
Casino jug, 36s	250.00	400.00	175.00	425.00
Casino jug, 42s	300.00	450.00	200.00	500.00
Casino teacup	100.00	150.00	65.00	175.00
Don beaker	200.00	325.00	140.00	350.00
Don beaker, one handle	200.00	325.00	140.00	350.00
Don mug, one handle	150.00	250.00	100.00	275.00
Don mug, two handles	150.00	250.00	100.00	275.00

FINE WHITE CHINA
Teacup   Very Rare

Kissing Under the Mistletoe
(without mistletoe)

KISSING UNDER THE MISTLETOE
Second Version, Without Mistletoe

Design No.:   HW11R
Designer: Barbara Vernon
Issued: By 1947 - by 1967
Combined with: *Cycling*, HW15R
                  Family at Breakfast, HW12
                  Feeding the Baby, HW13
                  Medicine Time, SF1
                  Proposal, HW11
                  Reading the Times, HW2R

Shape	USD	CAD	GBP	AUD
Casino jug, 42s				
with signature	150.00	225.00	100.00	225.00
without signature	100.00	150.00	70.00	150.00
Casino teacup				
with signature	75.00	125.00	50.00	125.00
without signature	50.00	75.00	35.00	75.00
Don beaker				
with signature	150.00	250.00	110.00	275.00
without signature	45.00	75.00	30.00	75.00
Don beaker, one handle				
with signature	150.00	250.00	110.00	275.00

Shape	USD	CAD	GBP	AUD
Don beaker, one handle				
without signature	45.00	75.00	30.00	75.00
Don mug, one handle				
with signature	100.00	150.00	70.00	150.00
without signature	35.00	55.00	25.00	60.00
Don mug, two handles				
with signature	100.00	150.00	70.00	150.00
without signature	35.00	55.00	25.00	60.00

FINE WHITE CHINA
Rex mug, small, 2 ½"   Very Rare

LAMBETH WALK
First Version, Lambeth Walk on Music Sheet

Design No.: HW16
Designer: Barbara Vernon
Issued: By 1937 - by 1949
Combined with: *Family at Breakfast*, HW12
Footballer, HW13R
Leapfrog, HW12R
Raising Hat, Style One, HW16R
Top Hat, HW14R

Lambeth Walk, First Version (HW16)

Shape	USD	CAD	GBP	AUD
Baby plate, round, small	75.00	125.00	50.00	125.00
Candle holder	2,000.00	3,000.00	1,250.00	4,000.00
Casino jug, 30s	300.00	475.00	200.00	475.00
Casino jug, 36s	250.00	400.00	175.00	425.00
Casino saucer	75.00	125.00	50.00	125.00
Casino teacup	75.00	125.00	50.00	125.00
Don beaker	150.00	250.00	110.00	275.00
Don mug, one handle	100.00	150.00	70.00	150.00
Don mug, two handles	100.00	150.00	70.00	150.00
Jam pot	1,500.00	2,500.00	1,000.00	3,000.00
Lid of hot water plate	150.00	225.00	100.00	250.00

FINE WHITE CHINA

Rex mug, small, 2 ½"	Very Rare
Saucer	Very Rare

Note: 1. This design should appear with the Barbara Vernon facsimile signature.
2. A Rex mug combines *Footballer* (HW13R) and *Lambeth Walk*, first version (HW16)

A rare Bunnykins vegetable tureen
Family at Breakfast, (HW12); *Lambeth Walk* (HW16)

Lambeth Walk, Second Version (HW16)

LAMBETH WALK,
Second Version, Musical Score on Music Sheet, Bird Sits Atop Sheet

After 1949 the words Lambeth Walk were replaced by a musical score, and a small bird sat atop the music sheet.

Design No.: HW16
Designer: Barbara Vernon
Issued: By 1949 - 1967
Combined with: *Bedtime with Dollies*, EC125
Footballer, HW13R
Going Shopping, SF10
Leapfrog, HW12R
Playing with Dolls, EC123
Raising Hat, Style One, HW16R
Santa Claus, SF9
Sleeping in a Rocking Chair, EC1
Soldiers Marching, HW18R
Top Hat, HW14R

Shape	USD	CAD	GBP	AUD
Baby plate, round, small				
with signature	45.00	75.00	30.00	90.00
without signature	20.00	30.00	15.00	30.00
Candle holder	2,000.00	3,000.00	1,250.00	4,000.00
Casino jug, 30s				
with signature	200.00	300.00	150.00	300.00
without signature	150.00	250.00	100.00	250.00
Casino jug, 36s				
with signature	150.00	225.00	100.00	225.00
without signature	125.00	200.00	85.00	200.00
Casino jug, 42s				
with signature	125.00	200.00	90.00	200.00
without signature	100.00	150.00	70.00	150.00
Casino saucer				
with signature	15.00	25.00	10.00	25.00
without signature	7.50	12.00	5.00	12.00
Casino sugar bowl, 30s				
with signature	150.00	225.00	100.00	250.00
without signature	125.00	200.00	85.00	225.00
Casino teacup				
with signature	15.00	25.00	10.00	25.00
without signature	7.50	12.00	5.00	12.00
Casino teapot, 24s				
with signature	275.00	400.00	175.00	450.00
without signature	175.00	275.00	125.00	325.00

Shape	USD	CAD	GBP	AUD
Don beaker				
with signature	75.00	125.00	50.00	150.00
without signature	50.00	75.00	35.00	75.00
Don beaker, one handle				
with signature	75.00	125.00	50.00	150.00
without signature	50.00	75.00	35.00	75.00
Don mug, one handle				
with signature	50.00	75.00	35.00	85.00
without signature	30.00	50.00	20.00	55.00
Don mug, two handles				
with signature	50.00	75.00	35.00	85.00
without signature	30.00	50.00	20.00	55.00
Egg cup				
Style One	40.00	60.00	25.00	65.00
Style Two	80.00	125.00	50.00	150.00
Style Three	7.50	12.50	5.00	12.50
Jam pot	1,500.00	2,500.00	1,000.00	3,000.00
Lid of hot water plate				
with signature	125.00	200.00	85.00	225.00
without signature	100.00	150.00	70.00	175.00
Plate, 6 ½"				
with signature	35.00	55.00	25.00	55.00
without signature	20.00	30.00	15.00	30.00
Sugar bowl with handles		Extremely rare		

LASSO GAMES / LASSOING

Design No.:	Front — HW117 Lasso Games
	Reverse — HW117R Lassoing
Designer:	Walter Hayward
Issued:	1959 - 1967
Combined with:	*Hobby Horse*, Style Two, EC121

Shape	USD	CAD	GBP	AUD
Casino teacup	50.00	75.00	35.00	75.00
Don beaker	85.00	135.00	60.00	150.00
Don beaker, one handle	85.00	135.00	60.00	150.00
Don mug, one handle	35.00	55.00	25.00	60.00
Don mug, two handles	35.00	55.00	25.00	60.00
Jaffa fruit saucer (plain)	60.00	95.00	40.00	100.00
Lid of hot water plate	100.00	150.00	75.00	175.00
Plate, 6 ½"	40.00	65.00	25.00	70.00

Lasso Games (HW117)

LEAPFROG

Design No.:	HW12R
Designer:	Barbara Vernon
Issued:	By 1937 - by 1952
Combined with:	

Asleep in the Open Air, HW10	*Convalescing*, SF5
Chicken Pulling a Cart, SF8	*Embracing at a Window*, HW5
Family at Breakfast, HW12	*Feeding the Baby*, HW13
Fixing Braces, HW3	*Gardener with Wheelbarrow*, HW9R
Gardening, Style One, HW9	*Lambeth Walk*, HW16
Pressing Trousers, HW14	*Proposal*, HW11

Family Going out on Washing Day, HW8
Family with Pram, Style One, HW15
Washing in the Open Air, HW10R

Lassoing (HW117R)

Shape	USD	CAD	GBP	AUD
Casino jug, 36s				
with signature	300.00	475.00	200.00	475.00
without signature	250.00	400.00	175.00	400.00
Casino jug, 42s				
with signature	250.00	400.00	175.00	400.00
without signature	200.00	325.00	150.00	325.00
Casino sugar bowl, 30s				
with signature	200.00	325.00	125.00	350.00
without signature	150.00	225.00	100.00	225.00
Casino teacup				
with signature	75.00	125.00	50.00	125.00
without signature	50.00	75.00	35.00	75.00
Don beaker				
with signature	150.00	250.00	110.00	275.00
without signature	125.00	200.00	90.00	225.00
Don beaker, one handle				
with signature	150.00	250.00	110.00	275.00
without signature	125.00	200.00	90.00	225.00
Don mug, one handle				
with signature	100.00	150.00	70.00	150.00
without signature	75.00	125.00	50.00	125.00
Jam pot	1,500.00	2,500.00	1,000.00	3,000.00

FINE WHITE CHINA

Saucer		Very rare
Teacup		Very rare

Leapfrog (HW12R)

Letterbox (SF13)

LETTERBOX

Design No.:	SF13
Designer:	Walter Hayward after Barbara Vernon
Issued:	By 1952 - by 1998

Shape	USD	CAD	GBP	AUD
Baby plate, round, small				
with signature	45.00	75.00	30.00	90.00
without signature	20.00	30.00	15.00	30.00
Cake stand	150.00	250.00	100.00	300.00
Casino saucer				
with signature	15.00	25.00	10.00	25.00
without signature	7.50	12.00	5.00	12.00
Casino teapot, 24s				
with signature	275.00	400.00	175.00	450.00
without signature	175.00	275.00	125.00	325.00
Cereal / oatmeal bowl				
with signature	25.00	40.00	15.00	45.00
without signature	10.00	15.00	7.50	15.00
Hot water plate				
with signature	175.00	275.00	125.00	325.00
without signature	125.00	200.00	85.00	225.00
Jaffa fruit saucer (plain)				
with signature	50.00	75.00	35.00	80.00
without signature	15.00	25.00	10.00	25.00
Plate, 6 ½"				
with signature	35.00	55.00	25.00	55.00
without signature	20.00	30.00	15.00	30.00
Plate, 7 ½"				
with signature	35.00	55.00	25.00	55.00
without signature	20.00	30.00	15.00	30.00
Plate, 8"	25.00	40.00	18.00	40.00

Note: A money box in the same shape of a post box was modelled but not put into production. Two examples have been recorded, one in the Royal Doulton Archives and another in a private collection. A Money Box was produced for the Millennium Bunnykins Extravaganza. For illustration of post box see page 198.

BUNNYKINS

DB1   DB2   DB3   DB4

DB5   DB6   DB7   DB8

DB9   DB10   DB11   DB12

BUNNYKINS

DB13   DB14   DB15   DB16

DB17   DB18   DB19   DB20

DB21   DB22   DB23   DB24

BUNNYKINS

DB25

DB26A

DB26B

DB27

DB28A

DB28B

DB29A

DB29B

DB30

DB31

DB32

DB40

Note: DB33 to 39 are Music Boxes

BUNNYKINS

DB41

DB42

DB43

DB45

DB46

DB47

DB48

DB49

DB50

DB51

DB52

DB54

Note: DB44 Ballet Bunnykins not issued; DB53 Carol Singer Music Box

BUNNYKINS

DB55

DB56

DB57

DB58

DB59

DB60

DB61

DB62

DB63

DB64

DB65

DB66

BUNNYKINS

DB67

DB68

DB69

DB70

DB71

DB72

DB73

DB74A

DB74B

DB75

DB76

DB77

BUNNYKINS

DB78

DB79

DB80

DB81

DB82

DB83

DB84

DB85

DB86

DB87

DB88

DB89

BUNNYKINS

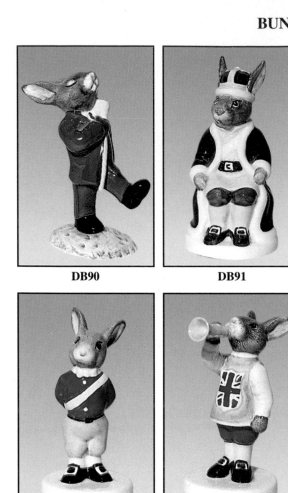

DB90

DB91

DB92

DB93

DB94

DB95

DB96

DB97

DB98

DB99

DB100

DB101

MEDICINE TIME

Design No.:	SF1
Designer:	Barbara Vernon
Issued:	By 1937 - by 1952
Combined with:	*Frightening Spider*, SF4
	Kissing Under the Mistletoe, HW11R

Shape	USD	CAD	GBP	AUD
Baby plate, round, small				
with signature	125.00	200.00	90.00	200.00
without signature	100.00	150.00	70.00	175.00
Baby plate, round, large				
with signature	300.00	450.00	200.00	500.00
without signature	250.00	375.00	175.00	375.00
Candle holder	2,000.00	3,000.00	1,250.00	4,000.00
Casino jug, 30s				
with signature	500.00	800.00	350.00	950.00
without signature	400.00	700.00	300.00	850.00
Casino saucer				
with signature	100.00	150.00	65.00	175.00
without signature	75.00	125.00	50.00	125.00
Casino teapot, 30s				
with signature	400.00	600.00	275.00	700.00
without signature	300.00	450.00	200.00	500.00
Cereal / oatmeal bowl				
with signature	110.00	175.00	75.00	200.00
without signature	90.00	150.00	60.00	175.00
Hot water plate				
with signature	175.00	275.00	125.00	325.00
without signature	125.00	200.00	85.00	225.00
Plate, 6 ½"				
with signature	90.00	150.00	60.00	175.00
without signature	60.00	100.00	40.00	100.00
Plate, 7"				
with signature	90.00	150.00	60.00	175.00
without signature	60.00	100.00	40.00	100.00
Plate, 8"	75.00	125.00	50.00	135.00

Medicine Time (SF1)

FINE WHITE CHINA

Night light	
Plate	Very Rare
Plate, 6"	Very Rare
Plate, 7"	Very Rare
Shallow bowl	Very Rare

MERRY CHRISTMAS FROM BUNNYKINS — *Walter Hayward*

Merry Christmas from Bunnykins,
Style One (SF137)

Style One

The reverse decoration on this plate has a single holly leaf wreath border and a 1936 copyright date.

Design No.:	Front — SF137 Merry Christmas from Bunnykins
	Reverse — Inscription
Designer:	Walter Hayward
Issued:	1981 - 1989
Rhyme:	'Bunnykins are just like you
	For they love Christmas too,
	They sing and dance as you can see
	And play around the Christmas tree,
	And each year they always say
	We wish it were Christmas every day'

Shape	USD	CAD	GBP	AUD
Plate, 8"	25.00	40.00	18.00	40.00

Reverse Inscription (SF137)

MERRY CHRISTMAS FROM BUNNYKINS — Colin Twinn

Style Two
First Variation, Large Size

The reverse decoration on this plate has a multiple holly leaf wreath border.

Design No.:	Front — CT39 Merry Christmas from Bunnykins		
	Reverse — CT66 Inscription		
Designer:	Colin Twinn		
Issued:	1990 - 1993		
Rhyme:	'Bunnykins are just like you		
	For they love Christmas too.		
	They sing and dance as you can see		
	And play around the Christmas tree		
	And each year they always say		
	"We wish it were Christmas every day."		

Shape	USD	CAD	GBP	AUD
Plate, 8"	25.00	40.00	18.00	40.00

Merry Christmas from Bunnykins
First Variation (CT39)

Merry Christmas from Bunnykins
Second Variation (CT43)

Style Two
Second Variation, Small Size

Design No.:	Front — CT43 Merry Christmas from Bunnykins		
	Reverse — CT44 Inscription		
Designer:	Colin Twinn		
Issued:	1992 - 1994		

Shape	USD	CAD	GBP	AUD
Hug-a-mug, one handle	10.00	15.00	7.50	15.00

Family Christmas Scene, First Version (CT72)

Style Three
FAMILY CHRISTMAS SCENE
First Version, Large Size

Design No.:	CT72 Family Christmas Scene
	CT73 Christmas Inscription
Designer:	Colin Twinn
Issued:	1993 - 1994
Inscription:	´Bunnykins are just like you
	For they love Christmas too.
	They sing and dance as you can see
	And play around the Christmas tree
	And each year they always say
	"We wish it were Christmas every day."

Shape	USD	CAD	GBP	AUD
Plate, 8"	25.00	40.00	18.00	40.00

Christmas Inscription, First Version (CT73)

Merry Christmas from Bunnykins,
Second Version (CT74)

Style Three
FAMILY CHRISTMAS SCENE
Second Version, Small Size

Design No.:	Front — CT74 Family Christmas Scene
	Reverse — CT75 Merry Christmas from Bunnykins
	Inscription
Designer:	Colin Twinn
Issued:	1993 - 1994

Shape	USD	CAD	GBP	AUD
Hug-a-mug, one handle	10.00	15.00	7.50	15.00
Money ball	10.00	15.00	7.50	15.00

Merry Christmas Inscription,
Second Version (CT75)

MR. PIGGLY'S STORES

Design No.:	SF14
Designer:	Walter Hayward after Barbara Vernon
Issued:	By 1952 - by 1998
Combined with:	*Fishing in the Goldfish Bowl*, HW3R
	Playing on the River, SF16
	See-saw, Style One, SFS17
	Toast for Tea Today, SF23

Mr. Piggly's Stores (SF14)

Shape	USD	CAD	GBP	AUD
Baby plate, small, round				
with signature	45.00	75.00	30.00	90.00
without signature	20.00	30.00	15.00	30.00
Bread and butter plate				
with signature	200.00	325.00	125.00	350.00
without signature	125.00	200.00	85.00	225.00
Casino jug, 24s				
with signature	300.00	475.00	200.00	475.00
without signature	175.00	275.00	125.00	300.00
Casino saucer				
with signature	15.00	25.00	10.00	25.00
without signature	7.50	12.00	5.00	12.00
Casino sugar, 30s				
with signature	150.00	225.00	100.00	250.00
without signature	100.00	150.00	65.00	175.00
Casino teapot, 30s				
with signature	250.00	375.00	165.00	400.00
without signature	150.00	225.00	100.00	250.00
Cereal / oatmeal bowl				
with signature	25.00	40.00	15.00	45.00
without signature	10.00	15.00	7.50	15.00
Hot water plate				
with signature	175.00	275.00	125.00	325.00
without signature	125.00	200.00	85.00	225.00
Jaffa fruit saucer (plain)				
with signature	50.00	75.00	35.00	80.00
without signature	15.00	25.00	10.00	25.00
Picture plaque, large	20.00	30.00	12.50	30.00
Plate, 6 ½"				
with signature	35.00	55.00	25.00	55.00
without signature	20.00	30.00	15.00	30.00
Plate, 7 ½"				
with signature	35.00	55.00	25.00	55.00
without signature	20.00	30.00	15.00	30.00
Plate, 8 ½"				
with signature	35.00	55.00	25.00	60.00
without signature	25.00	40.00	18.00	40.00
Porridge bowl				
with signature	90.00	150.00	60.00	175.00
without signature	70.00	110.00	45.00	125.00

Mrs. Moppet's Tea Room (LF6)

MRS. MOPPET'S TEA ROOM

Design No.:   LF6
Designer: Barbara Vernon
Issued: By 1940 - by 1952

Shape	USD	CAD	GBP	AUD
Baby plate, oval, large				
with signature	400.00	625.00	275.00	650.00
without signature	300.00	475.00	200.00	500.00
Baby plate, round, large				
with silver rim		Rare		
with signature	300.00	450.00	200.00	500.00
without signature	250.00	375.00	175.00	375.00
Bread / butter plate, handles				
with signature	500.00	800.00	325.00	900.00
without signature	400.00	625.00	275.00	650.00
Cereal / oatmeal bowl				
with signature	110.00	175.00	75.00	200.00
without signature	90.00	150.00	60.00	175.00
Plate, 8 ½"				
with signature	115.00	175.00	80.00	175.00
without signature	75.00	125.00	50.00	135.00
Porridge bowl				
with signature	125.00	200.00	80.00	225.00
without signature	100.00	100.00	65.00	175.00

Style One Egg Cup, *Trumpeter* (EC5),
with Barbara Vernon facsimile signature on side and backstamp/base.

NETTING A CRICKET

Design No.: HW6
Designer: Barbara Vernon
Issued: By 1937 - by 1952
Combined with: *Artist*, HW1
Cuddling under a Mushroom, HW4
Dunce, HW1R
Family Going out on Washing Day, HW8
Fishing in the Goldfish Bowl, HW3R
Gardener with Wheelbarrow, HW9R
Pressing Trousers, HW14
Proposal, HW11
Pulling Trousers, HW2
Reading the Times, HW2R

Netting a Cricket (HW6)

Shape	USD	CAD	GBP	AUD
Casino jug, 24s				
with signature	600.00	950.00	425.00	975.00
without signature	500.00	800.00	350.00	825.00
Casino sugar bowl, 30s				
with signature	250.00	375.00	175.00	400.00
without signature	175.00	275.00	125.00	325.00
Casino sugar bowl, 36s				
with signature	200.00	325.00	125.00	350.00
without signature	150.00	225.00	100.00	250.00
Casino teacup				
with signature	100.00	150.00	65.00	175.00
without signature	75.00	125.00	50.00	125.00
Don beaker				
with signature	200.00	325.00	140.00	350.00
without signature	175.00	275.00	125.00	300.00
Don beaker, one handle				
with signature	200.00	325.00	140.00	350.00
without signature	175.00	275.00	125.00	300.00
Don mug, one handle				
with signature	150.00	250.00	100.00	275.00
without signature	125.00	200.00	90.00	225.00
Don mug, two handles				
with signature	150.00	250.00	100.00	275.00
without signature	125.00	200.00	90.00	225.00
Jaffa fruit saucer				
plain rim	100.00	150.00	75.00	175.00
wavy rim	100.00	150.00	75.00	175.00
Jam pot	1,500.00	2,500.00	1,000.00	3,000.00
Plate, 6 ½"				
with signature	90.00	150.00	60.00	175.00
without signature	60.00	100.00	40.00	100.00

Note: Retirement dates are all approximate. When a design is retired all remaining stocks of the retired litho prints are used until exhausted.

NEW ARRIVAL THEME — Colin Twinn

Family Group with Father Standing (CT97)

FAMILY GROUP WITH FATHER STANDING

Design No.: CT97 Family Group with Father Standing
Designer: Colin Twinn
Issued: 1995 - 1997

Shape	USD	CAD	GBP	AUD
Baby plate, round, small	20.00	30.00	15.00	30.00
Plate, 8"	25.00	40.00	18.00	40.00

Family Group with Father Kneeling (CT98)

FAMILY GROUP WITH FATHER KNEELING

Design No.: Front — CT98 Family Group with Father Kneeling
             Reverse — CT99 New Arrival Inscription
Designer: Colin Twinn
Issued: 1995 - 1997

Shape	USD	CAD	GBP	AUD
Hug-a-mug, one handle	10.00	15.00	7.50	15.00
Money ball	10.00	15.00	7.50	15.00

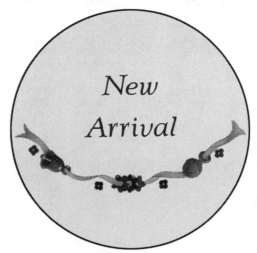

New Arrival Inscription (CT99)

NEW BABY THEME — *Frank Endersby*

SHOWING BABY AT WINDOW

Design No.:	40 Showing Baby at Window
Designer:	Frank Endersby
Issued:	1996 to the present

Shape	USD	CAD	GBP	AUD
Plate, 6 ½"	N/I	25.00	8.00	34.95
Plate, 8"	N/I	35.00	11.00	49.95

Showing Baby at Window (40)

Pushing Pram (41)

PUSHING PRAM / PLAYING WITH BALL

Design No.:	Front — 41 Pushing Pram
	Reverse — 42 Playing with Ball
Designer:	Frank Endersby
Issued:	1996 to the present
Combined with:	*Decorating the Cake*, (9)
	Playing and reading, (15)

Shape	USD	CAD	GBP	AUD
Hug-a-mug, one handle	30.00	33.00	11.00	49.95
Hug-a-mug, two handles	32.50	39.00	12.00	56.95
Divider dish	50.00	75.00	35.00	75.00
Malvern beaker	15.00	25.00	10.00	25.00
Money ball	33.75	40.00	15.00	62.95
Stratford teacup	7.50	12.00	5.00	12.00

* Indicates scene on divider dish.

Playing with Ball (42)

NURSERY THEME — Colin Twinn

Nursery, First Version (CT19)

NURSERY
First Version, Small Size

Design No.:	CT19 Nursery
Designer:	Colin Twinn
Issued:	1990 - 1993
Combined with:	*Family with Pram*, Style Two, CT14
	Standing by Pram, CT6

Shape	USD	CAD	GBP	AUD
Albion jug, 1 pint	150.00	225.00	100.00	225.00
Baby plate, round, small	20.00	30.00	15.00	30.00
Cake stand	150.00	250.00	100.00	300.00
Cereal / oatmeal bowl	35.00	55.00	25.00	55.00
Lamp	100.00	150.00	65.00	175.00
Money ball	10.00	15.00	7.50	15.00
Picture plaque, large	20.00	30.00	12.50	30.00
Plate, 6 ½"	20.00	30.00	15.00	30.00
Plate, 8"	25.00	40.00	18.00	40.00

Nursery, Second Version (CT28)

NURSERY
Second Version, Large Size /
BUNNY ON ROCKING HORSE

Design No.:	Front — CT28 Nursery
	Reverse — CT29 Bunny on Rocking Horse
Designer:	Colin Twinn
Issued:	1990 - 1993
Combined with:	*Family with Pram*, Style Two, CT14
	Father Bunnykins with Fishing Rod, (CT27)

Shape	USD	CAD	GBP	AUD
Albion cream jug	50.00	75.00	35.00	75.00
Albion jug, ½ pint	100.00	150.00	70.00	150.00
Albion jug, 1 pint	150.00	225.00	100.00	225.00
Albion teapot	50.00	85.00	35.00	95.00
Egg cup				
Style Three	7.50	12.50	5.00	12.50
Hug-a-mug, one handle	10.00	15.00	7.50	15.00
Hug-a-mug, two handles	10.00	15.00	7.50	15.00
Money ball	10.00	15.00	7.50	15.00
Picture plaque, small	20.00	30.00	12.50	30.00
Savings book	15.00	22.50	10.00	22.50
Stratford straight beaker	15.00	25.00	10.00	25.00
Stratford teacup	7.50	12.00	5.00	12.00

Bunny on Rocking Horse (CT29)

BUNNY WITH MIRROR

Design No.:   Front — CT35 Bunny with Mirror
Designer: Colin Twinn
Issued: 1990 - 1993
Combined with: *Bunnies in the Bath*, Second Version, CT34
      Classroom Scene, Style Two, First version, CT36
      Classroom Scene, Style Two, Second version, CT16
      Picking Daisies, CT4

Shape	USD	CAD	GBP	AUD
Albion cream jug	50.00	75.00	35.00	75.00
Albion sugar bowl	30.00	50.00	20.00	50.00
Divider dish	75.00	125.00	50.00	125.00
Egg cup				
Style Three	7.50	12.50	5.00	12.50

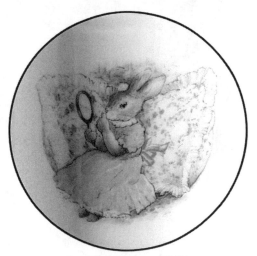

Bunny with Mirror (CT35)

China eggcups, *Pushing the Wheelbarrow* (CT3)
and *Bunnies in the Bath,* second version (CT34).

Orange Vendor (SF12)

ORANGE VENDOR

Design No.:	SF12
Designer:	Walter Hayward after Barbara Vernon
Issued:	By 1952 - 1967

Shape	USD	CAD	GBP	AUD
Baby plate, round, small				
with signature	45.00	75.00	30.00	90.00
without signature	20.00	30.00	15.00	30.00
Baby plate, round, large				
with signature	75.00	125.00	50.00	150.00
without signature	50.00	75.00	35.00	85.00
Casino jug, 30s				
with signature	200.00	300.00	150.00	300.00
without signature	150.00	250.00	100.00	250.00
Casino saucer				
with signature	15.00	25.00	10.00	25.00
without signature	7.50	12.00	5.00	12.00
Casino teapot, 30s				
with signature	250.00	375.00	165.00	400.00
without signature	150.00	225.00	100.00	250.00
Cereal / oatmeal bowl				
with signature	25.00	40.00	15.00	45.00
without signature	10.00	15.00	7.50	15.00
Hot water plate				
with signature	175.00	275.00	125.00	325.00
without signature	125.00	200.00	85.00	225.00
Jaffa fruit saucer (plain)				
with signature	25.00	40.00	15.00	40.00
without signature	20.00	30.00	12.50	30.00
Plate, 6 ½"				
with signature	35.00	55.00	25.00	55.00
without signature	20.00	30.00	15.00	30.00
Plate, 7 ½"				
with signature	35.00	55.00	25.00	55.00
without signature	20.00	30.00	15.00	30.00
Plate, 8 ½"				
with signature	35.00	55.00	25.00	60.00
without signature	25.00	40.00	18.00	40.00

Note: Retirement dates are all approximate. When a design is retired all remaining stocks of retired litho prints are used until exhausted.

PICNIC
Style One, First Version (without trees)

Design No.:   Unknown
Designer: Walter Hayward after Barbara Vernon
Issued: 1940

Shape	USD	CAD	GBP	AUD
Baby plate, oval, small		Rare		
Baby plate, round, large	450.00	675.00	325.00	700.00
Plate, 8 ½"	300.00	475.00	200.00	500.00

Note: This design should appear with the Barbara Vernon facsimile signature.

Picnic, Style One, First Version

Picnic, Style One, Second Version (LF10)

PICNIC
Style One, Second Version (with trees)

This scene was redrawn to better fit, or conform to round shapes.

Design No.:   LF10
Designer: Walter Hayward after Barbara Vernon
Issued: By 1940 - 1970
Combined with: *Game of Golf*, SF11

Shape	USD	CAD	GBP	AUD
Baby plate, oval, large				
with signature	200.00	325.00	150.00	325.00
without signature	150.00	225.00	100.00	225.00
Baby plate, round, large				
with signature	150.00	250.00	100.00	275.00
without signature	125.00	200.00	85.00	225.00
Bread and butter plate				
with signature	250.00	400.00	175.00	400.00
without signature	200.00	325.00	150.00	325.00
Casino teapot, 30s				
with signature	200.00	325.00	125.00	350.00
without signature	150.00	225.00	100.00	250.00
Cereal / oatmeal bowl				
with signature	110.00	175.00	75.00	200.00
without signature	90.00	150.00	60.00	175.00
Hot water plate				
with signature	150.00	225.00	100.00	250.00
without signature	125.00	200.00	85.00	225.00
Plate, 8 ½"				
with signature	115.00	175.00	80.00	175.00
without signature	75.00	125.00	50.00	135.00
Porridge bowl				
with signature	110.00	175.00	70.00	200.00
without signature	85.00	125.00	55.00	150.00

PICNIC CAKE STALL THEME — Colin Twinn

Picnic and Cake Stall (CT2)

PICNIC AND CAKE STALL

Design No.:	CT2 Picnic and Cake Stall
Designer:	Colin Twinn
Issued:	1989 - 1993

Shape	USD	CAD	GBP	AUD
Plate, 8"	30.00	45.00	20.00	50.00
Plate 10 ½"	35.00	55.00	25.00	60.00

Cake Stall (CT12)

CAKE STALL / PICKING DAISIES

Design No.:	Front — CT12 Cake Stall
	Reverse — CT4 Picking Daisies
Designer:	Colin Twinn
Issued:	1989 - 1993
Combined with:	*Bunny with Mirror*, CT35
	Classroom Scene, Style Two, Second Version, CT16
	Ice Cream Seller, Second Variation, CT11
	Pushing the Wheelbarrow, CT3
	Queen of the May, First Variation, CT7
	Queen of the May, Second Variation, CT13
	Standing by Pram, CT6

Shape	USD	CAD	GBP	AUD
Albion cream jug	50.00	75.00	35.00	75.00
Albion jug, ½ pint	100.00	150.00	70.00	150.00
Albion jug, 1 pint	150.00	225.00	100.00	225.00
Albion teapot	50.00	85.00	35.00	95.00
Hug-a-mug, one handle	10.00	15.00	7.50	15.00
Hug-a-mug, two handles	10.00	15.00	7.50	15.00
Malvern beaker	15.00	25.00	10.00	25.00
Stratford straight beaker	15.00	25.00	10.00	25.00
Stratford teacup	7.50	12.00	5.00	12.00

Note: *Cake Stall*, (CT12) is combined with *Standing by Pram*, (CT6) on Albion, ½ and 1 pint jugs.

Picking Daisies (CT4)

PICNIC THEME — Frank Endersby

PICNIC
Style Two

Design No.:	16 Picnic		
Designer:	Frank Endersby		
Issued:	1995 to the present		

Shape	USD	CAD	GBP	AUD
Baby plate, round, small	N/I	46.00	14.00	62.95
Cereal / oatmeal bowl	N/I	33.00	11.00	49.95
Plate, 6 ½"	N/I	25.00	8.00	34.95
Plate, 8"	N/I	35.00	11.00	49.95

Picnic, Style Two (16)

Playing Badminton (17)

PLAYING BADMINTON / RESTING, *Style One*

Design No.:	Front —17 Playing Badminton		
	Reverse — 18 Resting, Style One		
Designer:	Frank Endersby		
Issued:	1995 to the present		

Shape	USD	CAD	GBP	AUD
Hug-a-mug, one handle	30.00	33.00	11.00	49.95
Hug-a-mug, two handles	32.50	39.00	12.00	56.95
Money ball	33.75	40.00	15.00	62.95
Stratford straight beaker	15.00	25.00	10.00	25.00
Stratford teacup	7.50	12.00	5.00	12.00

Resting (18)

Note: It is unusual to find the Stratford beaker with this design as this shape was officially withdrawn in 1993, two years before this Frank Endersby design was introduced.

Pillow Fight (SF7)

PILLOW FIGHT
Style One

Design No.: SF7
Designer: Barbara Vernon
Issued: By 1940 - by 1952
Combined with: *Chicken Pulling a Cart*, SF8

Shape	USD	CAD	GBP	AUD
Baby plate, oval, small				
with signature	200.00	325.00	150.00	325.00
without signature	150.00	225.00	100.00	225.00
Casino teapot, 24s				
with signature	375.00	550.00	250.00	600.00
without signature	300.00	450.00	200.00	500.00
Cereal / oatmeal bowl				
with signature	50.00	80.00	35.00	80.00
without signature	35.00	55.00	25.00	55.00
Hot water plate				
with signature	175.00	275.00	125.00	325.00
without signature	125.00	200.00	85.00	225.00
Plate, 6 ½"				
with signature	60.00	95.00	40.00	100.00
without signature	40.00	65.00	25.00	70.00
Plate, 7 ½"				
with signature	60.00	95.00	49.00	100.00
without signature	40.00	65.00	25.00	70.00

PLAYING ON THE RIVER

Design No.:   SF16
Designer: Walter Hayward after Barbara Vernon
Issued: By 1952 - by 1998
Combined with: *Mr. Piggly's Stores*, SF14

Shape	USD	CAD	GBP	AUD
Baby plate, round, small				
with signature	45.00	75.00	30.00	75.00
without signature	20.00	30.00	15.00	30.00
Cake stand	150.00	250.00	100.00	300.00
Casino saucer				
with signature	15.00	25.00	10.00	25.00
without signature	7.50	12.00	5.00	12.00
Casino teapot, 30s				
with signature	250.00	375.00	165.00	400.00
without signature	150.00	225.00	100.00	250.00
Cereal / oatmeal bowl				
with signature	25.00	40.00	15.00	45.00
without signature	10.00	15.00	7.50	15.00
Hot water plate				
with signature	175.00	275.00	125.00	325.00
without signature	125.00	200.00	85.00	225.00
Jaffa fruit saucer (plain)				
with signature	50.00	75.00	35.00	80.00
without signature	15.00	25.00	10.00	25.00
Picture plaque, large	20.00	30.00	12.50	30.00
Plate, 6 ½"				
with signature	35.00	55.00	25.00	55.00
without signature	20.00	30.00	15.00	30.00
Plate, 7 ½"				
with signature	.35.00	55.00	25.00	55.00
without signature	20.00	30.00	15.00	30.00
Plate, 8"				
with signature	35.00	55.00	25.00	60.00
without signature	25.00	40.00	18.00	40.00

Playing on the River (SF16)

Playing with Cup and Spoon (EC6)

PLAYING WITH CUP AND SPOON

Design No.:	EC6
Designer:	Barbara Vernon
Issued:	1937 to the present
Combined with:	*Bedtime with Dollies*, EC125
	Daisy Chains, HW25
	Drummer, EC2
	Drummer and Bugler, EC126
	Fishing in the Goldfish Bowl, HW3R
	Hikers, EC124
	Hobby Horse, Style Two, EC121
	Holding Hat and Coat, EC4
	Playing with Doll and Pram, EC123
	Raising Hat, Style Two, EC7
	Reading, EC122
	Sheltering Under an Umbrella, EC3
	Sleeping in a Rocking Chair, EC1
	Trumpeter, EC5

Shape	USD	CAD	GBP	AUD
Albion sugar bowl	30.00	50.00	20.00	50.00
Beaker cover	85.00	135.00	50.00	150.00
Casino teacup				
with signature	15.00	25.00	10.00	25.00
without signature	7.50	12.00	5.00	12.00
Egg cup				
Style One	40.00	60.00	25.00	65.00
Style Two	80.00	125.00	50.00	135.00
Style Three	N/I	15.00	5.00	19.95
Lid of hot water plate	100.00	150.00	70.00	175.00
Money ball	**33.75**	**40.00**	**15.00**	**62.95**

FINE WHITE CHINA

Night light	Very Rare
Saucer	Very Rare
Teacup	Very Rare

PLAYING WITH DOLL AND PRAM

Design No.:	EC123
Designer:	Walter Hayward
Issued:	1959 to the present
Combined with:	*Bedtime with Dollies*, EC125
	Building Sand Castles, HW138
	Dancing with Doll, HW115R
	Drummer, EC2
	Drummer and Bugler, EC126
	Hikers, EC124
	Hobby Horse, Style Two, EC121
	Holding Hat and Coat, EC4
	Playing with Cup and Spoon, EC6
	Playing with Dolls and Prams, HW115
	Reading, EC122
	Sailing Boats, HW138R
	Sheltering Under an Umbrella, EC3
	Sleeping in a Rocking Chair, EC1

Playing with Doll and Pram (EC123)

Shape	USD	CAD	GBP	AUD
Albion cream jug	50.00	75.00	35.00	75.00
Albion jug, ½ pint	100.00	150.00	70.00	150.00
Albion jug, 1 pint	150.00	225.00	100.00	225.00
Albion sugar bowl	30.00	50.00	20.00	50.00
Beaker cover	85.00	135.00	50.00	150.00
Egg cup				
Style One	40.00	60.00	25.00	65.00
Style Two	80.00	125.00	50.00	135.00
Style Three	**N/I**	**15.00**	**5.00**	**19.95**
Lid of hot water plate	100.00	150.00	70.00	175.00

Playing with Dolls and Prams (HW115)

Dancing with Doll (HW115R)

PLAYING WITH DOLLS AND PRAMS / DANCING WITH DOLL

Design No.:	Front — HW115 Playing with Dolls and Prams
	Reverse — HW115R Dancing with Doll
Designer:	Walter Hayward
Issued:	1959 - by 1998
Combined with:	*Broken Umbrella*, HW27R
	Disturbing Sleeping Father, HW118
	Hikers, EC124
	Ice Cream on the Beach, HW136R
	Lunch Break, HW29R
	Playing with Doll and Pram, EC123
	*Playing with Doll and Teddy, HW120R
	*Roller Skating Arm in Arm, HW137R
	Serving Tea, HW116R
	Trying on Hats, HW28R

Shape	USD	CAD	GBP	AUD
Albion cream jug	50.00	75.00	35.00	75.00
Albion jug, ½ pint	100.00	150.00	70.00	150.00
Albion jug, 1 pint	150.00	225.00	100.00	225.00
Albion teapot	50.00	85.00	35.00	95.00
Casino saucer	7.50	12.00	5.00	12.00
Casino teacup	7.50	12.00	5.00	12.00
Divider dish	50.00	75.00	35.00	75.00
Don beaker	35.00	55.00	25.00	60.00
Don beaker, one handle	35.00	55.00	25.00	60.00
Don mug, one handle	20.00	30.00	15.00	30.00
Don mug, two handles	20.00	30.00	15.00	30.00
Egg box				
small	225.00	350.00	150.00	400.00
medium	300.00	450.00	200.00	500.00
large	375.00	550.00	250.00	600.00
Hug-a-mug, one handle	10.00	15.00	7.50	15.00
Hug-a-mug, two handles	10.00	15.00	7.50	15.00
Jaffa fruit saucer (plain)	10.00	15.00	7.50	15.00
Lamp	100.00	150.00	65.00	175.00
Lid of hot water plate	100.00	150.00	70.00	175.00
Money ball	10.00	15.00	7.50	15.00
Picture plaque, small	20.00	30.00	12.50	20.00
Plate, 6 ½"	20.00	30.00	15.00	30.00
Savings book	15.00	22.50	10.00	22.50
Stratford straight beaker	15.00	25.00	10.00	25.00
Stratford teacup	7.50	12.00	5.00	12.00

* Indicates scene on divider dish.

Note: The savings book can have a combined design of *Dancing with Doll* (HW115R) and *Trying on Hats* (HW28R) or *Dancing with Doll* (HW115R) and *Lunch Break* (HW29R)

PLAYTIME THEME — *Frank Endersby*

SEE-SAW
Style Two

Design No.:	52 See-saw
Designer:	Frank Endersby
Issued:	1995 to the present

Shape	USD	CAD	GBP	AUD
Baby plate, round, small	N/I	46.00	14.00	62.95
Plate, 6 ½"	N/I	25.00	8.00	34.95
Plate, 8"	N/I	35.00	11.00	49.95

See-saw, Style Two (52)

Pushing Swing (53)

PUSHING SWING / BUNNY ON SWING

Design No.:	Front — 53 Pushing Swing
	Reverse — 54 Bunny on Swing
Designer:	Frank Endersby
Issued:	1995 to the present

Shape	USD	CAD	GBP	AUD
Hug-a-mug, one handle	30.00	33.00	11.00	49.95
Hug-a-mug, two handles	32.50	39.00	12.00	56.95

Bunny on Swing (54)

Portrait Painter (SF20)

PORTRAIT PAINTER

Design No.:   SF20
Designer: Walter Hayward
Issued: 1954 - by 1998

Shape	USD	CAD	GBP	AUD
Baby plate, round, small				
with signature	45.00	75.00	30.00	80.00
without signature	20.00	30.00	15.00	30.00
Cake stand	150.00	250.00	100.00	300.00
Casino saucer				
with signature	15.00	25.00	10.00	25.00
without signature	7.50	12.00	5.00	12.00
Casino teapot, 30s				
with signature	250.00	375.00	165.00	400.00
without signature	150.00	225.00	100.00	250.00
Cereal / oatmeal bowl				
with signature	25.00	40.00	15.00	45.00
without signature	10.00	15.00	7.50	15.00
Hot water plate				
with signature	150.00	225.00	100.00	250.00
without signature	125.00	200.00	85.00	225.00
Jaffa fruit saucer (plain)				
with signature	50.00	110.00	45.00	125.00
without signature	15.00	25.00	10.00	25.00
Plate, 6 ½"				
with signature	25.00	40.00	18.00	40.00
without signature	20.00	30.00	15.00	30.00
Plate, 7 ½"				
with signature	25.00	40.00	18.00	40.00
without signature	20.00	30.00	15.00	30.00
Plate, 8"	25.00	40.00	18.00	40.00

POST OFFICE THEME — Frank Endersby

POSTING LETTERS

Design No.:	28 Posting Letters		
Designer:	Frank Endersby		
Issued:	1995 to the present		

Shape	USD	CAD	GBP	AUD
Cereal bowl	N/I	33.00	11.00	49.95
Plate, 6 ½"	N/I	25.00	8.00	34.95
Plate, 8"	N/I	35.00	11.00	49.95

Posting Letters (28)

Letter Box (29)

LETTER BOX / CARRYING LETTER

Design No.:	Front — 29 Letter Box
	Reverse — 30 Carrying Letter
Designer:	Frank Endersby
Issued:	1995 to the present
Combined with:	*Playing with Balloons*, (33)
	Trying on Hat, (12)

Shape	USD	CAD	GBP	AUD
Hug-a-mug, one handle	30.00	33.00	11.00	49.95
Hug-a-mug, two handles	32.50	39.00	12.00	56.95
Divider dish	50.00	75.00	35.00	75.00
Stratford teacup	7.50	12.00	5.00	12.00

* Indicates scene on divider dish.

Carrying Letter (30)

Postman Delivering Letters (HW19)

Writing Letters (HW19R)

POSTMAN DELIVERING LETTERS / WRITING LETTERS

Design No.:   Front — HW19 Postman Delivering Letters
              Reverse — HW19R Writing Letters
Designer: Walter Hayward after Barbara Vernon
Issued: By 1952 - 1967

Shape	USD	CAD	GBP	AUD
Baby plate, round, small				
with signature	125.00	200.00	90.00	200.00
without signature	100.00	150.00	70.00	175.00
Casino jug, 24s				
with signature	600.00	950.00	425.00	975.00
without signature	500.00	800.00	350.00	825.00
Casino jug, 36s				
with signature	400.00	600.00	275.00	700.00
without signature	350.00	550.00	225.00	650.00
Casino jug, 42s				
with signature	300.00	450.00	200.00	500.00
without signature	250.00	375.00	175.00	400.00
Casino saucer				
with signature	100.00	150.00	65.00	175.00
without signature	75.00	125.00	50.00	125.00
Casino sugar bowl, 30s				
with signature	250.00	375.00	175.00	400.00
without signature	175.00	275.00	125.00	325.00
Casino teacup				
with signature	100.00	150.00	65.00	175.00
without signature	75.00	125.00	50.00	125.00
Casino teapot, 24s				
with signature	500.00	800.00	350.00	950.00
without signature	400.00	700.00	300.00	850.00
Casino teapot, 30s				
with signature	400.00	600.00	275.00	700.00
without signature	300.00	450.00	200.00	500.00
Don beaker				
with signature	200.00	325.00	140.00	350.00
without signature	125.00	200.00	80.00	225.00
Don beaker, one handle				
with signature	200.00	325.00	140.00	350.00
without signature	125.00	200.00	80.00	225.00
Don mug, one handle				
with signature	150.00	250.00	100.00	275.00
without signature	65.00	100.00	45.00	100.00
Don mug, two handles				
with signature	150.00	250.00	100.00	275.00
without signature	65.00	100.00	45.00	100.00
Lid of hot water plate				
with signature	150.00	225.00	100.00	250.00
without signature	100.00	150.00	70.00	175.00
Plate, 6 ½"				
with signature	90.00	150.00	60.00	175.00
without signature	60.00	100.00	40.00	100.00

PRESSING TROUSERS

Pressing Trousers (HW14)

Design No.:	HW14			
Designer:	Barbara Vernon			
Issued:	By 1937 - 1967			
Combined with:	*Cycling*, HW15R			
	Dunce, HW1R			
	Feeding the Baby, HW13			
	Fishing in the Gold Fish Bowl, HW3R			
	Footballer, HW13R			
	Frightening Spider, SF4			

Golfer, HW4R
Leapfrog, HW12R
Netting a Cricket, HW6
Raising Hat, Style One, HW16R
Santa Claus, SF9
Top Hat, HW14R
Watering the Flowers, SF15
Wedding, LFd

Shape	USD	CAD	GBP	AUD
Baby plate, round, small				
with signature	75.00	125.00	50.00	125.00
without signature	50.00	80.00	35.00	80.00
Casino jug, 24s				
with signature	400.00	625.00	275.00	650.00
without signature	350.00	550.00	250.00	550.00
Casino jug, 30s				
with signature	300.00	475.00	200.00	475.00
without signature	225.00	325.00	150.00	325.00
Casino saucer				
with signature	75.00	125.00	50.00	125.00
without signature	50.00	75.00	35.00	75.00
Casino teacup				
with signature	75.00	125.00	50.00	125.00
without signature	50.00	75.00	35.00	75.00
Casino teapot, 30s				
with signature	325.00	500.00	225.00	550.00
without signature	250.00	400.00	175.00	450.00
Casino teapot, 36s				
with signature	250.00	375.00	165.00	400.00
without signature	225.00	350.00	150.00	400.00
Don beaker				
with signature	150.00	250.00	110.00	275.00
without signature	85.00	135.00	60.00	150.00
Don beaker, one handle				
with signature	150.00	250.00	110.00	275.00
without signature	85.00	135.00	60.00	150.00

Shape	USD	CAD	GBP	AUD
Don mug, one handle				
with signature	100.00	150.00	70.00	150.00
without signature	35.00	55.00	25.00	60.00
Don mug, two handles				
with signature	100.00	150.00	70.00	150.00
without signature	35.00	55.00	25.00	60.00
Jaffa fruit saucer				
plain rim	60.00	95.00	40.00	100.00
wavy rim	70.00	110.00	45.00	125.00
Lid of hot water plate				
with signature	125.00	200.00	85.00	225.00
without signature	100.00	150.00	70.00	175.00
Plate, 6 ½"				
with signature	60.00	95.00	40.00	100.00
without signature	40.00	65.00	25.00	70.00

FINE WHITE CHINA

Shape				
Baby bowl			Very Rare	
Cereal/oatmeal bowl			Very Rare	
Rex mug, small, 2 ½"				
with signature			Very Rare	
without signature			Very Rare	
Saucer			Very Rare	
Shallow bowl			Very Rare	
Sugar bowl			Very Rare	
Teacup			Very Rare	

Proposal (HW11)

PROPOSAL

Design No.:	HW11
Designer:	Barbara Vernon
Issued:	By 1937 - by 1967
Combined with:	*Cycling*, HW15R
	Dress Making, HW26
	Dunce, HW1R
	Family at Breakfast, HW12
	Family with Pram, Style One, HW15
	Footballer, HW13R
	Golfer, HW4R
	Holding Hat and Coat, EC4
	Kissing Under the Mistletoe, HW11R
	Leapfrog, HW12R
	Netting a Cricket, HW6
	Pulling on Trousers, HW2
	Raising Hat, Style One, HW16R
	Santa Claus, SF9
	Wedding, LFd

Shape	USD	CAD	GBP	AUD
Baby plate, round, small				
with signature	75.00	125.00	50.00	125.00
without signature	50.00	80.00	35.00	80.00
Candle holder	2,000.00	3,000.00	1,250.00	4,000.00
Casino jugs, 36s				
with signature	300.00	475.00	200.00	475.00
without signature	250.00	400.00	175.00	400.00
Casino jug, 42s				
with signature	250.00	400.00	175.00	400.00
without signature	200.00	325.00	150.00	325.00
Casino saucer				
with signature	75.00	125.00	50.00	125.00
without signature	50.00	75.00	35.00	75.00
Casino sugar bowl, 30s				
with signature	200.00	325.00	125.00	350.00
without signature	150.00	225.00	100.00	250.00
Casino sugar bowl, 36s				
with signature	175.00	275.00	125.00	325.00
without signature	125.00	200.00	85.00	225.00
Casino teacup				
with signature	75.00	125.00	50.00	125.00
without signature	50.00	75.00	35.00	75.00
Casino teapot, 24s				
with signature	375.00	550.00	250.00	600.00
without signature	300.00	450.00	200.00	500.00
Casino teapot, 30s				
with signature	325.00	500.00	225.00	550.00
without signature	250.00	400.00	175.00	450.00
Cereal/oatmeal bowl				
with signature	50.00	80.00	35.00	80.00
without signature	35.00	55.00	25.00	55.00

Shape	USD	CAD	GBP	AUD
Don beaker				
with signature	150.00	250.00	110.00	275.00
without signature	85.00	135.00	60.00	150.00
Don beaker, one handle				
with signature	150.00	250.00	110.00	275.00
without signature	85.00	135.00	60.00	150.00
Don mug, one handle				
with signature	100.00	150.00	70.00	150.00
without signature	35.00	55.00	25.00	60.00
Don mug, two handles				
with signature	100.00	150.00	70.00	150.00
without signature	35.00	55.00	25.00	60.00
Jaffa fruit saucer				
plain rim	60.00	95.00	40.00	100.00
wavy rim	70.00	110.00	45.00	125.00
Jam pot	1,500.00	2,500.00	1,000.00	3,000.00
Lid of hot water plate				
with signature	150.00	225.00	100.00	250.00
without signature	100.00	150.00	70.00	175.00
Plate, 6 ½"				
with signature	60.00	95.00	40.00	100.00
without signature	40.00	65.00	25.00	70.00

FINE WHITE CHINA

Shape	USD	CAD	GBP	AUD
Baby bowl			Very rare	
Beaker			Very rare	
Plate			Very rare	
Prince sugar bowl			Very rare	
Rex mug, small, 2 ½"			Very rare	
Saucer			Very rare	
Teacup			Very rare	

Note: *Proposal* (HW111) is combined with *Golfer* (HW4R) and also *Dunce* on Rex mugs.

PULLING ON TROUSERS

Design No.:	HW2
Designer:	Barbara Vernon
Issued:	By 1937 - by 1952
Combined with:	*Artist*, HW1
	Bedtime in Bunks, SF3
	Family at Breakfast, HW12
	Family with Pram, Style One, HW15
	Feeding the Baby, HW
	Fishing in the Goldfish Bowl, HW3R
	Game of Golf, SF11
	Golfer, HW4R
	Holding Hat and Coat, EC4
	Netting a Cricket, HW6
	Proposal, HW11
	Raising Hat, Style One, HW16R
	Reading the Times, HW2R

Pulling on Trousers (HW2)

Shape	USD	CAD	GBP	AUD
Casino jug, 30s				
with signature	300.00	475.00	200.00	475.00
without signature	225.00	325.00	150.00	325.00
Casino jug, 36s				
with signature	300.00	475.00	200.00	475.00
without signature	250.00	400.00	175.00	400.00
Casino jug, 42s				
with signature	250.00	400.00	175.00	400.00
without signature	200.00	325.00	150.00	325.00
Casino saucer				
with signature	75.00	125.00	50.00	75.00
without signature	50.00	75.00	35.00	25.00
Casino sugar bowl, 30s				
with signature	200.00	325.00	125.00	350.00
without signature	150.00	225.00	100.00	250.00
Casino teacup				
with signature	75.00	125.00	50.00	75.00
without signature	50.00	75.00	35.00	25.00
Cup / mug, large		Rare		
Don beaker				
with signature	150.00	250.00	110.00	275.00
without signature	125.00	200.00	90.00	225.00

Shape	USD	CAD	GBP	AUD
Don beaker, one handle				
with signature	150.00	250.00	110.00	275.00
without signature	125.00	200.00	90.00	225.00
Don mug, one handle				
with signature	100.00	150.00	70.00	150.00
without signature	75.00	125.00	50.00	125.00
Don mug, two handles				
with signature	100.00	150.00	70.00	150.00
without signature	75.00	125.00	50.00	225.00
Jaffa fruit saucer				
plain rim	70.00	110.00	45.00	125.00
wavy rim	70.00	110.00	45.00	125.00
Jam pot	1,500.00	2,500.00	1,000.00	3,000.00
Lid of hot water plate				
with signature	150.00	225.00	100.00	250.00
without signature	100.00	150.00	70.00	175.00
Plate, 6 ½"				
with signature	60.00	95.00	40.00	100.00
without signature	40.00	65.00	25.00	70.00
FINE WHITE CHINA				
Teacup		Very rare		

Punch and Judy Show (HW136)

Ice Cream on the Beach (HW136R)

PUNCH AND JUDY SHOW /
ICE CREAM ON THE BEACH

Design No.: Front — HW136 Punch and Judy Show
Reverse — HW136R Ice Cream on the Beach
Designer: Walter Hayward
Issued: 1967 - by 1998
Combined with: *Cowboy on Rocking Horse, HW140R
Playing with Dolls and Prams, HW115
*Roller Skating, HW137R
Sailing Boats, HW138R
Serving Tea, HW116R
To the Station, HW17R

Shape	USD	CAD	GBP	AUD
Albion cream jug	50.00	75.00	35.00	75.00
Albion jug, ½ pint	100.00	150.00	70.00	150.00
Albion jug, 1 pint	150.00	225.00	100.00	225.00
Albion teapot	50.00	85.00	35.00	95.00
Cake stand	150.00	250.00	100.00	300.00
Casino saucer	7.50	12.00	5.00	12.00
Casino teacup	7.50	12.00	5.00	12.00
Casino teapot, 30s	150.00	225.00	100.00	250.00
Divider dish	50.00	75.00	35.00	75.00
Don beaker	35.00	55.00	25.00	60.00
Don beaker, one handle	35.00	55.00	25.00	60.00
Don mug, one handle	20.00	30.00	15.00	30.00
Don mug, two handles	20.00	30.00	15.00	30.00
Egg box				
small	225.00	350.00	150.00	400.00
medium	300.00	450.00	200.00	500.00
large	375.00	550.00	250.00	600.00
Hug-a-mug, one handle	10.00	15.00	7.50	15.00
Hug-a-mug, two handles	10.00	15.00	7.50	15.00
Jaffa fruit saucer (plain)	15.00	25.00	10.00	25.00
Lamp	100.00	150.00	65.00	175.00
Malvern beaker	15.00	25.00	10.00	25.00
Money ball	10.00	15.00	7.50	15.00
Picture plaque, small	20.00	30.00	12.50	30.00
Savings book	15.00	22.50	10.00	22.50
Stratford straight beaker	15.00	25.00	10.00	25.00
Stratford teacup	7.50	12.00	5.00	12.00

* Indicates scene on divider dish.

QUEEN OF THE MAY — *Colin Twinn*

First Variation, Small Size

Design No.:	Front — CT7 Queen of the May		
	Reverse — CT8 Counting Motif		
Designer:	Colin Twinn		
Issued:	1988 - 1993		
Combined with:	*Picking Daisies*, CT4		

Shape	USD	CAD	GBP	AUD
Albion cream jug	50.00	75.00	35.00	75.00
Albion jug, ½ pint	100.00	150.00	70.00	150.00
Albion jug, 1 pint	150.00	225.00	100.00	225.00
Hug-a-mug, one handle	10.00	5.00	7.50	15.00
Hug-a-mug, two handles	10.00	5.00	7.50	15.00
Picture plaque, small	20.00	30.00	12.50	30.00
Malvern beaker	15.00	25.00	10.00	25.00
Money ball				
Spring 1992	10.00	15.00	7.50	15.00
Fall 1992	10.00	15.00	7.50	15.00

Queen of the May, First Variation (CT7)

Note: Two money balls were issued for the U.S. Special Events Tour in 1992. This design was featured on the Spring tour with no special inscription. *Happy Birthday from Bunnykins* (CT60) was featured on the Fall tour. *Queen of the May* (CT17) is combined with *Picking Daisies* (CT4) on a one handled, hug-a-mug.

Counting Motif (CT8)

Queen of the May, Second Variation (CT13)

Second Variation, Large Size

Design No.:	CT13 Queen of the May		
Designer:	Colin Twinn		
Issued:	1989- 1993		
Combined with:	*Picking Daisies*, CT13		

Shape	USD	CAD	GBP	AUD
Albion jug, 1 pint	150.00	225.00	100.00	225.00
Cake stand	150.00	250.00	100.00	300.00
Cereal / oatmeal bowl	10.00	15.00	7.50	15.00
Lamp	100.00	150.00	65.00	175.00
Picture plaque, small	20.00	30.00	12.50	30.00
Picture plaque, large	20.00	30.00	12.50	30.00
Plate, 8"	25.00	40.00	18.00	40.00

Raft (SF111)

RAFT

Design No.: SF111
Designer: Walter Hayward after Penelope Hollinshead
Issued: 1959 to the present

Shape	USD	CAD	GBP	AUD
Baby plate, round, small	**N/I**	**46.00**	**14.00**	**62.95**
Casino saucer	7.50	12.00	5.00	12.00
Casino teapot, 30s	150.00	225.00	100.00	250.00
Cereal / oatmeal bowl	10.00	15.00	7.50	15.00
Coupe plate, 6 ¾"		Very Rare		
Hot water plate	125.00	200.00	85.00	225.00
Jaffa fruit saucer (plain)	15.00	25.00	10.00	25.00
Picture plaque, large	20.00	30.00	12.50	30.00
Plate, 6 ½"	20.00	30.00	15.00	30.00
Plate, 7 ½"	20.00	30.00	15.00	30.00
Plate, 8"	25.00	40.00	18.00	40.00

Note: Retirement dates are all approximate. When a design is retired all remaining stocks of the retired litho prints are used until exhausted.

RAISING HAT
Style One

Design No.:   HW16R
Designer: Barbara Vernon
Issued: By 1937 - by 1952
Combined with: *Family at Breakfast*, HW12
                  Family with Pram, Style One, HW15
                  Feeding the Baby, HW13
                  Lambeth Walk, HW16
                  Pressing Trousers, HW14
                  Proposal, HW11
                  Pulling on Trousers, HW2
                  Sleeping in a Rocking Chair, EC1
                  Wedding, LFd

Raising Hat, Style One (HW16R)

Shape	USD	CAD	GBP	AUD
Casino jug, 42s				
with signature	250.00	400.00	175.00	400.00
without signature	200.00	325.00	150.00	325.00
Casino teacup				
with signature	75.00	125.00	50.00	125.00
without signature	50.00	75.00	35.00	75.00
Casino teapot, 30s				
with signature	325.00	500.00	225.00	550.00
without signature	250.00	400.00	175.00	450.00
Casino teapot, 36s				
with signature	250.00	375.00	175.00	400.00
without signature	225.00	350.00	150.00	375.00
Don beaker				
with signature	150.00	250.00	110.00	275.00
without signature	125.00	200.00	90.00	225.00
Don beaker, one handle				
with signature	150.00	250.00	110.00	275.00
without signature	125.00	200.00	90.00	225.00
Don mug, one handle				
with signature	100.00	150.00	70.00	150.00
without signature	75.00	125.00	50.00	125.00
Jam pot	1,500.00	2,500.00	1,000.00	3,000.00
Lid of hot water plate				
with signature	150.00	225.00	100.00	250.00
without signature	100.00	150.00	85.00	225.00

Note: *Raising Hat* (HW16R) is combined with *Family with Pram*, Style One, (HW15) on a large round and an oval baby plate, and also a 7 ½″ plate. For an illustration see page 71.

Raising Hat, Style Two (EC7)

RAISING HAT
Style Two

Design No.:	EC7
Designer:	Barbara Vernon
Issued:	1937 to the present
Combined with:	*Bedtime with Dollies*, EC125
	Drummer, EC2
	Drummer and Bugler, EC126
	Engine Pulling a Carriage, HW17
	Family with Pram, Style One, HW15
	Hikers, EC124
	Hobby Horse, Style Two, EC121
	Holding Hat and Coat, EC4
	Playing with Cup and Spoon, EC6
	Reading, EC122
	Sheltering Under an Umbrella, EC3
	Sleeping in a Rocking Chair, EC1
	To the Station, HW17R
	Trumpeter, EC5

Shape	USD	CAD	GBP	AUD
Albion sugar bowl	30.00	50.00	20.00	50.00
Beaker cover	85.00	135.00	50.00	150.00
Casino sugar bowl, 30s	150.00	225.00	100.00	250.00
Egg cup				
Style One	40.00	60.00	25.00	65.00
Style Two	80.00	125.00	50.00	135.00
Style Three	**N/I**	**15.00**	**5.00**	**19.95**
Lid of hot water plate	100.00	150.00	70.00	175.00

READING

Design No.:	EC122
Designer:	Walter Hayward
Issued:	1959 to the present
Combined with:	*Bedtime with Dollies*, EC125
	The Doll's House, HW120
	Drummer, EC2
	Drummer and Bugler, EC126
	Hikers, EC124
	Hobby Horse, Style Two, EC121
	Playing with Cup and Spoon, EC6
	Playing with Doll and Pram, EC123
	Raising Hat, Style Two, EC7
	Sheltering Under an Umbrella, EC3
	Sledging, Style One, HW141
	Sleeping in a Rocking Chair, EC1
	Trumpeter, EC5

Shape	USD	CAD	GBP	AUD
Albion sugar bowl	30.00	50.00	20.00	50.00
Beaker cover	125.00	175.00	75.00	175.00
Egg cup				
Style One	40.00	60.00	25.00	65.00
Style Two	80.00	125.00	50.00	135.00
Style Three	**N/I**	**15.00**	**5.00**	**19.95**
Lid of hot water plate	100.00	150.00	70.00	175.00
Money ball	10.00	15.00	7.50	15.00

Reading (EC122)

READING THE TIMES

Design No.:	HW2R
Designer:	Barbara Vernon
Issued:	By 1937 - by 1952
Combined with:	*Cycling*, HW15R
	Footballer, HW13R
	Golfer, HW4R
	Kissing Under the Mistletoe, HW11R
	Netting a Cricket, HW6
	Pulling on Trousers, HW2
	Smoking in the Doorway, SF2

Reading the Times (HW2R)

Shape	USD	CAD	GBP	AUD
Casino jug, 42s	300.00	450.00	200.00	500.00
Casino teacup	100.00	150.00	65.00	175.00
Cup / mug, large		Rare		
Don beaker	200.00	325.00	140.00	350.00
Don beaker, one handle	200.00	325.00	140.00	350.00
Don mug, one handle	150.00	250.00	100.00	275.00
Don mug, two handles	150.00	250.00	100.00	275.00

Note: This design should appear with the Barbara Vernon facsimile signature.

RING-A-RING O'ROSES

Design No.:	SF21
Designer:	Walter Hayward
Issued:	1954 - by 1998

Ring-a-Ring o'Roses (SF21)

Shape	USD	CAD	GBP	AUD
Baby plate, round, small				
with signature	45.00	75.00	30.00	75.00
without signature	20.00	30.00	15.00	30.00
Cake stand	150.00	250.00	100.00	300.00
Casino saucer				
with signature	15.00	25.00	10.00	25.00
without signature	7.50	12.00	5.00	12.00
Casino teapot, 24s				
with signature	275.00	400.00	175.00	450.00
without signature	175.00	275.00	125.00	325.00
Cereal / oatmeal bowl				
with signature	25.00	40.00	15.00	45.00
without signature	10.00	15.00	7.50	15.00
Hot water plate				
with signature	175.00	275.00	125.00	325.00
without signature	125.00	200.00	85.00	225.00
Jaffa fruit saucer (plain)				
with signature	70.00	110.00	45.00	125.00
without signature	15.00	25.00	10.00	45.00
Picture plaque, large	20.00	30.00	12.50	30.00
Plate, 6 ½"				
with signature	35.00	55.00	25.00	55.00
without signature	20.00	30.00	15.00	30.00
Plate, 7 ½"				
with signature	35.00	55.00	25.00	55.00
without signature	20.00	30.00	15.00	30.00
Plate, 8"				
with signature	35.00	55.00	25.00	60.00
without signature	25.00	40.00	18.00	40.00

Rocking Horse (HW24)

Hobby Horse (HW24R)

ROCKING HORSE / HOBBY HORSE, Style One

Design No.:	Front — HW24 Rocking Horse
	Reverse — HW24R Hobby Horse
Designer:	Walter Hayward after Barbara Vernon
Issued:	1954 - 1967
Combined with:	*Trumpeter*, EC5

Shape	USD	CAD	GBP	AUD
Casino teacup				
with signature	75.00	125.00	50.00	125.00
without signature	50.00	75.00	35.00	75.00
Don beaker				
with signature	150.00	200.00	110.00	275.00
without signature	85.00	135.00	60.00	150.00
Don beaker, one handle				
with signature	150.00	200.00	110.00	275.00
without signature	85.00	135.00	60.00	150.00
Don mug, one handle				
with signature	100.00	150.00	70.00	150.00
without signature	35.00	55.00	25.00	60.00
Don mug, two handles				
with signature	100.00	150.00	70.00	150.00
without signature	35.00	55.00	25.00	60.00
Jaffa fruit saucer (plain)				
with signature	100.00	150.00	75.00	165.00
without signature	60.00	95.00	40.00	100.00
Lamp	100.00	150.00	65.00	175.00
Lid of hot water plate				
with signature	150.00	225.00	100.00	250.00
without signature	100.00	150.00	70.00	175.00
Money ball	10.00	15.00	7.50	15.00
Plate, 6 ½"				
with signature	60.00	95.00	40.00	100.00
without signature	40.00	65.00	25.00	70.00

ROLLER SKATING RACE /
ROLLER SKATING ARM IN ARM

Design No.:	Front — HW137 Roller Skating Race
	Reverse — HW137R Roller Skating Arm in Arm
Designer:	Walter Hayward
Issued:	1967 - by 1998
Combined with:	*Building Sand Castles*, HW138
	Dancing with Doll, HW115R
	Playing with Dolls and Prams, HW115
	Sailing Boats, HW138R

Roller Skating Race (HW137)

Shape	USD	CAD	GBP	AUD
Albion cream jug	50.00	75.00	35.00	75.00
Albion jug, 1 pint	150.00	225.00	100.00	225.00
Albion teapot	50.00	85.00	35.00	95.00
Cake stand	150.00	250.00	100.00	300.00
Casino teacup	7.50	12.00	5.00	12.00
Divider dish	50.00	75.00	35.00	75.00
Don beaker	35.00	55.00	25.00	60.00
Don beaker, one handle	35.00	55.00	25.00	60.00
Don mug, one handle	15.00	25.00	10.00	25.00
Don mug, two handles	15.00	25.00	10.00	25.00
Egg box				
small	225.00	350.00	150.00	400.00
medium	300.00	450.00	200.00	500.00
large	375.00	550.00	250.00	600.00
Hug-a-mug, one handle	10.00	15.00	7.50	15.00
Hug-a-mug, two handles	10.00	15.00	7.50	15.00
Jaffa fruit saucer (plain)	15.00	25.00	10.00	25.00
Lamp	100.00	150.00	65.00	175.00
Malvern beaker	15.00	25.00	10.00	25.00
Money ball	10.00	15.00	7.50	15.00
Picture plaque, small	20.00	30.00	12.50	30.00
Plate, 6 ½"	20.00	30.00	15.00	30.00
Savings book	15.00	22.50	10.00	22.50
Stratford straight beaker	15.00	25.00	10.00	25.00
Stratford teacup	7.50	12.00	5.00	12.00

Roller Skating Arm in Arm (HW137R)

ROW BOAT / NIPPED BY A CRAB

Row Boat (HW21)   Nipped by a Crab (HW21R)

Design No.: Front — HW21 Row Boat
Reverse — HW21R Nipped by a Crab
Designer: Walter Hayward
Issued: By 1952 - by 1998

Combined with: *Cricketer*, HW22R
Family with Pram, Style One, HW15
Hikers, EC124
Swinging, HW20
Wheelbarrow Race, Style One, HW22

Shape	USD	CAD	GBP	AUD
Albion jug, ½ pint	100.00	150.00	70.00	150.00
Albion jug, 1 pint	150.00	225.00	100.00	225.00
Albion teapot	50.00	85.00	35.00	95.00
Casino jug, 36s				
with signature	175.00	275.00	125.00	275.00
without signature	125.00	200.00	85.00	200.00
Casino saucer				
with signature	15.00	25.00	10.00	25.00
without signature	7.50	12.00	5.00	12.00
Casino teacup				
with signature	15.00	25.00	10.00	25.00
without signature	7.50	12.00	5.00	12.00
Casino teapot, 24s				
with signature	275.00	400.00	175.00	450.00
without signature	175.00	275.00	125.00	325.00
Divider dish	50.00	75.00	35.00	75.00
Don beaker				
with signature	75.00	125.00	50.00	150.00
without signature	35.00	55.00	25.00	60.00
Don beaker, one handle				
with signature	75.00	125.00	50.00	150.00
without signature	35.00	55.00	25.00	60.00
Don mug, one handle				
with signature	65.00	100.00	45.00	75.00
without signature	15.00	25.00	10.00	25.00

Shape	USD	CAD	GBP	AUD
Don mug, two handles				
with signature	65.00	100.00	45.00	75.00
without signature	15.00	25.00	10.00	25.00
Egg box				
small	225.00	350.00	150.00	400.00
medium	300.00	450.00	200.00	500.00
large	375.00	550.00	250.00	600.00
Hug-a-mug, one handle	10.00	15.00	7.50	15.00
Hug-a-mug, two handles	10.00	15.00	7.50	15.00
Jaffa fruit saucer (plain)				
with signature	70.00	110.00	45.00	125.00
without signature	15.00	25.00	10.00	25.00
Lamp	100.00	150.00	65.00	175.00
Lid of hot water plate				
with signature	150.00	225.00	100.00	250.00
without signature	100.00	150.00	70.00	175.00
Malvern beaker	15.00	25.00	10.00	25.00
Money ball	10.00	15.00	7.50	15.00
Picture plaque, small	20.00	30.00	12.50	30.00
Plate, 6 ½"				
with signature	35.00	55.00	25.00	55.00
without signature	20.00	30.00	15.00	30.00
Savings book	15.00	22.50	10.00	22.50
Stratford straight beaker	15.00	25.00	10.00	25.00
Stratford teacup	7.50	12.00	5.00	12.00

Note: A Casino jug combines *Rowboat* (HW21), with *Swinging* (HW20).

SANTA BUNNYKINS
CHRISTMAS TREE ORNAMENT

Design No.:	Front — CT68 Santa Bunnykins
	Reverse — CT69 Christmas 1991
Designer:	Colin Twinn
Issued:	1991 - 1991
Series:	Christmas Tree Ornaments

Shape	USD	CAD	GBP	AUD
Christmas Tree Ornament	40.00	65.00	25.00	70.00

Note: For other Christmas tree ornaments in this series see
pages 42, 44, 80, and 165.

Santa Bunnykins Christmas Tree Ornament (CT68)

Santa Bunnykins Christmas Tree Ornament (CT69)

Santa Claus (SF9)

SANTA CLAUS

Design No.: SF9
Designer: Barbara Vernon
Issued: By 1940 - by 1952
Combined with: *Feeding the Baby*, HW13
Pressing Trousers, HW14
Proposal, HW11

Shape	USD	CAD	GBP	AUD
Baby plate, oval, small				
with signature	200.00	325.00	150.00	325.00
without signature	150.00	225.00	100.00	225.00
Baby plate, round, small				
with signature	75.00	125.00	50.00	125.00
without signature	50.00	80.00	35.00	80.00
Candle holder	2,000.00	3,000.00	1,250.00	4,000.00
Casino jug, 36s				
with signature	250.00	400.00	175.00	425.00
without signature	175.00	275.00	125.00	300.00
Casino teapot, 30s				
with signature	325.00	500.00	225.00	550.00
without signature	250.00	400.00	175.00	450.00
Cereal / oatmeal bowl				
with signature	50.00	80.00	35.00	80.00
without signature	35.00	55.00	25.00	55.00
Hot water plate				
with signature	175.00	275.00	125.00	325.00
without signature	125.00	200.00	85.00	225.00
Jaffa fruit saucer				
plain rim	100.00	160.00	75.00	165.00
wavy rim	70.00	110.00	45.00	125.00
Plate, 6 ½"				
with signature	60.00	95.00	40.00	100.00
without signature	40.00	65.00	25.00	70.00
Plate, 8 ½"				
with signature	70.00	115.00	45.00	125.00
without signature	45.00	70.00	30.00	75.00

FINE WHITE CHINA
Cereal bowl   Very rare
Plate, 7"   Very rare

SCHOOL THEME — Frank Endersby

MATHS LESSON

Design No.:	25 Maths Lesson
Designer:	Frank Endersby
Issued:	1995 to the present

Shape	USD	CAD	GBP	AUD
Baby plate, round, small	N/I	46.00	14.00	62.95
Plate, 6 ½"	N/I	25.00	8.00	34.95
Plate, 8"	N/I	35.00	11.00	49.95

Maths Lesson ((25)

Teacher Scolding (26)

TEACHER SCOLDING / BUNNY WITH BAG

Design No.:	Front — 26 Teacher Scolding
	Reverse — 27 Bunny with Bag
Designer:	Frank Endersby
Issued:	1995 to the present
Combined with:	*Carrying Letter, (30)*

Shape	USD	CAD	GBP	AUD
Hug-a-mug, one handle	30.00	33.00	11.00	49.95
Hug-a-mug, two handles	32.50	39.00	12.00	56.95
Divider dish	50.00	75.00	35.00	75.00

* Indicates scene on divider dish.

Bunny with Bag (27)

SCHOOL DINNER THEME — Colin Twinn

School Dinner, First Variation (CT17)

First Variation, Small Size

Design No.: CT17 School Dinner
Designer: Colin Twinn
Issued: 1990 - 1993

Shape	USD	CAD	GBP	AUD
Albion jug, 1 pint	150.00	225.00	100.00	225.00
Cake stand	150.00	250.00	100.00	300.00
Cereal / oatmeal bowl	10.00	15.00	7.50	15.00
Jaffa fruit saucer (plain)	10.00	15.00	7.50	15.00
Plate, 8"	25.00	40.00	18.00	40.00

School Dinner, Second Variation (CT30)

Second Variation, Large Size / COOK AND BUNNY

Design No.: Front — CT30 School Dinner
             Reverse — CT31 Cook and Bunny
Designer: Colin Twinn
Issued: 1990 - 1993

Shape	USD	CAD	GBP	AUD
Albion cream jug	50.00	75.00	35.00	75.00
Albion jug, 1 pint	150.00	225.00	100.00	225.00
Albion teapot	50.00	85.00	35.00	95.00
Hug-a-mug, one handle	10.00	15.00	7.50	15.00
Lamp	100.00	150.00	65.00	175.00
Malvern beaker	15.00	25.00	10.00	25.00
Money ball	10.00	15.00	7.50	15.00
Savings book	15.00	22.50	10.00	22.50
Stratford teacup	7.50	12.00	5.00	12.00

Cook and Bunny (CT31)

SCHOOL GATES THEME — Colin Twinn

First Variation, Large Size

Design No.:   CT20 School Gates
Designer: Colin Twinn
Issued: 1991 - 1993

Shape	USD	CAD	GBP	AUD
Albion jug, 1 pint	150.00	225.00	100.00	225.00
Cereal / oatmeal bowl	10.00	15.00	7.50	15.00
Lamp	100.00	150.00	65.00	175.00
Picture plaque, large	20.00	30.00	12.50	30.00
Plate, 6"	20.00	30.00	15.00	30.00
Plate, 8"	25.00	40.00	18.00	40.00

School Gates, First Variation (CT20)

School Gates, Second Variation (CT22)

SCHOOL GATES
Second Variation, Small Size / BUNNY ON TRIKE

Design No.:   Front — CT22 School Gates
Designer: Reverse — CT23 Bunny on Trike
Issued: 1991 - 1993
Combined with: *Bathtime Scene*, Style Two, Second Variation, CT24
              Bunnies in the Bath, First Version, CT25
              Classrooom Scene, Style Two, Second Version, CT16
              Ice Cream Seller, Second Variation, CT11

Shape	USD	CAD	GBP	AUD
Albion jug, ½ pint	100.00	150.00	70.00	150.00
Albion teapot	50.00	85.00	35.00	95.00
Hug-a-mug, one handle	10.00	15.00	7.50	15.00
Hug-a-mug, two handles	10.00	15.00	7.50	15.00
Lamp	100.00	150.00	65.00	175.00
Money ball	10.00	15.00	7.50	15.00
Picture plaque, small	20.00	30.00	12.50	30.00
Stratford straight beaker	15.00	25.00	10.00	25.00

Bunny on Trike (CT23)

See-saw, Style One (SF17)

SEE-SAW
Style One

Design No.:   SF17
Designer: Walter Hayward
Issued: By 1952 - by 1998
Combined with: *Engine Pulling a Carriage,* HW17
               Mr. Piggly's Stores, SF14

Shape	USD	CAD	GBP	AUD
Albion jug, ½ pint	100.00	150.00	70.00	150.00
Albion jug, 1 pint	150.00	225.00	100.00	225.00
Baby plate, round, small				
with signature	45.00	75.00	30.00	75.00
without signature	20.00	30.00	15.00	30.00
Cake stand	150.00	250.00	100.00	300.00
Cereal / oatmeal bowl				
with signature	25.00	40.00	15.00	45.00
without signature	10.00	15.00	7.50	15.00
Coupe plate, 6 ¾"			Very Rare	
Hot water plate				
with signature	175.00	275.00	125.00	325.00
without signature	125.00	200.00	85.00	225.00
Jaffa fruit saucer (plain)				
with signature	70.00	110.00	45.00	125.00
without signature	15.00	25.00	10.00	25.00
Picture plaque, large	20.00	30.00	12.50	30.00
Plate, 6 ½"				
with signature	35.00	55.00	25.00	55.00
without signature	20.00	30.00	15.00	30.00
Plate, 7 ½"				
with signature	35.00	55.00	25.00	55.00
without signature	20.00	30.00	15.00	30.00
Plate, 8"	25.00	40.00	18.00	40.00

SHELTERING UNDER AN UMBRELLA

Design No.: EC3
Designer: Barbara Vernon
Issued: 1937 to the present
Combined with: *Afternoon Tea*, HW116
Bedtime with Dollies, EC125
Drummer, EC2
Family Going Out on Washing Day, HW8
Fishing in the Goldfish Bowl, HW3R
Hikers, EC124
Hobby Horse, Style Two, EC121
Holding Hat and Coat, EC4
Playing with Cup and Spoon, EC6
Playing with Doll and Pram, EC123
Raising Hat, Style Two, EC7
Reading, EC122
Serving Tea, HW116R
Sleeping in a Rocking Chair, EC1
Trumpeter, EC5
Washing Day, HW8R

Sheltering Under an Umbrella (EC3)

Shape	USD	CAD	GBP	AUD
Albion sugar bowl	30.00	50.00	20.00	50.00
Beaker cover				
with signature	125.00	175.00	75.00	175.00
without signature	85.00	135.00	50.00	150.00
Casino sugar bowl, 30s				
with signature	150.00	225.00	100.00	250.00
without signature	125.00	200.00	85.00	225.00
Casino sugar bowl, 36s				
with signature	125.00	200.00	85.00	225.00
without signature	100.00	150.00	65.00	175.00
Egg cup				
Style One				
with signature	75.00	120.00	50.00	135.00
without signature	40.00	60.00	25.00	65.00
Style Two	80.00	125.00	50.00	135.00
Style Three	**N/I**	**15.00**	**5.00**	**19.95**
Lid of hot water plate				
with signature	125.00	200.00	85.00	225.00
without signature	100.00	150.00	70.00	175.00

FINE WHITE CHINA
Teacup   Very rare

SHOPPING THEME — Frank Endersby

Shopping (1)

SHOPPING

Design No.:	1 Shopping
Designer:	Frank Endersby
Issued:	1995 to the present

Shape	USD	CAD	GBP	AUD
Jaffa fruit saucer	10.00	15.00	7.50	15.00
Plate, 6 ½"	**N/I**	**25.00**	**8.00**	**34.95**
Plate, 8"	**N/I**	**35.00**	**11.00**	**49.95**

Vegetable Stall (2)

VEGETABLE STALL / EATING APPLES

Design No.:	Front — 2 Vegetable Stall
	Reverse — 3 Eating Apples
Designer:	Frank Endersby
Issued:	1995 to the present
Combined with:	*Resting, Style Two, (21)

Shape	USD	CAD	GBP	AUD
Hug-a-mug, one handle	**30.00**	**33.00**	**11.00**	**49.95**
Hug-a-mug, two handles	**32.50**	**39.00**	**12.00**	**56.95**
Divider dish	50.00	75.00	35.00	75.00
Stratford teacup	7.50	12.00	5.00	12.00

* Indicates scene on divider dish.

Note: 1. Bold type in the listing tables indicate a current design on a current shape.
    2. N/I, Not issued individually. The item(s) will be found only in boxed sets in that market.

Eating Apples (3)

SLEDGING, *Style One* / *SNOWBALL FIGHT*

Design No.:	Front — HW141 Sledging
	Reverse — HW141R Snowball Fight
Designer:	Walter Hayward
Issued:	1967 - by 1998
Combined with:	*Engine Pulling a Carriage*, HW17
	*Pea Shooter, HW118R
	Reading, EC122
	Serving Tea, HW116R

Shape	USD	CAD	GBP	AUD
Albion cream jug	50.00	75.00	35.00	75.00
Albion jug, ½ pint	100.00	150.00	70.00	150.00
Albion jug, 1 pint	150.00	225.00	100.00	225.00
Albion teapot	50.00	85.00	35.00	95.00
Casino teacup	7.50	12.00	5.00	12.00
Divider dish	50.00	75.00	35.00	75.00
Don beaker	35.00	55.00	25.00	60.00
Don beaker, one handle	35.00	55.00	25.00	60.00
Don mug, one handle	15.00	25.00	10.00	25.00
Don mug, two handles	15.00	25.00	10.00	25.00
Egg box				
small	225.00	350.00	150.00	400.00
medium	300.00	450.00	200.00	500.00
large	375.00	550.00	250.00	600.00
Hug-a-mug, one handle				
Christmas 1988 - 1991	10.00	15.00	7.50	15.00
regular issue	10.00	15.00	7.50	15.00
Hug-a-mug, two handles				
Christmas 1988 - 1991	10.00	15.00	7.50	15.00
regular issue	10.00	15.00	7.50	15.00
Jaffa fruit saucer (plain)	15.00	25.00	10.00	25.00
Lamp	100.00	15.00	65.00	175.00
Malvern beaker	15.00	25.00	10.00	25.00
Money ball	10.00	15.00	7.50	15.00
Picture plaque, small	20.00	30.00	12.50	30.00
Savings book	15.00	22.50	10.00	22.50
Stratford straight beaker	15.00	25.00	10.00	25.00
Stratford teacup	7.50	12.00	5.00	12.00

* Indicates scene on divider dish.

Sledging, Style One (HW141)

Snowball Fight (HW141R)

Note: A Merry Christmas from Bunnykins was added to the hug-a-mugs as part of the Christmas set issued between 1988 - 1991. *Sledging*, Style One (HW141) was combined with *Reading* (EC122) on a money ball and *Engine Pulling a Carriage* (HW17) is combined with *Snowball Fight* (HW141R) on a Don mug with two handles.

Sleeping in a Rocking Chair (EC1)

SLEEPING IN A ROCKING CHAIR

Design No.:	EC1
Designer:	Barbara Vernon
Issued:	1937 to the present
Combined with:	*Bugler with Toy Donkey*, HW26R
	Dress Making, HW26
	Drummer, EC2
	Drummer and Bugler, EC126
	Feeding the Baby, HW13
	Footballer, HW13R
	Haymaking, HW29
	Hikers, EC124
	Hobby Horse, Style Two, EC121
	Lambeth Walk, Second Version, HW16
	Lunch Break, HW29R
	Playing with Cup and Spoon, EC6
	Playing with Doll and Pram, EC123
	Raising Hat, Style One, HW16R
	Raising Hat, Style Two, EC7
	Reading, EC122
	Sheltering Under an Umbrella, EC3
	Skipping, HW20R
	Swinging, HW20
	Trumpeter, EC5

Shape	USD	CAD	GBP	AUD
Albion sugar bowl	30.00	50.00	20.00	50.00
Beaker cover				
with signature	125.00	175.00	75.00	175.00
without signature	85.00	135.00	50.00	150.00
Casino sugar bowl, 30s				
with signature	150.00	225.00	100.00	250.00
without signature	125.00	200.00	85.00	225.00
Egg cup				
Style One				
with signature	75.00	120.00	50.00	135.00
without signature	40.00	60.00	25.00	65.00
Style Two	80.00	125.00	50.00	135.00
Style Three	**N/I**	**15.00**	**5.00**	**19.95**
Lid of hot water plate				
with signature	125.00	200.00	85.00	225.00
without signature	100.00	150.00	70.00	175.00

SMOKING IN THE DOORWAY

Design No.: SF2
Designer: Barbara Vernon
Issued: 1937 - by 1952
Combined with: *Family at Breakfast*, HW12
Fixing Braces, HW3
Reading the Times, HW2R

Shape	USD	CAD	GBP	AUD
Baby plate, oval, small	400.00	625.00	275.00	650.00
Baby plate, round, small	125.00	200.00	90.00	200.00
Candle holder	2,000.00	3,000.00	1,250.00	4,000.00
Casino jug, 24s	600.00	950.00	425.00	975.00
Casino saucer	100.00	150.00	65.00	175.00
Casino teapot, 30s	400.00	600.00	275.00	700.00
Cereal / oatmeal bowl	85.00	135.00	60.00	150.00
Don beaker, one handle	200.00	325.00	140.00	350.00
Hot water plate	175.00	275.00	125.00	325.00
Jaffa fruit saucer				
plain rim	150.00	250.00	95.00	275.00
wavy rim	100.00	150.00	75.00	175.00
Plate, 6 ½"	90.00	150.00	60.00	175.00
Plate, 7 ½"	90.00	150.00	60.00	175.00
Porridge bowl	125.00	200.00	80.00	225.00

Smoking in the Doorway (SF2)

FINE WHITE CHINA

Plate, 7"   Very rare

Note: This design should appear with the Barbara Vernon
facsimile signature.

A very rare combination of a Bunnykins design
on a Series Ware shape.

SNOW SCENES THEME — Frank Endersby

Snow Scene, First Version (58)

SNOW SCENE

Design No.: 58 Snow Scene
Designer: Frank Endersby
Issued: 1995 to the present

Shape	USD	CAD	GBP	AUD
Jaffa fruit saucer	15.00	25.00	10.00	25.00
Plate, 6 ½"	**N/I**	**25.00**	**8.00**	**34.95**
Plate, 8"	**N/I**	**35.00**	**11.00**	**49.95**

Building Snowman (59)

BUILDING SNOWMAN / SLEDGING, STYLE TWO

Design No.: Front — 59 Building Snowman
Reverse — 60 Sledging
Designer: Frank Endersby
Issued: 1995 to the present
Combined with: *Resting in Wheelbarrow*, (57)

Shape	USD	CAD	GBP	AUD
Hug-a-mug, one handle	**30.00**	**33.00**	**11.00**	**49.95**
Hug-a-mug, two handles	**32.50**	**39.00**	**12.00**	**56.95**
Divider dish	50.00	75.00	35.00	75.00
Malvern beaker	15.00	25.00	10.00	25.00
Money ball	**33.75**	**40.00**	**15.00**	**62.95**
Stratford teacup	7.50	12.00	5.00	12.00

* Indicates scene on divider dish.

Note: 1. Bold type in the listing tables indicate a current design on a current shape.
2. N/I, Not issued individually. The item(s) will be found only in boxed sets in that market.

Sledging, Style Two (60)

SOLDIERS MARCHING TO THE MUSIC / SOLDIER MARCHING

Design No.:	Front — HW18 Soldiers Marching to the Music	
	Reverse — HW18R Soldier Marching	
Designer:	Walter Hayward after Barbara Vernon	
Issued:	By 1952 - 1967	
Combined with:	*Convalescing*, SF5	
	Lambeth Walk, Second Version, HW16	

Soldiers Marching to the Music (HW18)

Shape	USD	CAD	GBP	AUD
Casino jug, 30s				
with signature	300.00	475.00	200.00	475.00
without signature	200.00	325.00	150.00	325.00
Casino saucer				
with signature	75.00	125.00	50.00	125.00
without signature	50.00	75.00	35.00	75.00
Casino teacup				
with signature	75.00	125.00	50.00	125.00
without signature	50.00	75.00	35.00	75.00
Casino teapot, 36s				
with signature	250.00	375.00	165.00	400.00
without signature	225.00	350.00	150.00	400.00
Don beaker				
with signature	150.00	250.00	110.00	275.00
without signature	85.00	135.00	60.00	150.00
Don beaker, one handle				
with signature	150.00	250.00	110.00	275.00
without signature	85.00	135.00	60.00	150.00
Don mug, one handle				
with signature	100.00	150.00	70.00	150.00
without signature	35.00	55.00	25.00	60.00
Don mug, two handles				
with signature	100.00	150.00	70.00	150.00
without signature	35.00	55.00	25.00	60.00
Jaffa fruit saucer (plain)				
with signature	100.00	150.00	75.00	165.00
without signature	60.00	95.00	40.00	100.00
Lid of hot water plate				
with signature	150.00	225.00	100.00	250.00
without signature	100.00	150.00	70.00	175.00
Plate, 6 ½"				
with signature	60.00	95.00	40.00	100.00
without signature	40.00	65.00	25.00	70.00

Soldier Marching (HW18R)

Space Rocket Launch (SF132)

SPACE ROCKET LAUNCH

Design No.: SF132
Designer: Walter Hayward
Issued: 1967 - by 1998

Shape	USD	CAD	GBP	AUD
Albion cream jug	50.00	75.00	35.00	75.00
Baby plate, round, small	20.00	30.00	15.00	30.00
Cake stand	150.00	250.00	100.00	300.00
Casino saucer	7.50	12.00	5.00	12.00
Cereal / oatmeal bowl	10.00	15.00	7.50	15.00
Hot water plate	125.00	200.00	85.00	225.00
Jaffa fruit saucer (plain)	20.00	30.00	12.50	30.00
Picture plaque, large	20.00	30.00	12.50	30.00
Plate 6 ½"	20.00	30.00	15.00	30.00
Plate 7 ½"	20.00	30.00	15.00	30.00
Plate 8"	25.00	40.00	18.00	40.00

SPRING CLEANING

Design No.: LF14
Designer: Walter Hayward
Issued: By 1952 - 1970

Shape	USD	CAD	GBP	AUD
Baby plate, oval, large				
with signature	200.00	325.00	150.00	325.00
without signature	150.00	225.00	100.00	225.00
Baby plate, round, large				
with signature	150.00	250.00	100.00	275.00
without signature	125.00	200.00	85.00	225.00
Bread and butter plate				
with signature	250.00	400.00	175.00	400.00
without signature	200.00	325.00	150.00	325.00
Cereal / oatmeal bowl				
with signature	50.00	80.00	35.00	80.00
without signature	35.00	55.00	25.00	55.00
Hot water plate				
with signature	175.00	275.00	125.00	325.00
without signature	125.00	200.00	85.00	225.00
Plate, 8 ½"				
with signature	70.00	115.00	45.00	125.00
without signature	45.00	70.00	30.00	75.00
Porridge bowl				
with signature	110.00	175.00	70.00	200.00
without signature	85.00	125.00	55.00	150.00

Spring Cleaning (LF14)

SPRING CLEANING THEME — Frank Endersby

DUSTING

Design No.:	19 Dusting
Designer:	Frank Endersby
Issued:	1995 to the present

Shape	USD	CAD	GBP	AUD
Baby plate, round, small	N/I	**46.00**	**14.00**	**62.95**
Plate, 6 ½"	N/I	**25.00**	**8.00**	**34.95**
Plate, 8"	N/I	**35.00**	**11.00**	**49.95**

Dusting (19)

Beating Carpet (20)

BEATING CARPET / RESTING, Style Two

Design No.:	Front — 20 Beating Carpet
	Reverse — 21 Resting, Style Two
Designer:	Frank Endersby
Issued:	1995 to the present
Combined with:	*Eating Apples,* (3)

Shape	USD	CAD	GBP	AUD
Hug-a-mug, one handle	**30.00**	**33.00**	**11.00**	**49.95**
Hug-a-mug, two handles	**32.50**	**39.00**	**12.00**	**56.95**
Divider dish	50.00	75.00	35.00	75.00

* Indicates scene on divider dish.

Resting (21)

Note: 1. Bold type in the listing tables indicate a current design on a current shape.
2. N/I, Not issued individually. The item(s) will be found only in boxed sets in that market.

Storytime (SF110)

STORYTIME

Design No.:	SF110
Designer:	Walter Hayward
Issued:	1959 - 1967

Shape	USD	CAD	GBP	AUD
Baby plate, round, small	100.00	150.00	70.00	175.00
Casino saucer	75.00	125.00	50.00	125.00
Cereal / oatmeal bowl	90.00	150.00	60.00	175.00
Hot water plate	125.00	200.00	85.00	225.00
Plate 6 ½"	60.00	100.00	40.00	100.00
Plate 7 ½"	60.00	100.00	40.00	100.00
Plate 8"	75.00	125.00	50.00	135.00

Casino cup, *Fishing in the Goldfish Bowl* (HW3R)

SWINGING / SKIPPING

| Design No.: | Front — HW20 Swinging |
| Reverse — HW20R Skipping |
Designer:	Walter Hayward
Issued:	By 1952 - 1967
Combined with:	*Holding Hat and Coat*, EC4
Row Boat, HW21
Sleeping in a Rocking Chair, EC1

Shape	USD	CAD	GBP	AUD
Casino jug, 36s				
with signature	250.00	400.00	175.00	425.00
without signature	175.00	275.00	125.00	300.00
Casino saucer				
with signature	75.00	125.00	50.00	125.00
without signature	50.00	75.00	35.00	75.00
Casino sugar bowl, 36s				
with signature	175.00	275.00	125.00	325.00
without signature	125.00	200.00	85.00	225.00
Casino teacup				
with signature	75.00	125.00	50.00	125.00
without signature	50.00	75.00	35.00	75.00
Casino teapot, 36s				
with signature	250.00	375.00	165.00	400.00
without signature	225.00	350.00	150.00	375.00
Divider dish	50.00	75.00	35.00	75.00
Don beaker				
with signature	150.00	250.00	110.00	275.00
without signature	85.00	135.00	60.00	150.00
Don beaker, one handle				
with signature	150.00	250.00	110.00	275.00
without signature	85.00	135.00	60.00	150.00
Don mug, one handle				
with signature	100.00	150.00	70.00	150.00
without signature	35.00	55.00	25.00	60.00
Don mug, two handles				
with signature	100.00	150.00	70.00	150.00
without signature	35.00	55.00	25.00	60.00
Egg box				
small	225.00	350.00	150.00	400.00
Jaffa fruit saucer (plain)				
with signature	100.00	150.00	75.00	165.00
without signature	60.00	95.00	40.00	100.00
Lid of hot water plate				
with signature	150.00	225.00	100.00	250.00
without signature	100.00	150.00	70.00	175.00
Plate, 6 ½"				
with signature	60.00	95.00	40.00	100.00
without signature	40.00	65.00	25.00	70.00

Swinging (HW20)

Skipping (HW20R)

Note: A Casino jug combines *Swinging*, (HW20) with *Rowboat* (HW21).

Television Time (SF112)

TELEVISION TIME

Design No.:	SF112
Designer:	Walter Hayward
Issued:	1959 - by 1998

Shape	USD	CAD	GBP	AUD
Baby plate, round, small	20.00	30.00	15.00	30.00
Cake stand	150.00	250.00	100.00	300.00
Casino saucer	7.50	12.00	5.00	12.00
Cereal / oatmeal bowl	10.00	15.00	7.50	15.00
Hot water plate	125.00	200.00	85.00	225.00
Jaffa fruit saucer (plain)	15.00	25.00	10.00	25.00
Picture plaque, large	20.00	30.00	12.50	30.00
Plate, 6 ½"	20.00	30.00	15.00	30.00
Plate, 7 ½"	20.00	30.00	15.00	30.00

TENNIS

A boxed Bunnykins for Grown Ups Set containing a cereal bowl and a hug-a-mug with one handle with the *Aerobics/Jogging* design, a 6" plate with the *Aeroplane* design, an 8" plate with the *Breakfast Time* design and a cereal bowl with the *Tennis* design was distributed mainly in the U.S.A.

Design No.:	None
Designer:	Walter Hayward
Issued:	1986 - 1988
Series:	Bunnykins for Grown-Ups

Shape	USD	CAD	GBP	AUD
Cereal / oatmeal bowl	40.00	60.00	25.00	60.00
Complete set (M.I.B.)	200.00	300.00	100.00	300.00

Tennis

Note: See also *Aerobics / Jogging* and *Aeroplane* page 14 and *Breakfast Time* page 32.

TICKET QUEUE

Design No.:	SF109			
Designer:	Walter Hayward			
Issued:	1959 - by 1998			

Shape	USD	CAD	GBP	AUD
Baby plate, round, small	20.00	30.00	15.00	30.00
Casino saucer	7.50	12.00	5.00	12.00
Cereal / oatmeal bowl	10.00	15.00	7.50	15.00
Hot water plate	125.00	200.00	85.00	225.00
Picture plaque, large	20.00	30.00	12.50	30.00
Plate, 6 ½"	20.00	30.00	15.00	30.00
Plate, 7 ½"	20.00	30.00	15.00	30.00
Plate, 8"	25.00	40.00	18.00	40.00
Plate, 10 ½"	35.00	55.00	25.00	60.00

Ticket Queue (SF109)

Toast for Tea Today (SF23)

TOAST FOR TEA TODAY

Design No.:	SF23
Designer:	Walter Hayward
Issued:	1954 - 1967
Combined with:	*Dress Making*, HW26
	Dressing Up, First Version, SF22
	Haymaking, HW29
	Mr. Piggly's Stores, SF14
	Windy Day, HW27

Shape	USD	CAD	GBP	AUD
Baby plate, round, small				
with signature	75.00	125.00	50.00	125.00
without signature	50.00	80.00	35.00	80.00
Casino saucer				
with signature	75.00	125.00	50.00	125.00
without signature	50.00	80.00	35.00	80.00
Casino teapot, 24s				
with signature	375.00	550.00	250.00	600.00
without signature	300.00	450.00	200.00	500.00
Casino teapot, 30s				
with signature	325.00	500.00	225.00	550.00
without signature	250.00	400.00	175.00	450.00
Cereal / oatmeal bowl				
with signature	50.00	80.00	35.00	80.00
without signature	35.00	55.00	25.00	55.00
Hot water plate				
with signature	175.00	275.00	125.00	325.00
without signature	125.00	200.00	85.00	225.00
Jaffa fruit saucer (plain)				
with signature	100.00	150.00	75.00	165.00
without signature	60.00	95.00	40.00	100.00
Plate, 6 ½"				
with signature	60.00	95.00	40.00	100.00
without signature	40.00	65.00	25.00	40.00

Top Hat (HW14R)

TOP HAT

Design No.:	HW14R	
Designer:	Barbara Vernon	
Issued:	By 1937 - 1967	
Combined with:	*Embracing at a Window*, HW5	
	Feeding the Baby, HW13	
	Lambeth Walk, HW16	
	Pressing Trousers, HW14	

Shape	USD	CAD	GBP	AUD
Casino jug, 36s				
with signature	150.00	225.00	100.00	225.00
without signature	125.00	200.00	85.00	200.00
Casino jug, 42s				
with signature	125.00	200.00	90.00	200.00
without signature	100.00	150.00	70.00	150.00
Casino teacup				
with signature	15.00	25.00	10.00	25.00
without signature	7.50	12.00	5.00	12.00
Don beaker				
with signature	75.00	125.00	50.00	150.00
without signature	45.00	70.00	30.00	75.00
Don beaker, one handle				
with signature	75.00	125.00	50.00	150.00
without signature	45.00	70.00	30.00	75.00
Don mug, one handle				
with signature	50.00	75.00	35.00	85.00
without signature	30.00	50.00	20.00	55.00
Don mug, two handles				
with signature	50.00	75.00	35.00	85.00
without signature	30.00	50.00	20.00	55.00

FINE WHITE CHINA

Saucer	Very Rare
Teacup	Very Rare

TOPPLING THE FRUIT CART

Design No.:	SF134
Designer:	Walter Hayward
Issued:	1967 - by 1998

Shape	USD	CAD	GBP	AUD
Albion jug, 1 pint	150.00	225.00	100.00	225.00
Baby plate, round, small	20.00	30.00	15.00	30.00
Cake stand	150.00	250.00	100.00	300.00
Casino saucer	7.50	12.00	5.00	12.00
Cereal / oatmeal bowl	10.00	15.00	7.50	15.00
Hot water plate	125.00	200.00	85.00	225.00
Jaffa fruit saucer (plain)	15.00	25.00	10.00	25.00
Picture plaque, large	20.00	30.00	12.50	30.00
Plate, 6 ½"	20.00	30.00	15.00	30.00
Plate, 7 ½"	20.00	30.00	15.00	30.00
Plate, 8"	25.00	40.00	18.00	40.00

Toppling the Fruit Cart (SF134)

TOY SHOP

Design No.:	SF114
Designer:	Walter Hayward after Barbara Vernon
Issued:	1959 - 1967

Shape	USD	CAD	GBP	AUD
Baby plate, round, small	50.00	80.00	35.00	80.00
Casino saucer	50.00	75.00	35.00	75.00
Cereal / oatmeal bowl	35.00	55.00	25.00	55.00
Hot water plate	175.00	275.00	125.00	325.00
Jaffa fruit saucer (plain)	100.00	150.00	75.00	165.00
Plate, 6 ½"	40.00	65.00	25.00	70.00
Plate, 7 ½"	40.00	65.00	25.00	70.00

Toy Shop (SF114)

A busy Hug-a-mug

TRAIN STATION THEME — *Frank Endersby*

Waiting for Train (49)

WAITING FOR TRAIN

Design No.:	49 Waiting for Train
Designer:	Frank Endersby
Issued:	1995 to the present

Shape	USD	CAD	GBP	AUD
Baby plate, round, small	N/I	46.00	14.00	62.95
Jaffa fruit saucer	15.00	25.00	10.00	25.00
Plate, 6 ½″	N/I	25.00	8.00	34.95
Plate, 8″	N/I	35.00	11.00	49.95

Ticket Office (50)

TICKET OFFICE / SITTING ON SUITCASE

Design No.:	Front — 50 Ticket Office
	Reverse — 51 Sitting on Suitcase
Designer:	Frank Endersby
Issued:	1995 to the present

Shape	USD	CAD	GBP	AUD
Hug-a-mug, one handle	30.00	33.00	11.00	49.95
Hug-a-mug, two handles	32.50	39.00	12.00	56.95

Note: 1. Bold type in the listing tables indicate a current design on a current shape.
2. N/I, Not issued individually. The item(s) will be found only in boxed sets in that market.

Sitting on Suitcase (51)

TRIMMING THE TREE
CHRISTMAS TREE ORNAMENT

Design No.:	Front — CT80 Trimming the Tree
	Reverse — CT81 Christmas 1994
Designer:	Colin Twinn
Issued:	1994 - 1994
Series:	Christmas Tree Ornaments

Shape	USD	CAD	GBP	AUD
Christmas tree ornaments	40.00	65.00	25.00	70.00

Note: For other Christmas tree ornaments in this series see pages 42, 44, 80 and 143.

Trimming the Tree (CT80)

Trimming the Tree (CT81)

Trumpeter (EC5)

TRUMPETER

Design No.:	EC5
Designer:	Barbara Vernon
Issued:	1937 to the present
Combined with:	*Bedtime with Dollies*, EC125
	Drummer, EC2
	Drummer and Bugler, EC126
	Family Going out on Washing Day, HW8
	Feeding the Baby, HW13
	Hat Shop, HW28
	Hikers, EC124
	Hobby Horse, Style One, HW24R
	Hobby Horse, Style Two, EC121
	Holding Hat and Coat, EC4
	Playing with Cup and Spoon, EC6
	Raising Hat, Style Two, EC7
	Reading, EC122
	Rocking Horse, HW24
	Sheltering Under an Umbrella, EC3
	Sleeping in a Rocking Chair, EC1
	Washing Day, HW8R

Shape	USD	CAD	GBP	AUD
Albion sugar bowl	30.00	50.00	20.00	50.00
Beaker cover				
with signature	125.00	175.00	75.00	175.00
without signature	85.00	135.00	50.00	150.00
Casino sugar bowl, 36s				
with signature	125.00	200.00	85.00	225.00
without signature	100.00	150.00	65.00	175.00
Egg cup				
Style One				
with signature	75.00	120.00	50.00	135.00
without signature	40.00	60.00	25.00	65.00

Shape	USD	CAD	GBP	AUD
Egg cup				
Style Two				
with signature	150.00	225.00	100.00	250.00
without signature	80.00	125.00	50.00	135.00
Style Three	N/I	15.00	5.00	19.95
Lid of hot water plate				
with signature	150.00	225.00	100.00	250.00
without signature	100.00	150.00	70.00	175.00
Money ball	33.75	40.00	15.00	62.95

TUG OF WAR

Design No.:	LF1
Designer:	Barbara Vernon
Issued:	By 1937 - by 1952

Shape	USD	CAD	GBP	AUD
Bread / butter plate, handles				
with signature	800.00	1,250.00	500.00	1,600.00
without signature	600.00	1,000.00	400.00	1,100.00
Plate, 8 ½"				
with signature	300.00	475.00	200.00	500.00
without signature	250.00	400.00	175.00	425.00
Porridge bowl				
with signature	400.00	625.00	275.00	650.00
without signature	375.00	575.00	250.00	600.00

FINE WHITE CHINA

Bread and butter plate	Very Rare

Tug of War (LF1)

UNRAVELLING THE KNITTING /
TRYING ON KNITTING

Design No.:	Front — HW119 Unravelling the Knitting
	Reverse — HW119R Trying on Knitting
Designer:	Walter Hayward
Issued:	1959 - 1992
Combined with:	*Bedtime with Dollies*, EC125
	Broken Umbrella, HW27R
	Windy Day, HW27

Unravelling the Knitting (HW119)

Shape	USD	CAD	GBP	AUD
Albion cream jug	50.00	75.00	35.00	75.00
Albion jug, ½ pint	100.00	150.00	70.00	150.00
Albion jug, 1 pint	150.00	225.00	100.00	225.00
Albion teapot	50.00	85.00	35.00	95.00
Cake stand	150.00	250.00	100.00	300.00
Casino jug, 30s	150.00	250.00	100.00	275.00
Casino jug, 36s	125.00	200.00	85.00	225.00
Casino jug, 42s	100.00	150.00	70.00	175.00
Casino saucer	7.50	12.00	5.00	12.00
Casino sugar bowl, 36s	100.00	150.00	65.00	175.00
Casino teacup	7.50	12.00	5.00	12.00
Casino teapot, 30s	150.00	225.00	100.00	250.00
Don beaker	35.00	55.00	25.00	60.00
Don beaker, one handle	35.00	55.00	25.00	60.00
Don mug, one handle	15.00	25.00	10.00	25.00
Don mug, two handles	15.00	25.00	10.00	25.00
Egg box				
small	225.00	350.00	150.00	400.00
medium	300.00	450.00	200.00	500.00
large	375.00	550.00	250.00	600.00
Hug-a-mug, one handle	10.00	15.00	7.50	15.00
Hug-a-mug, two handles	10.00	15.00	7.50	15.00
Jaffa fruit saucer (plain)	15.00	25.00	10.00	25.00
Lamp	100.00	150.00	65.00	175.00
Lid of hot water plate	100.00	150.00	70.00	175.00
Malvern beaker / mug	15.00	25.00	10.00	25.00
Money ball	10.00	15.00	7.50	15.00
Picture plaque, small	20.00	30.00	12.50	30.00
Plate, 6 ½"	20.00	30.00	15.00	30.00
Savings book	15.00	22.50	10.00	22.50
Stratford straight beaker	15.00	25.00	10.00	25.00
Stratford teacup	7.50	12.00	5.00	12.00

Trying on Knitting (HW119R)

Note: Retirement dates are all approximate. When a design is retired all remaining stocks of retired litho prints are used until exhausted.

Visiting the Cottage, First Version (SF6a)

VISITING THE COTTAGE
First Version

Design No.:   SF6a
Designer: Barbara Vernon
Issued: By 1940 - c.1949

Shape	USD	CAD	GBP	AUD
Baby plate, round, small	275.00	425.00	200.00	450.00
Baby plate, round, large	450.00	675.00	325.00	700.00
Bread and butter plate	800.00	1,250.00	500.00	1,600.00
Hot water plate	375.00	600.00	250.00	625.00
Plate, 6 ½"	300.00	475.00	200.00	500.00
Plate, 7 ½"	300.00	475.00	200.00	500.00
Plate, 8 ½"	300.00	475.00	200.00	500.00
Porridge plate	400.00	625.00	275.00	650.00

Note: This design should appear with the Barbara Vernon facsimile signature.

VISITING THE COTTAGE
Second Version

Design No.:   SF6b
Designer: Barbara Vernon
Issued: c.1949 - 1952

Shape	USD	CAD	GBP	AUD
Baby plate, round, small	125.00	200.00	90.00	200.00
Baby plate, round, large	300.00	450.00	200.00	450.00
Bread / butter plate	500.00	800.00	325.00	900.00
Casino saucer	100.00	150.00	65.00	175.00
Casino jug, 24s	600.00	950.00	425.00	975.00
Cereal / oatmeal bowl	110.00	175.00	75.00	200.00
Jaffa fruit saucer				
plain rim	150.00	250.00	95.00	275.00
wavy rim	100.00	150.00	75.00	175.00
Plate, 6 ½"	90.00	150.00	60.00	175.00
Plate, 7 ½"	90.00	150.00	60.00	175.00
Plate, 8 ½"	115.00	175.00	80.00	175.00
Porridge plate	125.00	200.00	80.00	225.00

Visiting the Cottage, Second Version (SF6b)

Note: This design should appear with the Barbara Vernon facsimile signature.

WASHING DAY

Design No.:	HW8R
Designer:	Barbara Vernon
Issued:	By 1937 - by 1967
Combined with:	*Family at Breakfast*, HW12
	Family Going out on Washing Day, HW8
	Sheltering Under an Umbrella, EC3
	Trumpeter, EC5

Washing Day (HW8R)

Shape	USD	CAD	GBP	AUD
Casino sugar bowl, 36s				
with signature	175.00	275.00	125.00	325.00
without signature	125.00	200.00	85.00	225.00
Casino teacup				
with signature	75.00	125.00	50.00	125.00
without signature	50.00	75.00	35.00	25.00
Casino teapot, 30s				
with signature	325.00	500.00	225.00	550.00
without signature	250.00	400.00	175.00	450.00
Casino teapot, 36s				
with signature	250.00	375.00	165.00	400.00
without signature	225.00	350.00	150.00	375.00
Don beaker, one handle				
with signature	150.00	250.00	110.00	275.00
without signature	85.00	135.00	60.00	150.00
Don mug, one handle				
with signature	100.00	150.00	70.00	150.00
without signature	35.00	55.00	25.00	60.00
Don mug, two handles				
with signature	100.00	150.00	70.00	150.00
without signature	35.00	55.00	25.00	60.00

Washing in the Open Air (HW10R)

WASHING IN THE OPEN AIR

Design No.:	HW10R
Designer:	Barbara Vernon
Issued:	By 1937 - by 1967
Combined with:	*Asleep in the Open Air*, HW10
	Convalescing, SF5
	Family with Pram, Style One, HW15
	Feeding the Baby, HW13
	Gardening, Style One, HW9
	Leapfrog, HW12R

Shape	USD	CAD	GBP	AUD
Casino jug, 30s				
with signature	500.00	800.00	350.00	950.00
without signature	400.00	700.00	300.00	850.00
Casino jug, 36s				
with signature	400.00	600.00	275.00	700.00
without signature	350.00	550.00	225.00	650.00
Casino sugar bowl, 30s				
with signature	250.00	375.00	165.00	400.00
without signature	175.00	275.00	125.00	325.00
Casino teacup				
with signature	100.00	150.00	65.00	175.00
without signature	75.00	125.00	50.00	125.00
Don beaker, one handle				
with signature	200.00	325.00	140.00	350.00
without signature	125.00	200.00	80.00	225.00
Don mug, one handle				
with signature	150.00	250.00	100.00	275.00
without signature	65.00	100.00	45.00	100.00
Don mug, two handles				
with signature	150.00	250.00	100.00	275.00
without signature	65.00	100.00	45.00	100.00

WASHING UP THEME — Colin Twinn

First Variation, Large Size

Design No.:   CT15 Washing Up
Designer: Colin Twinn
Issued: 1990 - 1993

Shape	USD	CAD	GBP	AUD
Albion jug, 1 pint	150.00	225.00	100.00	225.00
Baby bowl, round, small	20.00	30.00	15.00	30.00
Cake stand	150.00	250.00	100.00	300.00
Picture plaque, large	20.00	30.00	12.50	30.00
Plate, 6½"	20.00	30.00	15.00	30.00
Plate, 8"	25.00	40.00	18.00	40.00

Washing Up, First Variation (CT15)

Washing Up, Second Variation (CT32)

Second Variation, Small Size
/ SPLASHING AT SINK

Design No.:   Front — CT32 Washing Up
               Reverse — CT33 Splashing at Sink
Designer: Colin Twinn
Issued: 1990 - 1993
Combined with: *Ice Cream Seller*, First Variation, CT5
                Pushing the Wheelbarrow, CT3

Shape	USD	CAD	GBP	AUD
Albion teapot	50.00	85.00	35.00	95.00
Divider dish	75.00	125.00	50.00	125.00
Hug-a-mug, two handles	10.00	15.00	7.50	15.00
Lamp	100.00	150.00	65.00	175.00
Malvern beaker	15.00	25.00	10.00	25.00
Money ball	10.00	15.00	7.50	15.00
Savings book	15.00	22.50	10.00	22.50

Splashing at Sink (CT33)

Watering the Flowers (SF15)

WATERING THE FLOWERS

Design No.: SF15
Designer: Walter Hayward after Barbara Vernon
Issued: By 1952 - 1967
Combined with: *Pressing Trousers*, HW14

Shape	USD	CAD	GBP	AUD
Baby plate, round, small				
with signature	75.00	125.00	50.00	125.00
without signature	50.00	80.00	35.00	80.00
Casino jug, 30s				
with signature	300.00	475.00	200.00	475.00
without signature	225.00	325.00	150.00	325.00
Casino saucer				
with signature	75.00	125.00	50.00	125.00
without signature	50.00	75.00	35.00	75.00
Casino teapot, 24s				
with signature	375.00	550.00	250.00	600.00
without signature	300.00	450.00	200.00	500.00
Cereal / oatmeal bowl				
with signature	50.00	80.00	35.00	80.00
without signature	35.00	55.00	25.00	55.00
Hot water plate				
with signature	175.00	275.00	125.00	325.00
without signature	125.00	200.00	85.00	225.00
Jaffa fruit saucer (plain)				
with signature	100.00	150.00	75.00	165.00
without signature	60.00	95.00	40.00	100.00
Plate, 6 ½"				
with signature	60.00	95.00	40.00	100.00
without signature	40.00	65.00	25.00	40.00
Plate, 7 ½"				
with signature	60.00	95.00	40.00	100.00
without signature	40.00	65.00	25.00	40.00

WEDDING

Design No.:	LFd
Designer:	Barbara Vernon
Issued:	1937 - by 1952
Combined with:	*Family at Breakfast*, HW12
	Pressing Trousers, HW14
	Proposal, HW11
	Raising Hat, Style One, HW16R

Shape	USD	CAD	GBP	AUD
Baby plate, round, large	450.00	675.00	325.00	700.00
Casino teapot, 24s	750.00	1,250.00	500.00	1,350.00
Casino teapot, 36s	550.00	850.00	375.00	950.00
Hot water plate	375.00	600.00	250.00	625.00
Plate, 7 ½"	300.00	475.00	200.00	500.00
Plate, 8 ½"	300.00	475.00	200.00	500.00
Porridge plate	400.00	625.00	275.00	650.00

FINE WHITE CHINA   Very Rare
Plate 7"

Wedding (LFd)

Note: This design should appear with the Barbara Vernon
facsimile signature.

The Casino teapot (24s), combining *Proposal* (HW11) and Wedding (LFd),
exists with a silver rimmed lid and a crackle finish, this is considered
extremely rare.

WHEELBARROW RACE , Style One / CRICKETER

Wheelbarrow Race, Style One (HW22)

Cricketer (HW22R)

Design No.:   Front — HW22 Wheelbarrow Race
                 Reverse — HW22R Cricketer
Designer: Walter Hayward
Issued: By 1952 - by 1998
Combined with: *Asleep in the Open Air*, HW10
                 Baking, SF19

Bedtime with Dollies, EC125
Drummer, EC2
Holding Hat and Coat, EC4
Nipped by a Crab, HW121R
Pea Shooter, HW118R
Row Boat, HW21

Shape	USD	CAD	GBP	AUD
Albion cream jug	50.00	75.00	35.00	75.00
Albion jug, ½ pint	100.00	150.00	70.00	150.00
Albion jug, 1 pint	150.00	225.00	100.00	225.00
Albion teapot	50.00	85.00	35.00	95.00
Casino jug, 24s				
with signature	300.00	475.00	200.00	475.00
without signature	175.00	275.00	125.00	300.00
Casino jug, 30s				
with signature	250.00	400.00	175.00	425.00
without signature	150.00	250.00	100.00	250.00
Casino jug, 42s				
with signature	150.00	225.00	100.00	225.00
without signature	100.00	150.00	70.00	150.00
Casino saucer				
with signature	15.00	25.00	10.00	25.00
without signature	7.50	12.00	5.00	12.00
Casino sugar bowl, 30s				
with signature	150.00	225.00	100.00	250.00
without signature	125.00	200.00	85.00	225.00
Casino teacup				
with signature	15.00	25.00	10.00	25.00
without signature	7.50	12.00	5.00	12.00
Casino teapot, 30s				
with signature	250.00	375.00	165.00	400.00
without signature	150.00	225.00	100.00	250.00
Casino teapot, 36s				
with signature	250.00	375.00	165.00	400.00
without signature	150.00	225.00	100.00	250.00
Divider dish	50.00	75.00	35.00	75.00

Shape	USD	CAD	GBP	AUD
Don beaker				
with signature	75.00	125.00	50.00	150.00
without signature	35.00	55.00	25.00	60.00
Don beaker, one handle				
with signature	75.00	125.00	50.00	150.00
without signature	35.00	55.00	25.00	60.00
Don mug, one handle				
with signature	65.00	100.00	45.00	75.00
without signature	15.00	25.00	10.00	25.00
Don mug, two handles				
with signature	65.00	100.00	45.00	75.00
without signature	15.00	25.00	10.00	25.00
Egg box				
small	225.00	350.00	150.00	400.00
medium	300.00	450.00	200.00	500.00
large	375.00	550.00	250.00	600.00
Hug-a-mug, one handle	10.00	15.00	7.50	15.00
Hug-a-mug, two handles	10.00	15.00	7.50	15.00
Jaffa fruit saucer (plain)	15.00	25.00	10.00	25.00
Lamp	100.00	150.00	65.00	175.00
Lid of hot water plate	100.00	150.00	70.00	175.00
Malvern beaker	15.00	25.00	10.00	25.00
Money ball	10.00	15.00	7.50	15.00
Picture plaque, small	20.00	30.00	12.50	30.00
Plate, 6 ½"				
with signature	35.00	55.00	25.00	55.00
without signature	20.00	30.00	15.00	30.00
Savings book	15.00	22.50	10.00	22.50
Stratford teacup	7.50	12.00	5.00	12.00

WHEELBARROW RACE
Style Two

Design No.: CT1
Designer: Colin Twinn
Issued: 1988 - 1993
Combined with: *Pushing the Wheelbarrow*, CT3

Shape	USD	CAD	GBP	AUD
Albion jug, ½ jug	100.00	150.00	70.00	150.00
Albion jug, 1 pint	150.00	225.00	100.00	225.00
Baby plate, round, small	20.00	30.00	15.00	30.00
Cake stand	150.00	250.00	100.00	300.00
Cereal / oatmeal bowl	10.00	15.00	7.50	15.00
Jaffa fruit saucer	30.00	45.00	20.00	50.00
Picture plaque, large	20.00	30.00	12.50	30.00
Plate, 6 ½"	20.00	30.00	15.00	30.00
Plate, 8"	25.00	40.00	18.00	40.00

Wheelbarrow Race, Style Two (CT1)

PUSHING THE WHEELBARROW

Pushing the Wheelbarrow (CT3)

Design No.: CT3
Designer: Colin Twinn
Issued: 1988 - 1993
Combined with: *Bunnies in the Bath*, Second Version, CT34
Ice Cream Seller, First Variation, CT5
Picking Daisies, CT4
Splashing at Sink, CT33
Washing Up, CT32
Wheelbarrow Race, Style Two, CT1

Shape	USD	CAD	GBP	AUD
Albion sugar bowl	30.00	50.00	20.00	50.00
Albion teapot	50.00	85.00	35.00	95.00
Egg cup				
Style Three	7.50	12.50	5.00	12.50
Hug-a-mug, one handle	10.00	15.00	7.50	15.00
Lamp	100.00	150.00	65.00	175.00
Malvern beaker	15.00	25.00	10.00	25.00
Stratford teacup	7.50	12.00	5.00	12.00

WINDY DAY / BROKEN UMBRELLA

Windy Day (HW27)

Broken Umbrella (HW27R)

Design No.:	Front — HW27 Windy Day
	Reverse — HW27R Broken Umbrella
Designer:	Walter Hayward
Issued:	1952 - by 1998
Combined with:	*Apple Picking*, SF25
	Dress Making, HW26

Drummer, EC2
Toast for Tea Today, SF23
Trying on Knitting, HW119R
Playing with Doll and Teddy, HW120R
Unravelling the Knitting, HW119

Shape	USD	CAD	GBP	AUD
Albion cream jug	50.00	75.00	35.00	75.00
Albion jug, 1 pint	100.00	150.00	70.00	150.00
Albion jug, ½ pint	150.00	225.00	100.00	225.00
Albion teapot	50.00	85.00	35.00	95.00
Casino jug, 36s				
with signature	175.00	275.00	125.00	275.00
without signature	125.00	200.00	85.00	200.00
Casino jug, 42s				
with signature	150.00	225.00	100.00	225.00
without signature	100.00	150.00	70.00	150.00
Casino saucer				
with signature	15.00	25.00	10.00	25.00
without signature	7.50	12.00	5.00	12.00
Casino teacup				
with signature	15.00	25.00	10.00	25.00
without signature	7.50	12.00	5.00	12.00
Casino teapot, 24s				
with signature	275.00	400.00	175.00	450.00
without signature	175.00	275.00	125.00	325.00
Casino teapot, 36s				
with signature	250.00	375.00	165.00	400.00
without signature	150.00	225.00	100.00	225.00
Divider dish	50.00	75.00	35.00	75.00
Don beaker				
with signature	75.00	125.00	50.00	150.00
without signature	35.00	55.00	25.00	60.00
Don beaker, one handle				
with signature	75.00	125.00	50.00	150.00

Shape	USD	CAD	GBP	AUD
Don Beaker, One handle				
without signature	35.00	55.00	25.00	60.00
Don mug, one handle				
with signature	65.00	100.00	45.00	75.00
without signature	15.00	25.00	10.00	25.00
Don mug, two handles				
with signature	65.00	100.00	45.00	75.00
without signature	15.00	25.00	10.00	25.00
Egg box				
small	225.00	350.00	150.00	400.00
medium	300.00	450.00	200.00	500.00
large	375.00	550.00	250.00	600.00
Hug-a-mug, one handle	10.00	15.00	7.50	15.00
Hug-a-mug, two handles	10.00	15.00	7.50	15.00
Jaffa fruit saucer (plain)				
with signature	70.00	110.00	45.00	125.00
without signature	15.00	25.00	10.00	25.00
Lamp	100.00	150.00	65.00	175.00
Lid of hot water plate	125.00	200.00	85.00	225.00
Malvern beaker	15.00	25.00	10.00	25.00
Money ball	10.00	15.00	7.50	15.00
Picture plaque, small	20.00	30.00	12.50	30.00
Plate, 6 ½"				
with signature	35.00	55.00	25.00	55.00
without signature	20.00	30.00	15.00	30.00
Savings book	15.00	22.50	10.00	22.50
Stratford straight beaker	15.00	25.00	10.00	25.00
Stratford teacup	7.50	12.00	5.00	12.00

Note: *Toast for Tea Today* (SF23) and *Dress Making* (HW25) are combined with *Windy Day* (HW27) on the Casino teapot.

WINNING POST

Design No.:	LF106			
Designer:	Walter Hayward after Barbara Vernon			
Issued:	1959 - 1970			

Shape	USD	CAD	GBP	AUD
Baby plate, round, small	100.00	150.00	70.00	175.00
Baby plate, round, large	250.00	375.00	125.00	375.00
Plate, 8 ½"	75.00	125.00	50.00	135.00
Porridge plate	100.00	150.00	65.00	175.00

Winning Post (LF106)

Xmas Menu (LF8)

XMAS MENU

Design No.:	LF8			
Designer:	Barbara Vernon			
Issued:	1940 - by 1952			

Shape	USD	CAD	GBP	AUD
Baby plate, oval , large				
with signature	600.00	1,000.00	400.00	1,100.00
without signature	500.00	800.00	350.00	950.00
Baby plate, round, large				
with signature	450.00	675.00	325.00	700.00
without signature	400.00	600.00	275.00	625.00
Bread and butter plate				
with signature	800.00	1,250.00	500.00	1,600.00
without signature	600.00	1,000.00	400.00	1,100.00
Cereal / oatmeal bowl				
with signature	225.00	350.00	150.00	375.00
without signature	200.00	325.00	125.00	350.00
Plate, 8 ½"				
with signature	300.00	475.00	200.00	500.00
without signature	250.00	400.00	175.00	425.00
Porridge plate				
with signature	400.00	625.00	275.00	650.00
without signature	375.00	575.00	250.00	600.00

FINE WHITE CHINA
Bread and butter plate   Very rare

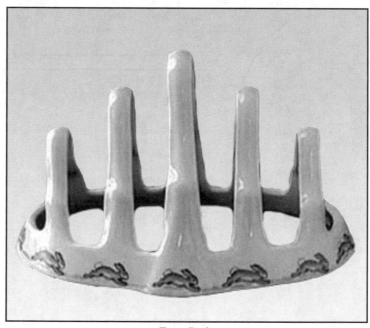

Toast Rack

BUNNYKINS BREAKFAST SET
Issues of 1939 - 1945

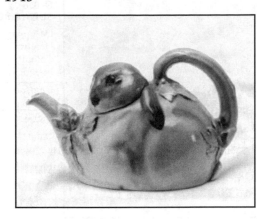

D6010
TEAPOT

Designer:	Charles Noke
Height:	4 ¾", 12.1 cm
Colour:	Brown rabbit; green leaves
Issued:	1939 - by 1945

Doulton	Price			
Number	USD	CAD	GBP	AUD
D6010	1,200.00	1,800.00	750.00	2,000.00

D6034
EGG CUP
Style One

Designer:	Charles Noke
Height:	1 ¾", 4.5 cm
Colour:	Brown rabbit
Issued:	1939 - by 1939

Doulton	Price			
Number	USD	CAD	GBP	AUD
D6034	2,250.00	3,000.00	1,500.00	3,500.00

D6040
SUGAR SIFTER

Designer:	Charles Noke
Height:	2 ¾", 7.0 cm
Colour:	Brown rabbit, blue sweater , red trousers
Issued:	1939 - by 1945

Doulton	Price			
Number	USD	CAD	GBP	AUD
D6040	6,000.00	9,000.00	4,000.00	10,000.00

Note: Designed by Charles Noke in 1939, this breakfast set comprises six pieces. Production started in 1940 but was soon halted due to wartime needs.

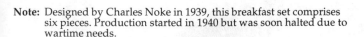

D6056
SUGAR BOWL

Designer: Charles Noke
Height: 1 ¾", 4.5 cm
Colour: Brown rabbit; green leaves
Issued: 1939 - by 1945

Doulton Number	Price USD	CAD	GBP	AUD
D6056	1,000.00	1,500.00	650.00	1,750.00

D6057
CREAM JUG

Designer: Charles Noke
Height: 2 ¾", 7.0 cm
Colour: Brown rabbit; green leaves
Issued: 1939 - by 1945

Doulton Number	Price USD	CAD	GBP	AUD
D6057	3,000.00	4,500.00	2,000.00	5,000.00

Note: The pieces comprising the Bunnykins Breakfast Set, due to the short production period, are scarce items and thus prices may vary. Prices listed above should be treated as indications only.

BUNNYKINS TEAPOTS
Issues of 1994 - 1998

D6966A
LONDON CITY GENT
BUNNYKINS TEAPOT

Designer:	Unknown
Modeller:	Martyn Alcock
Height:	8", 20.3 cm
Colour:	Brown and black
Issued:	1994 in a special edition of 2,500
Series:	Bunnykins Teapots of the World

Doulton		Price		
Number	USD	CAD	GBP	AUD
D6966	100.00	175.00	60.00	200.00

D6996B
U.S.A. PRESIDENT BUNNYKINS TEAPOT

Designer:	Unknown
Modeller:	Shane Ridge
Height:	8", 20.3 cm
Colour:	Red, white and blue
Issued:	1995 in a special edition of 2,500
Series:	Bunnykins Teapots of the World

Doulton		Price		
Number	USD	CAD	GBP	AUD
D6996	100.00	175.00	60.00	200.00

D7027
AUSSIE EXPLORER BUNNYKINS TEAPOT

Designer:	Unknown
Modeller:	Shane Ridge
Height:	7 ¾", 19.7 cm
Colour:	Brown bunny, yellow waistcoat, green hat, orange boomerang
Issued:	1996 in a special edition of 2,500
Series:	Bunnykins Teapots of the World

Photograph not available at press time

Doulton Number	Price			
	USD	CAD	GBP	AUD
D7027	125.00	175.00	75.00	200.00

D7126
JAPANESE BUNNYKINS TEAPOT
GEISHA GIRL

Designer:	Caroline Dadd
Modeller:	Martyn Alcock
Height:	7 ¾", 19.7 cm
Colour:	Brown bunny, lilac kimono with green and yellow sash, black hat, cream fan with red flowers
Issued:	1998 in a special edition of 2,500
Series:	Bunnykins Teapots of the World. The last of four.

Doulton Number	Price			
	USD	CAD	GBP	AUD
D7126	125.00	175.00	75.00	200.00

BUNNYKINS TEASET
Issues of 1998 - 2001

COOKIE JAR

Designer:	Unknown
Modeller:	Unknown
Height:	13 ½", 34.3 cm
Colour:	Brown bunny, blue dress, white collar and apron, pink hat, red flowers in basquet
Issued:	1998 - 2001

Description		Price		
	USD	CAD	GBP	AUD
Cookie jar	20.00	30.00	15.00	30.00

CREAMER

Designer:	Unknown
Modeller:	Unknown
Height:	4 ½", 11.9 cm
Colour:	Girl bunny - white dress with blue polka dots
	Boy bunny - deep pink jacket, pale pink jumper, brown trousers; white cow with black markings
Issued:	1998 - 2001

Description		Price		
	USD	CAD	GBP	AUD
Creamer	35.00	50.00	25.00	50.00

SALT AND PEPPER SET

Designer: Unknown
Modeller: Unknown
Height: Salt — 5 ¾", 14.6 cm
           Pepper — 6", 15.0 cm
Colour: Salt — Girl bunny wearing white dress with blue polka dots
           Pepper — Boy bunny wearing deep pink jacket, pink jumper
           brown trousers
Issued: 1998 - 2001

Description	USD	Price CAD	GBP	AUD
Salt and pepper set	35.00	50.00	25.00	50.00

SUGAR DISH

Designer: Unknown
Modeller: Unknown
Height: 5 ½", 14.0 cm
Colour: Brown bunny, blue dress, white collar and apron;
           brown sugar dish with white lid and spoon
Issued: 1998 - 2001

Description	USD	Price CAD	GBP	AUD
Sugar dish	20.00	30.00	15.00	30.00

TEAPOT

Designer: Unknown
Modeller: Unknown
Height: 9 ½", 24.0 cm
Colour: Brown bunny, green jacket, yellow shirt, deep pink bow tie,
           black belt and spectacles
Issued: 1998 - 2001

Description	USD	Price CAD	GBP	AUD
Teapot	20.00	30.00	15.00	30.00

Note: This set was released through Royal Doulton stores in the U.S.A.

BUNNYKINS TOBY JUGS
Issues of 1999 - 2001

D7157
FORTUNE TELLER BUNNYKINS™

Designer:	Kimberley Curtis
Modeller:	Warren Platt
Height:	5 ½", 14.0 cm
Colour:	Black, blue, brown, mauve, pink, white and yellow
Issued:	1999 in a limited edition of 1,500
Series:	Bunnykins Toby Jugs

Photograph not available at press time

Back		Price		
Stamp	USD	CAD	GBP	AUD
D-7157-Special	200.00	350.00	125.00	400.00

D7160
PARTY TIME BUNNYKINS™

Designer:	Caroline Dadd
Modeller:	Warren Platt
Height:	6", 15 cm
Colour:	Blue pants; yellow shirt; red hat and balloons
Issued:	2000 in a limited edition of 1,500
Series:	Bunnykins Toby Jugs

Royal Doulton®
PARTY-TIME BUNNYKINS
D7160
Modelled by WARREN PLATT
Designed by CAROLINE DADD
Second in the Series of Bunnykins Toby Jugs
PRODUCED EXCLUSIVELY FOR
U.K.I. CERAMICS LTD.
IN A WORLDWIDE
LIMITED EDITION OF 1,500
THIS IS No.
©2000 ROYAL DOULTON
AND U.K.I. CERAMICS LTD.

Back		Price		
Stamp	USD	CAD	GBP	AUD
D-7160-Special	200.00	350.00	125.00	400.00

D7166
WITCHING TIME BUNNYKINS™

Designer:	Caroline Dadd
Modeller:	Warren Platt
Height:	6", 15 cm
Colour:	Black, yellow and red
Issued:	2001 in a limited edition of 1,500
Series:	Bunnykins Toby Jugs

Photograph not available at press time

Back		Price		
Stamp	USD	CAD	GBP	AUD
D-7166-Special	200.00	350.00	125.00	400.00

Teapots
Aussie Explorer (D7027) London City Gent (D6966) U.S.A. President (D6996)

BUNNYKINS

DB102

DB103

DB104

DB105

DB106

DB107

DB108

DB109

DB115

DB116

DB117

DB118

Note: DB110 to 114 Royal Family not issued

BUNNYKINS

DB119

DB120

DB121

DB122

DB123

DB124

DB125

DB126

DB127

DB128

DB129

DB130

BUNNYKINS

DB131

DB132

DB133

DB134

DB135

DB136

DB137

DB142

DB143

DB144

DB145

DB146

Note: DB138 to 141 not issued

BUNNYKINS

DB147

DB148

DB149

DB150

DB151

DB152

DB153

DB154

DB155

DB156

DB157

DB158

BUNNYKINS

DB159

DB160

DB161

DB162

DB163

DB164

DB165

DB166

DB167

DB168

DB169

DB170

BUNNYKINS

DB171

DB172

DB173

DB174

DB175

DB176

DB177

DB178

DB179

DB180

DB181

DB182

BUNNYKINS

| DB183 | DB184 | DB185 | DB186 |

| DB187 | DB188 | DB189 | DB190 |

| DB191 | DB192 | DB193 | DB195 |

Note: DB194 Merry Christmas Tableau

BUNNYKINS

DB196

DB197

DB198

DB199

DB201

DB202

DB203

DB204

DB205

DB206

DB207

DB208

Note: DB200 Happy Millennium Tableau

PART TWO

BUNNYKINS BANKS
Issues of 1967 - 1981

BUNNYKINS COMMEMORATIVES
Issues of 1982 - 2002

Pillar Box; *Letterbox*, SF13, front; *Holding Hat and Coat*, EC4, back
From the Royal Doulton Archives.

BUNNYKINS BANKS
Issues of 1967 - 1981

D6615A
BUNNYBANK
First Version

Designer:	Unknown
Modeller:	John Bromley and David Biggs
Height:	8 ½", 21.6 cm
Colour:	Grey rabbit, green coat and hat, maroon drum
Issued:	1967 - 1977

Doulton	Price			
Number	USD	CAD	GBP	AUD
D6615A	200.00	325.00	125.00	350.00

D6615B
BUNNYBANK
Second Version

Designer:	Unknown
Modeller:	John Bromley and David Biggs
Height:	9 ¼", 23.5 cm
Colour:	Brown rabbit, green coat and hat, maroon drum
Issued:	1979 - 1981

Doulton		Price		
Number	USD	CAD	GBP	AUD
D6615B	200.00	325.00	125.00	350.00

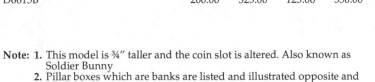

Note: 1. This model is ¾" taller and the coin slot is altered. Also known as Soldier Bunny
   2. Pillar boxes which are banks are listed and illustrated opposite and on page 195.

BUNNYKINS COMMEMORATIVES
Issues 1982 - 2002

Birth of the First Child of
T.R.H. The Prince and Princess of Wales 1982

TO CELEBRATE THE BIRTH OF THE FIRST CHILD OF T.R.H. THE PRINCE AND PRINCESS OF WALES 1982

The following is a list of designs known to appear on these shapes; more may exist.

Design No.: HW17, HW17R, HW22, HW22R, HW23, HW23R, HW26, HW26R, HW27R, HW137, HW137R, EC1, EC4, EC121, EC126

Issued: 1982

Shape	USD	CAD	GBP	AUD
Hug-a-mug, one handle	60.00	95.00	35.00	100.00
Hug-a-mug, two handles	75.00	110.00	50.00	125.00
Savings book	70.00	110.00	45.00	125.00

TO T.R.H. THE PRINCE AND PRINCESS OF WALES A SECOND CHILD 1984 IN JOYFUL CELEBRATION

The following is a list of designs known to appear on these shapes, more may exist.

Design No.: HW22R, HW23, HW27, HW27R, HW120R
Issued: 1984

Shape	USD	CAD	GBP	AUD
Hug-a-mug, one handle	35.00	60.00	20.00	65.00
Savings book	75.00	125.00	40.00	150.00

To T.R.H. The Prince and Princess of Wales
A Second Child 1984

BUNNYKINS CELEBRATE THEIR GOLDEN JUBILEE 1934 - 1984

Birthday Cake

Design No.: SF140 — Birthday Cake
Designer: Walter Hayward
Issued: 1984 - 1984
Backstamp: Golden Jubilee Celebration

Shape	USD	CAD	GBP	AUD
Baby plate, round, small				
with inscription	75.00	100.00	45.00	100.00
without inscription	50.00	75.00	30.00	75.00
Cereal bowl				
with inscription	75.00	100.00	45.00	100.00
without inscription	50.00	75.00	30.00	75.00
Plate, 8"				
with inscription	75.00	100.00	45.00	100.00
without inscription	50.00	75.00	30.00	75.00

Birthday Cake (SF140)

Note: The inscription was removed from the design after the Jubilee and the design was sold on baby plates, cereal bowls and the 8" plate.

Chicken Pulling a Cart (SF141)

CHICKEN PULLING A CART

This scene was first issued in 1940 and discontinued by 1952. It was reissued in 1984 to commemorate the fiftieth anniversary of Bunnykins and was issued in two variations, with and without the inscription.

Design No.: SF141 — Chicken Pulling a Cart
Designer: After a design by Barbara Vernon (SF8)
Issued: 1984 - 1984
Backstamp: Golden Jubilee Celebration.

Shape	USD	CAD	GBP	AUD
Plate, 8"				
with inscription	100.00	150.00	65.00	150.00
without inscription	85.00	135.00	50.00	135.00

Note: For the complete listing on SF141 see page 43.

Marriage of the Prince Andrew
with Miss Sarah Ferguson

TO CELEBRATE THE MARRIAGE OF THE PRINCE ANDREW WITH MISS SARAH FERGUSON WESTMINSTER ABBEY, WEDNESDAY, 23RD JULY 1986

The following is a list of designs known to appear on these shapes; more may exist.

Design No.:   HW27, HW29, HW29R,HW115, HW115R, HW116, HW119, HW119R, HW120, HW136, HW136R, HW139, HW139R
Issued: 1986

Shape	USD	CAD	GBP	AUD
Hug-a-mug, one handle.	75.00	110.00	40.00	125.00
Money ball	65.00	100.00	40.00	100.00

TO CELEBRATE AUSTRALIA' S BICENTENARY 1788-1988

Design No.:   None
Designer: Walter Hayward
Issued: 1987 - 1988
Backstamp: The Australian Bicentenary 1788-1988

Shape	USD	CAD	GBP	AUD
Plate, 8"	65.00	95.00	35.00	100.00

Bunnykins Celebrate Australia's
Bicentenary 1788 - 1988

To COMMEMORATE BUNNYKINS
60th ANNIVERSARY 1994

Dancing in the Moonlight
Second Version, First Variation, Large Size

Design No.: Front — CT91 Dancing in the Moonlight
Designer: Justin Clarke based on a design by
Barbara Vernon
Issued: 1994 - 1994
Backstamp: Dancing in the Moonlight Bunnykins 60th
Anniversary

Shape	USD	CAD	GBP	AUD
Baby plate, round, small	35.00	55.00	20.00	55.00
Plate, 8"	35.00	55.00	20.00	55.00

Note: See also *Dancing in the Moonlight*, Style One, page 53.

Dancing in the Moonlight, Second Version,
First Variation (CT91)

Dancing in the Moonlight, Second Version,
Second Variation (CT92)

Dancing in the Moonlight
Second Version, Second Variation, Small Size

Design No.: Front — CT92 Dancing in the Moonlight
Reverse — CT93 Bunnykins 60th Anniversary
inscription
Designer: Justin Clarke based on a design by Barbara
Vernon
Issued: 1994 - 1994

Shape	USD	CAD	GBP	AUD
Hug-a-mug, one handle	30.00	50.00	15.00	50.00
Money ball	30.00	50.00	20.00	50.00

Bunnykins 60th Anniversary Inscription (CT93)

TO CELEBRATE THE MILLENNIUM EXHIBITION HELD APRIL 15TH TO MAY 31ST, 2000 AT THE ROYAL DOULTON VISITORS' CENTRE

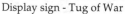

Display sign - Tug of War

Key fob - Tug of War

Desk clock - Sleeping in a Rocking Chair

Name:	**Display Sign**	**Key Fob**	**Desk Clock**
Designer:	Unknown	Unknown	Unknown
Modeller:	Unknown	Unknown	Unknown
Height:	2 ¼", 6 cm	2½" x 2", 6.4 x5.0 cm	4 ¼", 11 cm
Colour:	Multicoloured print	Multicoloured print	Multicoloured print
Issue:	1,250	1,250	1,000

Desk Clock Scenes:
Drummer, EC2
Drummer and Bugler, EC126
Hikers, EC124
Hobby Horse, EC121
*Playing with Cup and Spoo*n, EC6
Playing with Doll and Pram, EC123
Raising Hat, EC7
Reading, EC122
Sheltering Under an Umbrella, EC3
Sleeping in a Rocking Chair, EC1
Trumpeter, EC5

Shape	ISSUE PRICE GBP	USD	CAD	GBP	AUD
Desk clock	45.00	55.00	90.00	45.00	110.00
Display sign	15.00	25.00	50.00	15.00	60.00
Key Fob	5.00	10.00	15.00	5.00	20.00

Note: Please see DB200 which was also part of the exhibition (page 269).

TO COMMEMORATE THE AUSTRALIAN TOUR, 2000

Name:	Scenes:	Designer:	Height:	Colour:
Key Fob	*Trumpeter*, EC4	Barbara Vernon	2½" x 2", 6.4 x 5.0 cm	Cream/multicoloured print
Key Fob	*Drummer*, EC2	Barbara Vernon	2½" x 2", 6.4 x 5.0 cm	Cream/multicoloured print
Key Fob	*Drummer and Bugler*, EC126	Walter Hayward	2½" x 2", 6.4 c 5.0 cm	Cream/multicoloured print

Shape	ISSUE PRICE AUD	USD	CAD	GBP	AUD
Key fobs, set of three	30.00	60.00	100.00	40.00	100.00

ROYAL DOULTON BUNNYKINS EXTRAVAGANZA FAIR, OCTOBER 2001

Mantle clock	Pillar Money Box	Commemorative tray 2001

Name:	Mantle Clock	Piller Money Box	Commemorative Tray 2001
Designer:	Unknown	Unknown	Unknown
Modeller:	Unknown	Unknown	Unknown
Height/diameter:	4", 10.1 cm	5 ½", 14 cm	5 ¼", 13.5 cm
Colour:	Multicoloured print	Multicoloured print	Multicoloured print
Issue:	1,000	1,000	300
Scenes:	144 different combinations of 14 designs	*Posting Letters*, (28) *Sitting on Oil Drum*, (39)	*Letter Box*, (29)

Shape	ISSUE PRICE GBP	USD	CAD	GBP	AUD
Mantle clock	45.00	65.00	100.00	45.00	125.00
Pillar Money Box	45.00	65.00	100.00	45.00	125.00
Commemorative Tray	10.00	15.00	25.00	10.00	30.00

TO COMMEMORATE THE 65TH ANNIVERSARY OF NURSERY WARES HELD AT THE ROYAL DOULTON VISITORS' CENTRE, APRIL 2002

Rex mug

Commemorative tray 2002

Name:	**Rex Mug**	**Commemorative Tray**
Designer:	Unknown	Unknown
Modeller:	Unknown	Unknown
Height/Diameter:	3", 7.5 cm	5 ¼", 13.5 cm
Colour:	Multicoloured print	Multicoloured print
Issue:	325	700
Scenes:	Unknown	*Beating Carpet*, (20)

Shape	ISSUE PRICE GBP	USD	CAD	GBP	AUD
Rex mug	25.00	40.00	60.00	25.00	60.00
Commemorative tray	15.00	25.00	40.00	15.00	40.00

PART THREE

BUNNYKINS FIGURINES

EARTHENWARE
Issues of 1939 - 1940
Issues of 1972 - 2002

RESIN
Issues of 1996 - 1997

Mother Bunnykin, Farmer Bunnykin,
Bunnykins Breakfast Set Teapot
Mary Bunnykin, Reggie Bunnykin, Freddie Bunnykin, Billy Bunnykin

BUNNYKINS FIGURINE BACKSTAMPS

BK-1. COPR. (Date) DOULTON & CO. LIMITED
IN USE BETWEEN 1972 - 197

BK-1

BK-2. © ROYAL DOULTON TABLEWARE LTD (Date)
IN USE BETWEEN 1976 - 1984

BK-2

BK-1 was modified by replacing "COPR. (Date) DOULTON & CO. LIMITED" with © ROYAL DOULTON TABLEWARE LTD (Date) in the backstamp.

BK-3. © ROYAL DOULTON TABLEWARE LTD.
(Date) GOLDEN JUBILEE CELEBRATION 1984
IN USE FOR 1984

BK-3

"Golden Jubilee Celebration 1984" was added to BK-2 during 1984 for the 50th anniversary of Bunnykins.

Note: Flexibility must be allowed in dating by use of backstamps due to the over or under use of the backstamp lithos. Royal Doulton consumed all inventories of lithos before changing to a new style.

BK-4. © ROYAL DOULTON (U.K.) (Date) AND
© (Date) ROYAL DOULTON (U.K.) IN USE 1985 - 1986

BK-4a   **BK-4b**

BK-3 was modified for 1985 by the removal of "TABLEWARE LTD" and the insertion of "(U.K.)." A variation occurs with the date appearing after the copyright symbol.

BK-5. © (Date) ROYAL DOULTON
IN USE BETWEEN 1987 - 1997

BK-5a   **BK-5b**

BK-4a and 4b were modified in 1987 by the removal of "(U.K.)" from the copyright line.

BK-6. © (Date) ROYAL DOULTON AND YEAR CYPHER
IN USE FOR 1998 - 2000

BK-6a   **BK-6b**

In 1998 Royal Doulton added a dating cypher to the backstamp. See the following page for the year cyphers.

In 1999 Royal Doulton began issuing numbered limited edition Bunnykins figurines. BK-6b is the backstamp used.

BUNNYKINS FIGURINE BACKSTAMPS

BK-7. © 2000 ROYAL DOULTON, YEAR CYPHER AND MILLENNIUM STAMP - 2000

BK-7

For use on figurines produced in the year 2000.
A Millennium logo built around the Doulton logo.

BK-8. BUNNYKINS BY ROYAL DOULTON MADE IN ENGLAND © (Date) ROYAL DOULTON IN USE BETWEEN 2000 to 2002

BK-8a   **BK-8b**

An entirely new backstamp was designed in 2000. The copyright line MADE IN ENGLAND was added to © (Date) ROYAL DOULTON and the Crown, Lion and Doulton logo were removed. BK-8b is the numbered limited edition backstamp with the exception of the Doulton interlocking "D's"

BK-SPECIAL. ROYAL DOULTON BACKSTAMPS

BK-Special   **ICC Backstamp**

Adaptation of the generic BK-8a stamp to serve a special purpose; such as ICC, Event or Bunnykins of the year issues.

BK-Special Bunnykins of the Year backstamp

BK-EXC. COMMISSIONED FIGURINES IN USE BETWEEN 1972 - 2002

Over the years retailers have commissioned many different Bunnykins figurines. Each have a backstamp relating to them. The are all listed under "BK-EXC (LUSIVE)

ROYAL DOULTON YEAR CYPHERS

1998 Umbrella   1999 Top Hat

2000 Fob Watch   2001 Waistcoat   2002 Boot

BUNNYKIN FIGURINES BY SERIES

If you collect it is always a good idea to do so with a purpose or an objective in mind, only well thought out collections will have balance, allowing you to display your figurines with pride. You may decide to aquire the complete range, maybe only the marching bands, or build a collection around a theme which Bunnykins figurines may only be a part of, for example, the olympics. It is with this in mind that the following listing by Series may be of assistance to you.

AMERICAN HERITAGE

American Firefighter Bunnykins, third variation	DB268
Liberty Bell Bunnykins	DB257
Pilgrim Bunnykins	DB212
Statue of Liberty Bunnykins	DB198
Uncle Sam Bunnykins, second variation	DB175

AUSTRALIAN HERITAGE

Captain Cook Bunnykins	DB251
Digger Bunnykins	DB248
Federation Bunnykins	DB224
Sydney Bunnykins	DB195
Waltzing Matilda Bunnykins	DB236

BUNNYKINS FAMILY

Billy Bunnykin	D6001
Farmer Bunnykin	D6003
Freddie Bunnykin	D6024
Mary Bunnykin	D6002
Mother Bunnykin	D6004
Reggie Bunnykin	D6025

BUNNYKINS GAMES

Basketball Player Bunnykins	DB208
Gymnast Bunnykins	DB207
Runner Bunnykins	DB205
Soccer Player Bunnykins, second version	DB209
Swimmer Bunnykins	DB206

BUNNYKINS OF THE YEAR

1996	Father Bunnykins	DB154
1997	Sailor Bunnykins	DB166
1998	Seaside Bunnykins	DB177
1999	Mother Bunnykins	DB189
2000	Sundial Bunnykins	DB213
2001	Sands of Time Bunnykins	DB229
2002	Stop Watch Bunnykins	DB253

BUNNYKINS OF THE WORLD

Mandarin	DB252

CRICKET

Batsman Bunnykins	DB144
Bowler Bunnykins	DB145
Out For a Duck Bunnykins	DB160
Wicketkeeper Bunnykins	DB150

DANCERS OF THE WORLD

Flamenco Bunnykins	DB256
Morris Dancer Bunnykins	DB204
Tyrolean Dancer Bunnykins	DB242

FAIRY TALES

Cinderella Bunnykins	DB231
Little Red Riding Hood Bunnykins	DB230

FOOTBALLER / GOALKEEPER BUNNYKINS

First Variation

Footballer Bunnykins	DB117
Goalkeeper Bunnykins	DB116

Second Variation

Footballer Bunnykins	DB119
Goalkeeper Bunnykins	DB118

Third Variation

Footballer Bunnykins	DB121
Goalkeeper Bunnykins	DB120

Fourth Variation

Goalkeeper Bunnykins	DB122
Soccer Player Bunnykins	DB123

HOLIDAY OUTING

Father Bunnykins	DB154
Mother Bunnykins	DB189
Sailor Bunnykins	DB166
Seaside Bunnykins	DB177
Tourist Bunnykins	DB190

INTERNATIONAL COLLECTORS CLUB

ICC Members Exclusives

1987	Collector Bunnykins	DB54
1992	Master Potter Bunnykins	DB131
1995	Partners in Collecting Bunnykins	DB151
1999	Tourist Bunnykins	DB190
2000	Sightseer Bunnykins	DB215
2001	Choir Singer Bunnykins	DB223
2002	Cinderella Bunnykins	DB231

ICC Membership Gift

1999	Judge Bunnykins	DB188
2000	Lawyer Bunnykins	DB214
2001	Choir Singer Bunnykins	DB223
2002	Vicar Bunnykins	DB254

JAZZ BAND

Banjo Player Bunnykins	DB182
Clarinet Player Bunnykins	DB184
Double Bass Player Bunnykins	DB185
Drummer Player Bunnykins, Style Two	DB250
Saxaphone Player Bunnykins	DB186
Trumpet Player Bunnykins	DB210

MUSIC BOXES

Astro Bunnykins 'Rocket Man'	DB35
Happy Birthday Bunnykins	DB36
Jogging Bunnykins	DB37
Mr. Bunnybeat Strumming	DB38
Mrs. Bunnykins At the Easter Parade	DB39
Santa Bunnykins	DB34
Tally Ho! Bunnykins, First Variation	DB33A
Tally Ho! Bunnykins, Second Variation	DB33B

NURSERY RHYME

Jack and Jill Bunnykins	DB222
Little Bo Peep Bunnykins	DB220
Little Boy Blue Bunnykins	DB239
Little Jack Horner Bunnykins	DB221
Little Miss Muffet Bunnykins	DB240
Mary Mary Quite Contrary Bunnykins	DB247
Wee Willie Winkie	DB270

OOMPAH BANDS

First Variation - Red Band

Cymbals Bunnykins	DB25
Drum-major Bunnykins	DB27
Drummer Bunnykins, 50th Anniversary	DB26A
Drummer Bunnykins, Oompah Band	DB26B
Sousaphone Bunnykins	DB23
Trumpeter Bunnykins	DB24

Second Variation - Blue Band

Cymbals Bunnykins	DB88
Drum-major Bunnykins	DB90
Drummer Bunnykins	DB89
Sousaphone Bunnykins	DB86
Trumpeter Bunnykins	DB87

Third Variation - Green Band

Cymbals Bunnykins	DB107
Drum-major Bunnykins	DB109
Drummer Bunnykins	DB108
Sousaphone Bunnykins	DB105
Trumpeter Bunnykins	DB106

PUNCH AND JUDY

Mr. Punch Bunnykins	DB234
Judy Bunnykins	DB235

ROBIN HOOD

Friar Tuck Bunnykins	DB246
King Richard Bunnykins	DB258
Little John Bunnykins	DB243
Maid Marion Bunnykins	DB245
Prince John Bunnykins	DB266
Robin Hood Bunnykins	DB244
Sheriff of Nottingham Bunnykins	DB265
Will Scarlet Bunnykins	DB264

ROYAL FAMILY

First Variation

Harry the Herald	DB49
King John	DB45
Prince Frederick	DB48
Princess Beatrice	DB47
Queen Sophie	DB46

Second Variation

Harry the Herald	DB95
King John	DB91
Prince Frederick	DB94
Princess Beatrice	DB93
Queen Sophie	DB92

Third Variation

Harry the Herald	DB115

TIME

Sands of Time Bunnykins	DB229
Sundial Bunnykins	DB213
Stop Watch Bunnykins	DB253

TOUCHDOWN BUNNYKINS

Touchdown Bunnykins	DB29A
Boston College	DB29B
Cincinnati Bengals	DB98
Notre Dame College	DB99
Ohio State University	DB96
University of Indiana	DB100
University of Michigan	DB97

TRAVEL SERIES

Chocks Away Bunnykins	DB267
Day Trip Bunnykins	DB260
Dodgem Bunnykins	DB249

SPECIAL EVENTS

1986 Mrs. Bunnykins At the Easter Parade, 2nd Var.	DB52
1987 Storytime Bunnykins, 2nd Var.	DB59
1988 Family Photograph Bunnykins, 2nd Var.	DB67
1989 Billie and Buntie Bunnykins Sleigh Ride	DB81
1991 Bedtime Bunnykins	DB103
2000 Morris Dancer Bunnykins	DB204
2001 Little Red Riding Hood	DB230
2001 Tyrolean Dancer Bunnykins	DB242
2002 Flamenco Bunnykins	DB256

TABLEAU

Bath Night Bunnykins	DB241
Merry Christmas Bunnykins	DB194
Sandcastle Money Box	DB228

EARTHENWARE ISSUES
1939 - 1940

D6001
BILLY BUNNYKIN™

Designer:	Charles Noke
Height:	4 ½", 11.9 cm
Colour:	Red trousers, blue jacket, white bow tie with blue spots
Issued:	1939-c.1940

Doulton	Price			
Number	USD	CAD	GBP	AUD
D6001	2,000.00	3,000.00	1,500.00	3,250.00

D6002
MARY BUNNYKIN™

Designer:	Charles Noke
Height:	6 ½", 16.5 cm
Colour:	Red bodice, dark blue collar; pale blue skirt, white apron
Issued:	1939-c.1940

Doulton	Price			
Number	USD	CAD	GBP	AUD
D6002	2,250.00	3,500.00	1,500.00	4,000.00

D6003
FARMER BUNNYKIN™

Designer:	Charles Noke
Height:	7 ½", 19.1 cm
Colour:	Green coat, blue and white smock, yellow bow tie, red handkerchief with white dots
Issued:	1939-c.1940

Doulton	Price			
Number	USD	CAD	GBP	AUD
D6003	2,000.00	3,000.00	1,500.00	3,250.00

Note: Italicized prices are indications only.

D6004
MOTHER BUNNYKIN™

Designer: Charles Noke
Height: 7", 17.8 cm
Colour: Blue skirt, red jacket, white
           shawl with blue stripes
Issued: 1939-c.1940

| Doulton | Price | | | |
Number	USD	CAD	GBP	AUD
D6004	2,500.00	4,000.00	1,650.00	4,500.00

D6024
FREDDIE BUNNYKIN™

Designer: Charles Noke
Height: 3 ¾", 9.5 cm
Colour: Green trousers, red jacket
           and yellow bow tie
Issued: 1939-c.1940

| Doulton | Price | | | |
Number	USD	CAD	GBP	AUD
D6024	4,000.00	6,000.00	2,500.00	6,000.00

D6025
REGGIE BUNNYKIN™

Designer: Charles Noke
Height: 3 ¾", 9.5 cm
Colour: Blue smock; red bow tie
Issued: 1939-c.1940

| Doulton | Price | | | |
Number	USD	CAD	GBP	AUD
D6025	4,000.00	6,000.00	2,500.00	6,000.00

EARTHENWARE ISSUES
1972 to 2002

DB1
FAMILY PHOTOGRAPH BUNNYKINS™
First Variation

Designer:	Based on a design by Walter Hayward
Modeller:	Albert Hallam
Height:	4 ½", 11.9 cm
Colour:	Blue, white, burgundy and grey
Issued:	1972 - 1988
Varieties:	DB67; also called Father, Mother and Victoria Bunnykins, DB68

BUNNYKINS ®
"Family Photograph"
DB1
© ROYAL DOULTON
TABLEWARE LTD 1972

Back Stamp	Price			
	USD	CAD	GBP	AUD
BK-1	100.00	150.00	70.00	175.00
BK-2	100.00	150.00	70.00	175.00
BK-3	110.00	160.00	75.00	185.00

DB2
BUNTIE BUNNYKINS HELPING MOTHER™

Designer:	Based on a design by Walter Hayward
Modeller:	Albert Hallam
Height:	3 ½", 8.9 cm
Colour:	Rose-pink and yellow
Issued:	1972 - 1993

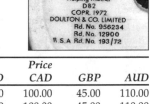

BUNTIE BUNNYKINS
"Helping Mother"
DB2
COPR. 1972
DOULTON & CO. LIMITED
Rd. No. 956234
Rd. No. 12900
R.S.A Rd. No. 193/72

Back Stamp	Price			
	USD	CAD	GBP	AUD
BK-1	65.00	100.00	45.00	110.00
BK-2	65.00	100.00	45.00	110.00
BK-3	70.00	115.00	50.00	125.00

DB3
BILLIE BUNNYKINS COOLING OFF™

Designer:	Based on a design by Walter Hayward
Modeller:	Albert Hallam
Height:	3 ¾", 9.5 cm
Colour:	Burgundy, yellow and green-grey
Issued:	1972 - 1987

BILLIE BUNNYKINS
"Cooling Off"
DB3
© ROYAL DOULTON
TABLEWARE LTD 1972

Back Stamp	Price			
	USD	CAD	GBP	AUD
BK-1	175.00	275.00	120.00	295.00
BK-2	175.00	275.00	120.00	295.00
BK-3	185.00	285.00	125.00	300.00

Note: Also found with blue pants and white boots.

DB4
BILLIE & BUNTIE BUNNYKINS
SLEIGH RIDE™
First Variation

Designer:	Based on a design by Walter Hayward
Modeller:	Albert Hallam
Height:	3 ¼", 8.3 cm
Colour:	Blue, maroon and yellow
Issued:	1972 - 1997
Varieties:	DB81

Back Stamp	Price			
	USD	CAD	GBP	AUD
BK-1	35.00	55.00	25.00	60.00
BK-2	35.00	55.00	25.00	60.00
BK-3	40.00	60.00	30.00	70.00

Note: Colour variations exist in Buntie's blue dress.

DB5
MR. BUNNYKINS AUTUMN DAYS™

Designer:	Based on a design by Walter Hayward
Modeller:	Albert Hallam
Height:	4", 10.1 cm
Colour:	Maroon, yellow and blue
Issued:	1972 - 1982

Back Stamp	Price			
	USD	CAD	GBP	AUD
BK-1	225.00	375.00	160.00	400.00
BK-2	225.00	375.00	160.00	400.00

DB6
MRS. BUNNYKINS CLEAN SWEEP™

Designer:	Based on a design by Walter Hayward
Modeller:	Albert Hallam
Height:	4", 10.1 cm
Colour:	Blue and white
Issued:	1972 - 1991

Back Stamp	Price			
	USD	CAD	GBP	AUD
BK-1	100.00	150.00	70.00	150.00
BK-2	100.00	150.00	70.00	150.00
BK-3	110.00	165.00	80.00	165.00

DB7
DAISIE BUNNYKINS SPRING TIME™

Designer:	Based on a design by Walter Hayward
Modeller:	Albert Hallam
Height:	3 ½", 8.9 cm
Colour:	Blue, white and yellow
Issued:	1972 - 1983

Back Stamp	Price			
	USD	CAD	GBP	AUD
BK-1	200.00	325.00	150.00	350.00
BK-2	200.00	325.00	150.00	350.00

DB8
DOLLIE BUNNYKINS PLAYTIME™
First Variation

Designer:	Based on a design by Walter Hayward
Modeller:	Albert Hallam
Height:	4", 10.1 cm
Colour:	White dress with pink design, blue dress
Issued:	1972 - 1993
Varieties:	DB80

Back Stamp	Price			
	USD	CAD	GBP	AUD
BK-1	60.00	100.00	40.00	110.00
BK-2	60.00	100.00	40.00	110.00
BK-3	65.00	110.00	50.00	120.00

DB9
STORYTIME BUNNYKINS™
First Variation

Designer:	Based on a design by Walter Hayward
Modeller:	Albert Hallam
Height:	3", 7.6 cm
Colour:	White dress with blue design, pink dress
Issued:	1972 - 1997
Varieties:	DB59; also called Partners in Collecting, DB151

Back Stamp	Price			
	USD	CAD	GBP	AUD
BK-1	35.00	55.00	25.00	60.00
BK-2	35.00	55.00	25.00	60.00
BK-3	40.00	60.00	30.00	70.00

DB10
BUSY NEEDLES BUNNYKINS™

Designer:	Based on a design by Walter Hayward
Modeller:	Albert Hallam
Height:	3 ¼", 8.3 cm
Colour:	White, green and maroon
Issued:	1973 - 1988
Varieties:	Also called Susan Bunnykins, DB70

Back Stamp	Price			
	USD	CAD	GBP	AUD
BK-1	85.00	150.00	60.00	165.00
BK-2	85.00	150.00	60.00	165.00
BK-3	95.00	160.00	65.00	175.00

DB11
RISE AND SHINE BUNNYKINS™

Designer:	Based on a design by Walter Hayward
Modeller:	Albert Hallam
Height:	3 ¾", 9.5 cm
Colour:	Maroon, yellow and blue
Issued:	1973 - 1988

Back Stamp	Price			
	USD	CAD	GBP	AUD
BK-1	125.00	200.00	90.00	220.00
BK-2	125.00	200.00	90.00	220.00
BK-3	135.00	225.00	95.00	250.00

DB12
TALLY HO! BUNNYKINS™
First Variation

Designer:	Based on a design by Walter Hayward
Modeller:	Albert Hallam
Height:	3 ¾", 9.5 cm
Colour:	Burgundy, yellow, blue, white and green
Issued:	1973 - 1988
Varieties:	DB78; also called William Bunnykins, DB69

Back Stamp	Price			
	USD	CAD	GBP	AUD
BK-1	95.00	150.00	65.00	175.00
BK-2	95.00	150.00	65.00	175.00
BK-3	100.00	165.00	75.00	200.00

DB13
THE ARTIST BUNNYKINS™

Designer:	Based on a design by Walter Hayward
Modeller:	Alan Maslankowski
Height:	3 ¾", 9.5 cm
Colour:	Burgundy, yellow and blue
Issued:	1975 - 1982

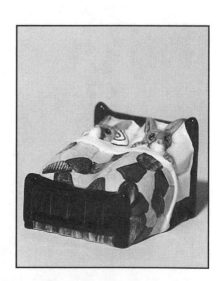

Back Stamp	Price			
	USD	CAD	GBP	AUD
BK-1	400.00	625.00	275.00	650.00
BK-2	400.00	625.00	275.00	650.00
BK-3	400.00	625.00	275.00	650.00

DB14
GRANDPA'S STORY BUNNYKINS™

Designer:	Based on a design by Walter Hayward
Modeller:	Alan Maslankowski
Height:	4", 10.1 cm
Colour:	Burgundy, grey, yellow blue and green
Issued:	1975 - 1983

Back Stamp	Price			
	USD	CAD	GBP	AUD
BK-1	400.00	625.00	275.00	650.00
BK-2	400.00	625.00	275.00	650.00

DB15
SLEEPYTIME BUNNYKINS™

Designer:	Based on a design by Walter Hayward
Modeller:	Alan Maslankowski
Height:	1 ¾", 4.7 cm
Colour:	Brown, white, yellow, blue and red
Issued:	1975 - 1993

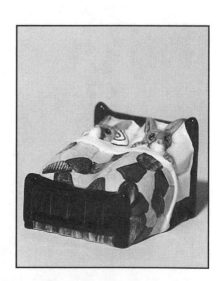

Back Stamp	Price			
	USD	CAD	GBP	AUD
BK-1	55.00	85.00	40.00	100.00
BK-2	55.00	85.00	40.00	100.00
BK-3	60.00	95.00	45.00	110.00

DB16
MR. BUNNYBEAT STRUMMING™

Designer: Harry Sales
Modeller: David Lyttleton
Height: 4 ½", 11.9 cm
Colour: Pink and yellow coat, blue and white stripped trousers, white with blue polka-dot neck bow
Issued: 1982 - 1988
Varieties: Also called Rock and Roll Bunnykins, DB124

Back Stamp	Price			
	USD	CAD	GBP	AUD
BK-2	175.00	250.00	110.00	300.00
BK-3	175.00	250.00	110.00	300.00

DB17
SANTA BUNNYKINS HAPPY CHRISTMAS™

Designer: Harry Sales
Modeller: David Lyttleton
Height: 4 ½", 11.9 cm
Colour: Red, white and brown
Issued: 1981 - 1996

Back Stamp	Price			
	USD	CAD	GBP	AUD
BK-2	40.00	65.00	30.00	70.00
BK-3	45.00	70.00	35.00	75.00

DB18
MR. BUNNYKINS
AT THE EASTER PARADE™
First Variation

Designer: Harry Sales
Modeller: David Lyttleton
Height: 5", 12.7 cm
Colour: Red, yellow, brown and yellow ribbon
Issued: 1982 - 1993
Varieties: DB51

Back Stamp	Price			
	USD	CAD	GBP	AUD
BK-2	70.00	100.00	50.00	110.00
BK-3	70.00	100.00	50.00	110.00

DB19
MRS. BUNNYKINS
AT THE EASTER PARADE™
First Variation

Designer:	Harry Sales
Modeller:	David Lyttleton
Height:	4 ½", 11.9 cm
Colour:	Pale blue and maroon
Issued:	1982 - 1996
Varieties:	DB52

Back Stamp	Price USD	CAD	GBP	AUD
BK-2	35.00	55.00	25.00	60.00
BK-3	40.00	55.00	30.00	60.00

DB20
ASTRO BUNNYKINS ROCKET MAN™

Designer:	Harry Sales
Modeller:	David Lyttleton
Height:	4 ¼", 10.8 cm
Colour:	White, red, blue and yellow
Issued:	1983 - 1988

Back Stamp	Price USD	CAD	GBP	AUD
BK-2	125.00	175.00	200.00	225.00
BK-3	125.00	175.00	200.00	225.00

DB21
HAPPY BIRTHDAY BUNNYKINS™

Designer:	Harry Sales
Modeller:	Graham Tongue
Height:	3 ¾", 9.5 cm
Colour:	Red and blue
Issued:	1983 - 1997

Back Stamp	Price USD	CAD	GBP	AUD
BK-2	35.00	55.00	25.00	65.00
BK-3	35.00	55.00	25.00	60.00

DB22
JOGGING BUNNYKINS™

Designer: Harry Sales
Modeller: David Lyttleton
Height: 2 ½", 6.4 cm
Colour: Yellow, blue and white
Issued: 1983 - 1989

Back Stamp	USD	Price CAD	GBP	AUD
BK-2	60.00	95.00	40.00	100.00
BK-3	65.00	95.00	45.00	100.00

DB23
SOUSAPHONE BUNNYKINS™
First Variation

Designer: Harry Sales
Modeller: David Lyttleton
Height: 3 ½", 8.9 cm
Colour: Red, blue and yellow
Issued: 1984 - 1990
Varieties: DB86, DB105
Series: Bunnykins Oompah Band

Back Stamp	USD	Price CAD	GBP	AUD
BK-2	125.00	195.00	90.00	200.00
BK-3	125.00	195.00	90.00	200.00
BK-4	125.00	195.00	90.00	200.00
Set DB23 - 27 (5pcs.)	500.00	800.00	350.00	1,000.00

DB24
TRUMPETER BUNNYKINS™
First Variation

Designer: Harry Sales
Modeller: David Lyttleton
Height: 3 ½", 8.9 cm
Colour: Red, blue and yellow
Issued: 1984 - 1990
Varieties: DB87, DB106
Series: Bunnykins Oompah Band

Back Stamp	USD	Price CAD	GBP	AUD
BK-2	125.00	195.00	90.00	200.00
BK-3	125.00	195.00	90.00	200.00
BK-4	125.00	195.00	90.00	200.00

DB25
CYMBALS BUNNYKINS™
First Variation

Designer:	Harry Sales
Modeller:	David Lyttleton
Height:	3 ½", 8.9 cm
Colour:	Red, blue and yellow
Issued:	1984 - 1990
Varieties:	DB88, DB107
Series:	Bunnykins Oompah Band

Back Stamp	Price			
	USD	CAD	GBP	AUD
BK-2	125.00	195.00	90.00	200.00
BK-3	125.00	195.00	90.00	200.00
BK-4	125.00	195.00	90.00	200.00

DB26A
DRUMMER BUNNYKINS™
Style One, First Variation, 50th Anniversary Edition

Designer:	Harry Sales
Modeller:	David Lyttleton
Height:	3 ½", 8.9 cm
Colour:	Blue, yellow, red and cream
Issued:	1984 - 1984
Series:	Bunnykins Oompah Band

Back Stamp	Price			
	USD	CAD	GBP	AUD
BK-3	125.00	200.00	90.00	225.00

DB26B
DRUMMER BUNNYKINS™
Style One, Second Variation, Bunnykins

Designer:	Harry Sales
Modeller:	David Lyttleton
Height:	3 ¾", 9.5 cm
Colour:	Blue, yellow, red and cream
Issued:	1984 - 1990
Varieties:	DB89, DB108
Series:	Bunnykins Oompah Band

Back Stamp	Price			
	USD	CAD	GBP	AUD
BK-2	125.00	200.00	90.00	225.00
BK-3	125.00	200.00	90.00	225.00
BK-4	125.00	200.00	90.00	225.00

DB27
DRUM-MAJOR BUNNYKINS™
First Variation

Designer:	Harry Sales
Modeller:	David Lyttleton
Height:	3 ½", 8.9 cm
Colour:	Red, blue and yellow
Issued:	1984 - 1990
Varieties:	DB90, DB109
Series:	Bunnykins Oompah Band

Back Stamp	Price			
	USD	CAD	GBP	AUD
BK-2	125.00	195.00	90.00	200.00
BK-3	125.00	195.00	90.00	200.00
BK-4	125.00	195.00	90.00	200.00

DB28A
OLYMPIC BUNNYKINS™
First Variation

Designer:	Harry Sales
Modeller:	David Lyttleton
Height:	3 ¾", 9.5 cm
Colour:	White and blue
Issued:	1984 - 1988

Back Stamp	Price			
	USD	CAD	GBP	AUD
BK-2	125.00	195.00	90.00	200.00
BK-3	125.00	195.00	90.00	200.00
BK-4	125.00	195.00	90.00	200.00

DB28B
OLYMPIC BUNNYKINS™
Second Variation

Designer:	Harry Sales
Modeller:	David Lyttleton
Height:	3 ½", 8.9 cm
Colour:	Gold and green
Issued:	1984 - 1984

Back Stamp	Price			
	USD	CAD	GBP	AUD
BK-Special	500.00	800.00	350.00	900.00

DB29A
TOUCHDOWN BUNNYKINS™
First Variation

Designer:	Harry Sales
Modeller:	David Lyttleton
Height:	3 ¼", 8.3 cm
Colour:	Blue and white
Issued:	1985 - 1988
Varieties:	DB29B, DB96, DB97, DB98, DB99, DB100

Back Stamp		Price		
	USD	CAD	GBP	AUD
BK-3	125.00	195.00	85.00	200.00
BK-4	125.00	195.00	85.00	200.00
BK-5a	125.00	195.00	85.00	200.00

DB29B
TOUCHDOWN BUNNYKINS™
Second Variation (Boston College)

Designer:	Harry Sales
Modeller:	David Lyttleton
Height:	3 ¼", 8.3 cm
Colour:	Maroon and gold
Issued:	1985 in a limited edition of 50
Varieties:	DB29A, DB96, DB97, DB98, DB99, DB100

Photograph not available at press time

Back Stamp		Price		
	USD	CAD	GBP	AUD
BK-4	*1750.00*	*2,250.00*	*1,000.00*	*2,250.00*

Note: Italicized prices are indications only.

DB30
KNOCKOUT BUNNYKINS™

Designer:	Harry Sales
Modeller:	David Lyttleton
Height:	4", 10.1 cm
Colour:	Yellow, green and white
Issued:	1984 - 1988

Back Stamp		Price		
	USD	CAD	GBP	AUD
BK-3	225.00	350.00	165.00	400.00
BK-4	225.00	350.00	165.00	400.00
BK-5a	225.00	350.00	165.00	400.00

DB31
DOWNHILL BUNNYKINS™

Designer:	Harry Sales
Modeller:	Graham Tongue
Height:	2 ½", 6.4 cm
Colour:	Yellow, green, maroon and grey
Issued:	1985 - 1988

DOWNHILL BUNNYKINS
DB 31
© ROYAL DOULTON
TABLEWARE LTD 1984

Back Stamp	Price			
	USD	CAD	GBP	AUD
BK-3	165.00	250.00	115.00	275.00
BK-4	165.00	250.00	115.00	275.00
BK-5a	165.00	250.00	115.00	275.00

DB32
BOGEY BUNNYKINS™

Designer:	Harry Sales
Modeller:	David Lyttleton
Height:	4", 10.1 cm
Colour:	Green, brown and yellow
Issued:	1984 - 1992

"BOGEY BUNNYKINS"
DB 32
© ROYAL DOULTON
TABLEWARE LTD 1984
20

Back Stamp	Price			
	USD	CAD	GBP	AUD
BK-2	100.00	160.00	70.00	175.00
BK-3	100.00	160.00	70.00	175.00
BK-4	100.00	160.00	70.00	175.00
BK-5a	100.00	160.00	70.00	175.00

DB33A
TALLY HO!™
Music Box
First Variation, Tally-Ho! Figurine

Designer:	Based on a design by Walter Hayward
Modeller:	Albert Hallam
Height:	7", 17.8 cm
Colour:	Red coat, yellow jumper
Issued:	1984 - 1993
Tune:	Rock A Bye Baby

Photograph not
available
at press time

Back Stamp	Price			
	USD	CAD	GBP	AUD
BK-3	150.00	235.00	100.00	250.00
BK-4	150.00	235.00	100.00	250.00
BK-5a	150.00	235.00	100.00	250.00

DB33B
TALLY HO!™
Music Box
Second Variation, William Bunnykins Figurine

Designer:	Based on a design by
	Walter Hayward
Modeller:	Albert Hallam
Height:	7", 17.8 cm
Colour:	Brown trousers, red coat and
	maroon tie
Issued:	1988 - 1991
Tune:	'Rock A Bye Baby'

Photograph not available at press time

Back		Price		
Stamp	USD	CAD	GBP	AUD
BK-4	150.00	235.00	100.00	250.00
BK-5a	150.00	235.00	100.00	250.00

DB34
SANTA BUNNYKINS™
Music Box

Designer:	Harry Sales
Modeller:	David Lyttleton
Height:	7 ¼", 18.4 cm
Colour:	Red, white and brown
Issued:	1984 - 1991
Tune:	'White Christmas'

Photograph not available at press time

Back		Price		
Stamp	USD	CAD	GBP	AUD
BK-3	150.00	235.00	100.00	250.00
BK-4	150.00	235.00	100.00	250.00
BK-5a	150.00	235.00	100.00	250.00

DB35
ASTRO BUNNYKINS 'ROCKET MAN'™
Music Box

Designer:	Harry Sales
Modeller:	David Lyttleton
Height:	7", 17.8 cm
Colour:	White, red and blue
Issued:	1984 - 1989
Tune:	'Fly Me To The Moon'

Photograph not available at press time

Back		Price		
Stamp	USD	CAD	GBP	AUD
BK-3	150.00	235.00	100.00	250.00
BK-4	150.00	235.00	100.00	250.00
BK-5a	150.00	235.00	100.00	250.00

DB36
HAPPY BIRTHDAY BUNNYKINS™
Music Box

Designer:	Harry Sales
Modeller:	Graham Tongue
Height:	7", 17.8 cm
Colour:	Red and white
Issued:	1984 - 1991
Tune:	'Happy Birthday To You'

Photograph not available at press time

Back Stamp	Price			
	USD	CAD	GBP	AUD
BK-3	150.00	235.00	100.00	250.00
BK-4	150.00	235.00	100.00	250.00
BK-5a	150.00	235.00	100.00	250.00

DB37
JOGGING BUNNYKINS™
Music Box

Designer:	Harry Sales
Modeller:	David Lyttleton
Height:	5 ½", 14.0 cm
Colour:	Yellow and blue
Issued:	1987 - 1989
Tune:	'King of the Road'

Photograph not available at press time

Back Stamp	Price			
	USD	CAD	GBP	AUD
BK-5a	150.00	235.00	100.00	250.00

DB38
MR. BUNNYBEAT STRUMMING™
Music Box

Designer:	Harry Sales
Modeller:	David Lyttleton
Height:	7 ½", 19.1 cm
Colour:	Pink, white and yellow
Issued:	1987 - 1989
Tune:	'Hey Jude'

Photograph not available at press time

Back Stamp	Price			
	USD	CAD	GBP	AUD
BK-5a	150.00	235.00	100.00	250.00

DB39
MRS. BUNNYKINS
AT THE EASTER PARADE™
Music Box

Designer:	Harry Sales
Modeller:	David Lyttleton
Height:	7", 17.8 cm
Colour:	Blue, yellow and maroon
Issued:	1987 - 1991
Tune:	'Easter Parade'

*Photograph not
available
at press time*

Back Stamp	Price			
	USD	CAD	GBP	AUD
BK-5a	125.00	200.00	90.00	225.00

DB40
AEROBIC BUNNYKINS™

Designer:	Harry Sales
Modeller:	David Lyttleton
Height:	2 ¾", 7.0 cm
Colour:	Yellow and pale blue
Issued:	1985 - 1988

Back Stamp	Price			
	USD	CAD	GBP	AUD
BK-4	150.00	250.00	100.00	275.00
BK-5a	150.00	250.00	100.00	275.00

DB41
FREEFALL BUNNYKINS™

Designer:	Harry Sales
Modeller:	David Lyttleton
Height:	2 ¼", 5.7 cm
Colour:	Grey, yellow and white
Issued:	1986 - 1989

Back Stamp	Price			
	USD	CAD	GBP	AUD
BK-4	300.00	475.00	200.00	500.00
BK-5a	300.00	475.00	200.00	500.00

Note: Different colour variations; dark grey suit, light grey suit.

DB42
ACE BUNNYKINS™

Designer:	Harry Sales	
Modeller:	David Lyttleton	
Height:	3 ¾", 9.5 cm	
Colour:	White and blue	
Issued:	1986 - 1989	

Back		Price		
Stamp	USD	CAD	GBP	AUD
BK-4	250.00	375.00	165.00	400.00
BK-5a	250.00	375.00	165.00	400.00

DB43
HOME RUN BUNNYKINS™
(1 on Back of Jersey)

Designer:	Harry Sales
Modeller:	David Lyttleton
Height:	4", 10.1 cm
Colour:	Blue, yellow and white
Issued:	1986 - 1993

Back		Price		
Stamp	USD	CAD	GBP	AUD
BK-4	100.00	135.00	60.00	150.00
BK-5a	100.00	135.00	60.00	150.00

DB44: Assigned to Ballet Bunnykins but not issued.

DB45
KING JOHN™
First Variation

Designer:	Harry Sales
Modeller:	David Lyttleton
Height:	4", 10.1 cm
Colour:	Red, yellow and blue
Issued:	1986 - 1990
Varieties:	DB91
Series:	Bunnykins Royal Family

Back		Price		
Stamp	USD	CAD	GBP	AUD
BK-4	100.00	165.00	70.00	175.00
BK-5a	100.00	165.00	70.00	175.00
Set DB45 - 49 (5pcs.)	500.00	800.00	450.00	900.00

DB46
QUEEN SOPHIE™
First Variation

Designer:	Harry Sales
Modeller:	David Lyttleton
Height:	4 ½", 11.9 cm
Colour:	Blue and red
Issued:	1986 - 1990
Varieties:	DB92
Series:	Bunnykins Royal Family

Back Stamp	Price			
	USD	CAD	GBP	AUD
BK-4	135.00	175.00	100.00	200.00
BK-5a	135.00	175.00	100.00	200.00

DB47
PRINCESS BEATRICE™
First Variation

Designer:	Harry Sales
Modeller:	David Lyttleton
Height:	3 ½", 8.9 cm
Colour:	Pale green
Issued:	1986 - 1990
Varieties:	DB93
Series:	Bunnykins Royal Family

Back Stamp	Price			
	USD	CAD	GBP	AUD
BK-4	135.00	175.00	100.00	200.00
BK-5a	135.00	175.00	100.00	200.00

DB48
PRINCE FREDERICK™
First Variation

Designer:	Harry Sales
Modeller:	David Lyttleton
Height:	3 ½", 8.9 cm
Colour:	Green, white and red
Issued:	1986 - 1990
Varieties:	DB94
Series:	Bunnykins Royal Family

Back Stamp	Price			
	USD	CAD	GBP	AUD
BK-4	135.00	175.00	100.00	200.00
BK-5a	135.00	175.00	100.00	200.00

DB49
HARRY THE HERALD™
First Variation

Designer: Harry Sales
Modeller: David Lyttleton
Height: 3 ½", 8.9 cm
Colour: Maroon, white and tan
Issued: 1986 - 1990
Varieties: DB95, DB115
Series: Bunnykins Royal Family

Back Stamp		Price		
	USD	CAD	GBP	AUD
BK-4	135.00	175.00	100.00	200.00
BK-5a	135.00	175.00	100.00	200.00

DB50
UNCLE SAM BUNNYKINS™
First Variation

Designer: Harry Sales
Modeller: David Lyttleton
Height: 4 ½", 11.9 cm
Colour: Blue, red and white
Issued: 1986 - 2001
Varieties: DB175

Back Stamp		Price		
	USD	CAD	GBP	AUD
BK-4	50.00	75.00	40.00	85.00
BK-5a	50.00	75.00	40.00	85.00

Note: Prototype exists with yellow bowtie.

DB51
MR. BUNNYKINS AT EASTER PARADE™
Second Variation

Designer: Harry Sales
Modeller: David Lyttleton
Height: 5", 12.7 cm
Colour: Blue tie and hat band, maroon coat,
            light grey trousers, pink ribbon
            on package
Issued: 1986 - 1986
Varieties: DB18

Back Stamp		Price		
	USD	CAD	GBP	AUD
BK-4	1,200.00	1,800.00	700.00	2,000.00

DB52
MRS. BUNNYKINS
AT THE EASTER PARADE™
Second Variation

Designer:	Harry Sales
Modeller:	David Lyttleton
Height:	4 ½", 11.9 cm
Colour:	Maroon dress, white collar, blue bow on bonnet, multicoloured bows on packages
Issued:	1986 - 1986
Varieties:	DB19
Series:	Special Events 1986

Photograph not available at press time

Back Stamp	USD	Price CAD	GBP	AUD
BK-Special	900.00	1,250.00	600.00	1,350.00

DB53
CAROL SINGER™
Music Box

Designer:	Harry Sales
Modeller:	David Lyttleton
Height:	7", 17.8 cm
Colour:	Red, yellow and green
Issued:	1986 - 1990
Tune:	'Silent Night'

Photograph not available at press time

Back Stamp	USD	Price CAD	GBP	AUD
BK-4	300.00	475.00	200.00	500.00
BK-5a	300.00	475.00	200.00	500.00

DB54
COLLECTOR BUNNYKINS™

Designer:	Harry Sales
Modeller:	David Lyttleton
Height:	4 ¼", 10.8 cm
Colour:	Brown, blue and grey
Issued:	1987 - 1987
Series:	ICC Members Exclusive

INTERNATIONAL COLLECTORS CLUB ROYAL DOULTON
COLLECTOR BUNNYKINS
DB54
EXCLUSIVELY FOR
COLLECTORS CLUB
© 1986 ROYAL DOULTON
MODELLED BY
D. Lyttleton

Back Stamp	USD	Price CAD	GBP	AUD
BK-Special	425.00	675.00	300.00	750.00

DB55
BEDTIME BUNNYKINS™
First Variation

Designer:	Graham Tongue
Modeller:	David Lyttleton
Height:	3 ¼", 8.3 cm
Colour:	Blue and white stripped pyjamas, brown teddy bear
Issued:	1987 - 1998
Varieties:	DB63, DB79, DB103

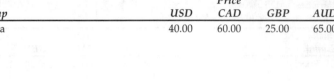

Back Stamp	Price			
	USD	CAD	GBP	AUD
BK-5a	40.00	60.00	25.00	65.00

DB56
BE PREPARED BUNNYKINS™

Designer:	Graham Tongue
Modeller:	David Lyttleton
Height:	4", 10.1 cm
Colour:	Dark green and grey
Issued:	1987 - 1996

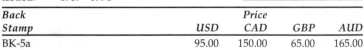

Back Stamp	Price			
	USD	CAD	GBP	AUD
BK-5a	45.00	70.00	30.00	75.00

DB57
SCHOOLDAYS BUNNYKINS™

Designer:	Graham Tongue
Modeller:	David Lyttleton
Height:	3 ½", 8.9 cm
Colour:	Dark green, white and yellow
Issued:	1987 - 1994

Back Stamp	Price			
	USD	CAD	GBP	AUD
BK-5a	95.00	150.00	65.00	165.00

DB58
AUSTRALIAN BUNNYKINS™

Designer:	Harry Sales
Modeller:	Warren Platt
Height:	4", 10.1 cm
Colour:	Gold and green
Issued:	1988 - 1988

Back Stamp	Price			
	USD	CAD	GBP	AUD
BK-Special	275.00	425.00	200.00	450.00

DB59
STORYTIME BUNNYKINS™
Second Variation

Designer:	Based on a design by Walter Hayward
Modeller:	Albert Hallam
Height:	3", 7.6 cm
Colour:	Left - green polka dots on white dress, yellow shoes Right - yellow dress, green shoes
Issued:	1987 - 1987
Varieties:	DB9; also called Partners in Collecting, DB151
Series:	Special Events 1987

Back Stamp	Price			
	USD	CAD	GBP	AUD
BK-5a	275.00	425.00	200.00	450.00

DB60
SCHOOLMASTER BUNNYKINS™

Designer:	Graham Tongue
Modeller:	Warren Platt
Height:	4", 10.1 cm
Colour:	Black, green and white
Issued:	1987 - 1996

Back Stamp	Price			
	USD	CAD	GBP	AUD
BK-5a	45.00	70.00	30.00	75.00

DB61
BROWNIE BUNNYKINS™

Designer:	Graham Tongue
Modeller:	Warren Platt
Height:	4", 10.1 cm
Colour:	Brown uniform, yellow neck-tie
Issued:	1987 - 1993

Back	Price			
Stamp	USD	CAD	GBP	AUD
BK-5a	125.00	175.00	85.00	200.00

Note: Models with unpainted belts exist.

DB62
SANTA BUNNYKINS HAPPY CHRISTMAS™
Christmas Tree Ornament

Designer:	Harry Sales
Modeller:	David Lyttleton
Height:	3 ¾", 9.5 cm
Colour:	Red and white
Issued:	1987 in a limited edition of 1,551

Back	Price			
Stamp	USD	CAD	GBP	AUD
BK-5a	1,000.00	1,500.00	500.00	1,500.00

Note: Unpainted models exist.

DB63
BEDTIME BUNNYKINS™
Second Variation

Designer:	Graham Tongue
Modeller:	David Lyttleton
Height:	3 ¼", 8.3 cm
Colour:	Red and white stripped pyjamas, white teddy bear
Issued:	1987 - 1987
Varieties:	DB55, DB79, DB103

Back	Price			
Stamp	USD	CAD	GBP	AUD
BK-Comm	300.00	450.00	150.00	500.00

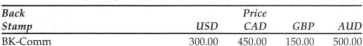

DB64
POLICEMAN BUNNYKINS™

Designer:	Graham Tongue
Modeller:	Martyn Alcock
Height:	4 ¼", 10.8 cm
Colour:	Dark blue uniform
Issued:	1988 - 2000

Back Stamp	USD	Price CAD	GBP	AUD
BK-5a	35.00	55.00	25.00	60.00

DB65
LOLLIPOPMAN BUNNYKINS™

Designer:	Graham Tongue
Modeller:	Martyn Alcock
Height:	3 ¾", 9.5cm
Colour:	White and yellow
Issued:	1988 - 1991

Back Stamp	USD	Price CAD	GBP	AUD
BK-5a	225.00	325.00	125.00	325.00

Note: Two sign varieties exist, one with a red rim, the other with a white rim.

DB66
SCHOOLBOY BUNNYKINS™

Designer:	Graham Tongue
Modeller:	Martyn Alcock
Height:	4", 10.1 cm
Colour:	Blue, white and grey
Issued:	1988 - 1991

Back Stamp	USD	Price CAD	GBP	AUD
BK-5a	225.00	325.00	150.00	325.00

DB67
FAMILY PHOTOGRAPH BUNNYKINS™
Second Variation

Designer:	Based on a design by Walter Hayward
Modeller:	Albert Hallam
Height:	4 ½", 11.9 cm
Colour:	Pink, black and white
Issued:	1988 - 1988
Varieties:	DB1; also called Father, Mother and Victoria Bunnykins, DB68
Series:	Special Events 1988

Back Stamp	Price			
	USD	CAD	GBP	AUD
BK-Special	225.00	325.00	150.00	325.00

DB68
FATHER, MOTHER & VICTORIA
BUNNYKINS™

Designer:	Based on design Family Photograph by Walter Hayward
Modeller:	Martyn Alcock
Height:	4 ½", 11.9 cm
Colour:	Blue, grey, maroon and yellow
Issued:	1988 - 1996
Varieties:	Also called Family Photograph Bunnykins, DB1, DB67

Back Stamp	Price			
	USD	CAD	GBP	AUD
BK-5a	75.00	100.00	50.00	100.00

DB69
WILLIAM BUNNYKINS™

Designer:	Based on a design by Walter Hayward
Modeller:	Martyn Alcock
Height:	4", 10.1 cm
Colour:	Red and white
Issued:	1988 - 1993
Varieties:	Also called Tally Ho! Bunnykins, DB12, DB78

Back Stamp	Price			
	USD	CAD	GBP	AUD
BK-5a	100.00	135.00	60.00	150.00

DB70
SUSAN BUNNYKINS™

Designer:	Based on the design Busy Needles by Walter Hayward
Modeller:	Martyn Alcock
Height:	3 ¼", 8.3 cm
Colour:	White, blue and yellow
Issued:	1988 - 1993
Varieties:	Also called Busy Needles Bunnykins, DB10

Back Stamp	Price			
	USD	CAD	GBP	AUD
BK-5a	115.00	150.00	75.00	175.00

DB71
POLLY BUNNYKINS™

Designer:	Graham Tongue
Modeller:	Martyn Alcock
Height:	3 ½", 8.9 cm
Colour:	Pink
Issued:	1988 - 1993

Back Stamp	Price			
	USD	CAD	GBP	AUD
BK-5a	100.00	135.00	60.00	150.00

DB72
TOM BUNNYKINS™

Designer:	Graham Tongue
Modeller:	Martyn Alcock
Height:	3", 7.6 cm
Colour:	Browns, white and blue
Issued:	1988 - 1993

Back Stamp	Price			
	USD	CAD	GBP	AUD
BK-5a	100.00	135.00	60.00	150.00

DB73
HARRY BUNNYKINS™

Designer: Graham Tongue
Modeller: Martyn Alcock
Height: 3", 7.9 cm
Colour: Blue, brown, white and yellow
Issued: 1988 - 1993

Back Stamp		Price		
	USD	CAD	GBP	AUD
BK-5a	50.00	75.00	35.00	85.00

DB74A
NURSE BUNNYKINS™
First Variation (Red Cross)

Designer: Graham Tongue
Modeller: Martyn Alcock
Height: 4 ¼", 10.8 cm
Colour: Dark and light blue and white, red cross
Issued: 1989 - 1994
Varieties: DB74B

Back Stamp		Price		
	USD	CAD	GBP	AUD
BK-5a	200.00	300.00	150.00	325.00

DB74B
NURSE BUNNYKINS™
Second Variation (Green Cross)

Designer: Graham Tongue
Modeller: Martyn Alcock
Height: 4 ¼", 10.8 cm
Colour: Dark and light blue and white, green cross
Issued: 1994 - 2000
Varieties: DB74A

Back Stamp		Price		
	USD	CAD	GBP	AUD
BK-5a	40.00	55.00	22.00	65.00

DB75
FIREMAN BUNNYKINS™
First Variation

Designer:	Graham Tongue
Modeller:	Martyn Alcock
Height:	4 ¼", 10.8 cm
Colour:	Dark blue and yellow
Issued:	1989 - 2001
Varieties:	DB183; Also called American
	Firefighter Bunnykins, DB268

Back Stamp	Price			
	USD	CAD	GBP	AUD
BK-5a	35.00	55.00	25.00	60.00

DB76
POSTMAN BUNNYKINS™

Designer:	Graham Tongue
Modeller:	Martyn Alcock
Height:	4 ½", 11.9 cm
Colour:	Dark blue and red
Issued:	1989 - 1993

Back Stamp	Price			
	USD	CAD	GBP	AUD
BK-5a	115.00	175.00	85.00	200.00

DB77
PAPERBOY BUNNYKINS™

Designer:	Graham Tongue
Modeller:	Martyn Alcock
Height:	4", 10.1 cm
Colour:	Green, yellow, red and white
Issued:	1989 - 1993

Back Stamp	Price			
	USD	CAD	GBP	AUD
BK-5a	100.00	165.00	70.00	175.00

DB78
TALLY HO! BUNNYKINS™
Second Variation

Designer:	Based on a design by Walter Hayward
Modeller:	Albert Hallam
Height:	4", 10.1 cm
Colour:	Light blue coat and white rocking horse, yellow sweater
Issued:	1988 - 1988
Varieties:	DB12; also called William Bunnykins, DB69

Back Stamp		Price		
	USD	CAD	GBP	AUD
BK-Comm	150.00	250.00	100.00	275.00

DB79
BEDTIME BUNNYKINS™
Third Variation

Designer:	Graham Tonge
Modeller:	David Lyttleton
Height:	3 ¼", 8.3 cm
Colour:	Light blue and white
Issued:	1988 - 1988
Varieties:	DB55, DB63, DB103

Back Stamp		Price		
	USD	CAD	GBP	AUD
BK-Exc	500.00	800.00	350.00	900.00

DB80
DOLLIE BUNNYKINS PLAYTIME™
Second Variation

Designer:	Based on a design by Walter Hayward
Modeller:	Albert Hallam
Height:	4", 10.1 cm
Colour:	White and yellow
Issued:	1988 in a limited edition of 250
Varieties:	DB8

Back Stamp		Price			
		USD	CAD	GBP	AUD
BK-Exc	Higbee	150.00	200.00	85.00	225.00
BK-Exc	Holmes	150.00	200.00	85.00	225.00
BK-Exc	Hornes	150.00	200.00	85.00	225.00
BK-Exc	Strawbridge	150.00	200.00	85.00	225.00

DB81
BILLIE & BUNTIE BUNNYKINS SLEIGH RIDE™
Second Variation

Designer:	Based on a design by Walter Hayward
Modeller:	Albert Hallam
Height:	3 ½", 8.9 cm
Colour:	Green, yellow and red
Issued:	1989 - 1989
Varieties:	DB4
Series:	Special Events 1989

Back Stamp	Price			
	USD	CAD	GBP	AUD
BK-Special	150.00	225.00	100.00	250.00

DB82
ICE CREAM BUNNYKINS™

Designer:	Graham Tongue
Modeller:	Warren Platt
Height:	4 ½", 11.9 cm
Colour:	White, blue and green
Issued:	1990 - 1993

Back Stamp	Price			
	USD	CAD	GBP	AUD
BK-5a	175.00	275.00	125.00	300.00

DB83
SUSAN BUNNYKINS AS QUEEN OF THE MAY™

Designer:	Graham Tongue
Modeller:	Martyn Alcock
Height:	4", 10.1 cm
Colour:	White polka-dot dress, blue and brown chair
Issued:	1990 - 1992

Back Stamp	Price			
	USD	CAD	GBP	AUD
BK-5a	125.00	200.00	90.00	225.00

DB84
FISHERMAN BUNNYKINS™
Style One

Designer:	Graham Tongue
Modeller:	Warren Platt
Height:	4 ¼", 10.8 cm
Colour:	Maroon, yellow and grey
Issued:	1990 - 1993

Back Stamp	Price			
	USD	CAD	GBP	AUD
BK-5a	115.00	175.00	85.00	200.00

DB85
COOK BUNNYKINS™

Designer:	Graham Tongue
Modeller:	Warren Platt
Height:	4 ¼", 10.8 cm
Colour:	White and green
Issued:	1990 - 1994

Back Stamp	Price			
	USD	CAD	GBP	AUD
BK-5a	60.00	95.00	45.00	100.00

DB86
SOUSAPHONE BUNNYKINS™
Second Variation

Designer:	Harry Sales
Modeller:	David Lyttleton
Height:	3 ½", 8.9 cm
Colour:	Blue uniform and yellow sousaphone
Issued:	1990 in a limited edition of 250
Varieties:	DB23, DB105
Series:	Bunnykins Oompah Band

Back Stamp	Price			
	USD	CAD	GBP	AUD
BK-Exc	500.00	750.00	300.00	800.00
DB86 to 90 (5pcs.)	2,500.00	4,000.00	1,650.00	4,000.00

DB87
TRUMPETER BUNNYKINS™
Second Variation

Designer:	Harry Sales
Modeller:	David Lyttleton
Height:	3 ¾", 9.5 cm
Colour:	Blue uniform and yellow trumpet
Issued:	1990 in a limited edition of 250
Varieties:	DB24, DB106
Series:	Bunnykins Oompah Band

Back Stamp	Price			
	USD	CAD	GBP	AUD
BK-Exc	500.00	750.00	300.00	800.00

DB88
CYMBALS BUNNYKINS™
Second Variation

Designer:	Harry Sales
Modeller:	David Lyttleton
Height:	3 ½", 8.9 cm
Colour:	Blue uniform and yellow cymbals
Issued:	1990 in a limited edition of 250
Varieties:	DB25, DB107
Series:	Bunnykins Oompah Band

Back Stamp	Price			
	USD	CAD	GBP	AUD
BK-Exc	500.00	750.00	300.00	800.00

DB89
DRUMMER BUNNYKINS™
Style One, Third Variation

Designer:	Harry Sales
Modeller:	David Lyttleton
Height:	3 ¾", 9.5 cm
Colour:	Blue trousers and sleeves, yellow vest, cream and red drum
Issued:	1990 in a limited edition of 250
Varieties:	DB26B, DB108
Series:	Bunnykins Oompah Band

Back Stamp	Price			
	USD	CAD	GBP	AUD
BK-Exc	500.00	750.00	300.00	800.00

DB90
DRUM-MAJOR BUNNYKINS™
Second Variation

Designer:	Harry Sales
Modeller:	David Lyttleton
Height:	3 ¾", 9.5 cm
Colour:	Blue and yellow uniform
Issued:	1990 in a limited edition of 250
Varieties:	DB27, DB109
Series:	Bunnykins Oompah Band

Back Stamp		Price		
	USD	CAD	GBP	AUD
BK-Exc	500.00	750.00	300.00	800.00

DB91
KING JOHN™
Second Variation

Designer:	Harry Sales
Modeller:	David Lyttleton
Height:	4", 10.1 cm
Colour:	Purple, yellow and white
Issued:	1990 in a limited edition of 250
Varieties:	DB45
Series:	Bunnykins Royal Family

Back Stamp	Price			
	USD	CAD	GBP	AUD
BK-Exc	500.00	750.00	300.00	800.00
Set DB91 - 95 (5 pcs.)	2,500.00	4,000.00	1,650.00	4,000.00

DB92
QUEEN SOPHIE™
Second Variation

Designer:	Harry Sales
Modeller:	David Lyttleton
Height:	4 ½", 11.9 cm
Colour:	Pink and purple
Issued:	1990 in a limited edition of 250
Varieties:	DB46
Series:	Bunnykins Royal Family

Back Stamp		Price		
	USD	CAD	GBP	AUD
BK-Exc	500.00	750.00	300.00	800.00

DB93
PRINCESS BEATRICE™
Second Variation

Designer:	Harry Sales
Modeller:	David Lyttleton
Height:	3 ½″, 8.9 cm
Colour:	Yellow and gold
Issued:	1990 in a limited edition of 250
Varieties:	DB47
Series:	Bunnykins Royal Family

Back Stamp	Price			
	USD	CAD	GBP	AUD
BK-Exc	500.00	750.00	300.00	800.00

DB94
PRINCE FREDERICK™
Second Variation

Designer:	Harry Sales
Modeller:	David Lyttleton
Height:	3 ½″, 8.9 cm
Colour:	Red, blue and yellow
Issued:	1990 in a limited edition of 250
Varieties:	DB48
Series:	Bunnykins Royal Family

Back Stamp	Price			
	USD	CAD	GBP	AUD
BK-Exc	500.00	750.00	300.00	800.00

DB95
HARRY THE HERALD™
Second Variation

Designer:	Harry Sales
Modeller:	David Lyttleton
Height:	3 ½″, 8.9 cm
Colour:	Blue, red and yellow
Issued:	1990 in a limited edition of 250
Varieties:	DB49, DB115
Series:	Bunnykins Royal Family

Back Stamp	Price			
	USD	CAD	GBP	AUD
BK-Exc	500.00	750.00	300.00	800.00

DB96
TOUCHDOWN BUNNYKINS™
Third Variation (Ohio State University)

Designer:	Harry Sales
Modeller:	David Lyttleton
Height:	3 ¼", 8.3 cm
Colour:	Grey and orange
Issued:	1990 in a limited edition of 200
Varieties:	DB29A, DB29B, DB97, DB98, DB99, DB100

Back Stamp	Price			
	USD	CAD	GBP	AUD
BK-5a	750.00	1,250.00	500.00	1,250.00
Set DB96-100 (5 pcs.)	4,000.00	6,000.00	2,750.00	6,000.00

DB97
TOUCHDOWN BUNNYKINS™
Fourth Variation (University of Michigan)

Designer:	Harry Sales
Modeller:	David Lyttleton
Height:	3 ¼", 8.3 cm
Colour:	Yellow and blue
Issued:	1990 in a limited edition of 200
Varieties:	DB29A, DB29B, DB96, DB98, DB99, DB100

Back Stamp	Price			
	USD	CAD	GBP	AUD
BK-5a	750.00	1,250.00	500.00	1,250.00

DB98
TOUCHDOWN BUNNYKINS™
Fifth Variation (Cincinnati Bengals)

Designer:	Harry Sales
Modeller:	David Lyttleton
Height:	3 ½", 8.9 cm
Colour:	Orange and black
Issued:	1990 in a limited edition of 200
Varieties:	DB29A, DB29B, DB96, DB97, DB99, DB100

Back Stamp	Price			
	USD	CAD	GBP	AUD
BK-5a	750.00	1,250.00	500.00	1,250.00

DB99
TOUCHDOWN BUNNYKINS™
Sixth Variation (Notre Dame College)

Designer:	Harry Sales
Modeller:	David Lyttleton
Height:	3 ½", 8.9 cm
Colour:	Green and yellow
Issued:	1990 in a limited edition of 200
Varieties:	DB29A, DB29B, DB96, DB97, DB98, DB100

Back Stamp	Price			
	USD	CAD	GBP	AUD
BK-5a	750.00	1,250.00	500.00	1,250.00

DB100
TOUCHDOWN BUNNYKINS™
Seventh Variation (University of Indiana)

Designer:	Harry Sales
Modeller:	David Lyttleton
Height:	3 ½", 8.9 cm
Colour:	White and red
Issued:	1990 in a limited edition of 200
Varieties:	DB29A, DB29B, DB96, DB97, DB98, DB99

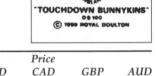

Back Stamp	Price			
	USD	CAD	GBP	AUD
BK-5a	750.00	1,250.00	500.00	1,250.00

DB101
BRIDE BUNNYKINS™

Designer:	Graham Tongue
Modeller:	Amanda Hughes-Lubeck
Height:	4", 10.1 cm
Colour:	Cream dress, grey, blue and white train
Issued:	1991 - 2001

Back Stamp	Price			
	USD	CAD	GBP	AUD
BK-5a	40.00	65.00	25.00	70.00

DB102
GROOM BUNNYKINS™

Designer:	Graham Tongue
Modeller:	Martyn Alcock
Height:	4 ½", 11.9 cm
Colour:	Grey and burgundy
Issued:	1991 - 2001

Back		Price		
Stamp	USD	CAD	GBP	AUD
BK-5a	40.00	60.00	30.00	65.00

DB103
BEDTIME BUNNYKINS™
Fourth Variation

Designer:	Graham Tongue
Modeller:	David Lyttleton
Height:	3 ¼", 8.3 cm
Colour:	Yellow and green striped pyjamas, brown teddy bear
Issued:	1991 - 1991
Varieties:	DB55, DB63, DB79
Series:	Special Events Tour 1991

Back			Price		
Stamp	Colour	USD	CAD	GBP	AUD
BK-Special	Pale yellow	225.00	350.00	150.00	400.00
BK-Special	Daffodil yellow	225.00	350.00	150.00	400.00

DB104
CAROL SINGER BUNNYKINS™

Designer:	Harry Sales
Modeller:	David Lyttleton
Height:	4", 10.1 cm
Colour:	Dark green, red, yellow and white
Issued:	1991 in a special edition of 1,000

Back		Price		
Stamp	USD	CAD	GBP	AUD
BK-Exc, UK Backstamp - 700	300.00	450.00	200.00	550.00
BK-Exc, USA Backstamp - 300	450.00	650.00	300.00	700.00

DB105
SOUSAPHONE BUNNYKINS™
Third Variation

Designer:	Harry Sales
Modeller:	David Lyttleton
Height:	4", 10.1 cm
Colour:	Dark green, red and yellow
Issued:	1991 in a limited edition of 250
Varieties:	DB23, DB86
Series:	Bunnykins Oompah Band

Back Stamp	Price			
	USD	CAD	GBP	AUD
BK-Exc	600.00	900.00	400.00	900.00
Set DB105 to 109 (5 pcs.)	3,500.00	5,000.00	2,000.00	5,500.00

DB106
TRUMPETER BUNNYKINS™
Third Variation

Designer:	Harry Sales
Modeller:	David Lyttleton
Height:	3 ¾", 9.5 cm
Colour:	Dark green, red and yellow
Issued:	1991 in a limited edition of 250
Varieties:	DB24, DB87
Series:	Bunnykins Oompah Band

Back Stamp	Price			
	USD	CAD	GBP	AUD
BK-Exc	600.00	900.00	400.00	950.00

DB107
CYMBALS BUNNYKINS™
Third Variation

Designer:	Harry Sales
Modeller:	David Lyttleton
Height:	4", 10.1 cm
Colour:	Dark green, red and yellow
Issued:	1991 in a limited edition of 250
Varieties:	DB25, DB88
Series:	Bunnykins Oompah Band

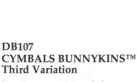

Back Stamp	Price			
	USD	CAD	GBP	AUD
BK-Exc	600.00	900.00	400.00	950.00

DB108
DRUMMER BUNNYKINS™
Style One, Fourth Variation

Designer:	Harry Sales
Modeller:	David Lyttleton
Height:	3 ½", 8.9 cm
Colour:	Dark green, red and white
Issued:	1991 in a limited edition of 250
Varieties:	DB26B, DB89
Series:	Bunnykins Oompah Band

Back		Price		
Stamp	USD	CAD	GBP	AUD
BK-Exc	600.00.	900.00	400.00	950.00

DB109
DRUM-MAJOR BUNNYKINS™
Third Variation

Designer:	Harry Sales
Modeller:	David Lyttleton
Height:	3 ½", 8.9 cm
Colour:	Dark green, red and yellow
Issued:	1991 in a limited edition of 250
Varieties:	DB27, DB90
Series:	Bunnykins Oompah Band

Back		Price		
Stamp	USD	CAD	GBP	AUD
BK-Exc	600.00	900.00	400.00	950.00

DB110 TO DB114 Not allocated

DB115
HARRY THE HERALD™
Third Variation

Designer:	Harry Sales
Modeller:	David Lyttleton
Height:	3 ½", 8.9 cm
Colour:	Yellow and dark green
Issued:	1991 in a limited edition of 300
Varieties:	DB49, DB95
Series:	Bunnykins Royal Family

Back		Price		
Stamp	USD	CAD	GBP	AUD
BK-Special	1,000.00	1,600.00	700.00	1,800.00

DB116
GOALKEEPER BUNNYKINS™
First Variation

Designer: Denise Andrews
Modeller: Warren Platt
Height: 4 ½", 11.9 cm
Colour: Green and black
Issued: 1991 in a special edition of 250
Varieties: DB118, DB120, DB122
Series: Footballers

Back Stamp	Price			
	USD	CAD	GBP	AUD
BK-Exc	500.00	800.00	350.00	900.00

DB117
FOOTBALLER BUNNYKINS™
First Variation

Designer: Denise Andrews
Modeller: Warren Platt
Height: 4 ½", 11.9 cm
Colour: Green and white
Issued: 1991 in a special edition of 250
Varieties: DB119, DB121; also called Soccer Player, DB123
Series: Footballers

Back Stamp	Price			
	USD	CAD	GBP	AUD
BK-Exc	500.00	800.00	350.00	900.00

DB118
GOALKEEPER BUNNYKINS™
Second Variation

Designer: Denise Andrews
Modeller: Warren Platt
Height: 4 ½", 11.9 cm
Colour: Red and black
Issued: 1991 in a special edition of 250
Varieties: DB116, DB120, DB122
Series: Footballers

Back Stamp	Price			
	USD	CAD	GBP	AUD
BK-Exc	500.00	800.00	350.00	900.00

DB119
FOOTBALLER BUNNYKINS™
Second Variation

Designer:	Denise Andrews
Modeller:	Warren Platt
Height:	4 ½", 11.9 cm
Colour:	Red
Issued:	1991 in a special edition of 250
Varieties:	DB117, DB121; also called Soccer Player, DB123
Series:	Footballers

Back Stamp	Price			
	USD	CAD	GBP	AUD
BK-Exc	500.00	800.00	350.00	900.00

DB120
GOALKEEPER BUNNYKINS™
Third Variation

Designer:	Denise Andrews
Modeller:	Warren Platt
Height:	4 ½", 11.9 cm
Colour:	Yellow and black
Issued:	1991 in a special edition of 250
Varieties:	DB116, DB118, DB122
Series:	Footballers

Back Stamp	Price			
	USD	CAD	GBP	AUD
BK-Exc	500.00	800.00	350.00	900.00

DB121
FOOTBALLER BUNNYKINS™
Third Variation

Designer:	Denise Andrews
Modeller:	Warren Platt
Height:	4 ½", 11.9 cm
Colour:	White and blue
Issued:	1991 in a special edition of 250
Varieties:	DB117, DB119; also called Soccer Player, DB123
Series:	Footballers

Back Stamp	Price			
	USD	CAD	GBP	AUD
BK-Exc	500.00	800.00	350.00	900.00

DB122
GOALKEEPER BUNNYKINS™
Fourth Variation

Designer:	Denise Andrews
Modeller:	Warren Platt
Height:	4 ½", 11.9 cm
Colour:	Yellow and black
Issued:	1991 in a special edition of 250
Varieties:	DB116, DB118, DB120
Series:	Footballers

Back Stamp	Price			
	USD	CAD	GBP	AUD
BK-Exc	500.00	800.00	350.00	900.00

DB123
SOCCER PLAYER BUNNYKINS™

Designer:	Denise Andrews
Modeller:	Warren Platt
Height:	4 ½", 11.9 cm
Colour:	Dark blue and white
Issued:	1991 in a special edition of 250
Varieties:	Also called Footballer Bunnykins, DB117, DB119, DB121
Series:	Footballers

Back Stamp	Price			
	USD	CAD	GBP	AUD
BK-Exc	500.00	800.00	350.00	900.00

DB124
ROCK AND ROLL BUNNYKINS™

Designer:	Harry Sales
Modeller:	David Lyttleton
Height:	4 ½", 11.9 cm
Colour:	White, blue and red
Issued:	1991 in a limited edition of 1,000
Varieties:	Also called Mr. Bunnybeat Strumming, DB16

Back Stamp	Price			
	USD	CAD	GBP	AUD
BK-Exc	500.00	800.00	350.00	900.00

DB125
MILKMAN BUNNYKINS™

Designer:	Graham Tongue
Modeller:	Amanda Hughes-Lubeck
Height:	4 ½", 11.9 cm
Colour:	White, green and grey
Issued:	1992 in a special edition of 1,000

Back		Price		
Stamp	USD	CAD	GBP	AUD
BK-Special	350.00	550.00	250.00	600.00

DB126
MAGICIAN BUNNYKINS™
First Variation

Designer:	Graham Tongue
Modeller:	Warren Platt
Height:	4 ½", 11.9 cm
Colour:	Black suit, yellow shirt, yellow table cloth with deeper yellow border
Issued:	1992 in a limited edition of 1,000
Varieties:	DB159

Back		Price		
Stamp	USD	CAD	GBP	AUD
BK-5a	225.00	350.00	165.00	375.00

DB127
GUARDSMAN BUNNYKINS™

Designer:	Denise Andrews
Modeller:	Warren Platt
Height:	4 ½", 11.9 cm
Colour:	Scarlet jacket, black trousers and bearskin hat
Issued:	1992 in a special edition of 1,000

Back		Price		
Stamp	USD	CAD	GBP	AUD
BK-Exc	350.00	550.00	250.00	600.00

DB128
CLOWN BUNNYKINS™
First Variation

Designer:	Denise Andrews
Modeller:	Warren Platt
Height:	4 ¼", 10.8 cm
Colour:	White costume with black stars and pompons, red square on trousers and red ruff at neck
Issued:	1992 in a special edition of 750
Varieties:	DB129

Back Stamp	Price			
	USD	CAD	GBP	AUD
BK-Exc	450.00	700.00	325.00	800.00

DB129
CLOWN BUNNYKINS™
Second Variation

Designer:	Denise Andrews
Modeller:	Warren Platt
Height:	4 ¼", 10.8 cm
Colour:	White costume with red stars and black pompons, black ruff around neck
Issued:	1992 in a special edition of 250
Varieties:	DB128

Back Stamp	Price			
	USD	CAD	GBP	AUD
BK-Exc	850.00	1,350.00	600.00	1,450.00

DB130
SWEETHEART BUNNYKINS™
First Variation

Designer:	Graham Tongue
Modeller:	Warren Platt
Height:	3 ¾", 9.5 cm
Colour:	Yellow sweater, blue trousers, red heart
Issued:	1992 - 1997
Varieties:	DB174

Back Stamp	Price			
	USD	CAD	GBP	AUD
BK-5a	40.00	60.00	30.00	60.00

DB131
MASTER POTTER BUNNYKINS™

Designer:	Graham Tongue
Modeller:	Warren Platt
Height:	3 ¾", 9.5 cm
Colour:	Blue white, green and brown
Issued:	1992 - 1993
Series:	ICC Members Exclusive

Back Stamp	Price			
	USD	CAD	GBP	AUD
BK-Special	175.00	275.00	125.00	300.00

DB132
HALLOWEEN BUNNYKINS™

Designer:	Graham Tongue
Modeller:	Martyn Alcock
Height:	3 ¼", 8.3 cm
Colour:	Orange and yellow pumpkin
Issued:	1993 - 1997

Back Stamp	Price			
	USD	CAD	GBP	AUD
BK-5a	50.00	75.00	35.00	85.00

DB133
AUSSIE SURFER BUNNYKINS™

Designer:	Graham Tongue
Modeller:	Martyn Alcock
Height:	4", 10.1 cm
Colour:	Gold and green outfit, white and blue base
Issued:	1994 - 1997

Back Stamp	Price			
	USD	CAD	GBP	AUD
BK-Special	95.00	150.00	60.00	150.00

DB134
JOHN BULL BUNNYKINS™

Designer:	Denise Andrews
Modeller:	Amanda Hughes-Lubeck
Height:	4 ½", 11.9 cm
Colour:	Grey, yellow, red white and blue Union Jack waistcoat
Issued:	1993 in a special edition of 1,000

Back Stamp	Price			
	USD	CAD	GBP	AUD
BK-Exc	350.00	550.00	250.00	650.00

DB135
MOUNTIE BUNNYKINS™

Designer:	Graham Tongue
Modeller:	Warren Platt
Height:	4", 10.1 cm
Colour:	Red jacket, dark blue trousers and brown hat
Issued:	1993 in a special edition of 750
Varieties:	DB136

Back Stamp	Price			
	USD	CAD	GBP	AUD
Bk-5b	500.00	800.00	350.00	900.00

DB136
SERGEANT MOUNTIE BUNNYKINS™

Designer:	Graham Tongue
Modeller:	Warren Platt
Height:	4", 10.1 cm
Colour:	Red jacket, yellow stripes on sleeve, dark blue trousers, brown hat
Issued:	1993 in a special edition of 250
Varieties:	DB135

Back Stamp	Price			
	USD	CAD	GBP	AUD
Bk-5b	850.00	1,400.00	625.00	1,500.00

DB137
60th ANNIVERSARY BUNNYKINS™

Designer:	Graham Tongue
Modeller:	Martyn Alcock
Height:	4 ½", 11.9 cm
Colour:	Lemon, yellow and white
Issued:	1994 - 1994

| Back | | Price | | |
Stamp	USD	CAD	GBP	AUD
BK-5a	70.00	100.00	50.00	100.00

Note: Numbers DB138 to DB141 not issued.

DB142
CHEERLEADER BUNNYKINS™
First Variation

Designer:	Denise Andrews
Modeller:	Warren Platt
Height:	4 ½", 11.9 cm
Colour:	Red
Issued:	1994 in a special edition of 1,000
Varieties:	DB143

| Back | | Price | | |
Stamp	USD	CAD	GBP	AUD
BK-Exc	200.00	325.00	150.00	350.00

DB143
CHEERLEADER BUNNYKINS™
Second Variation

Designer:	Denise Andrews
Modeller:	Warren Platt
Height:	4 ½", 11.9 cm
Colour:	Yellow
Issued:	1994 in a special edition of 1,000
Varieties:	DB142

| Back | | Price | | |
Stamp	USD	CAD	GBP	AUD
BK-Exc	200.00	325.00	150.00	350.00

DB144
BATSMAN BUNNYKINS™

Designer: Denise Andrews
Modeller: Amanda Hughes-Lubeck
Height: 4", 10.1 cm
Colour: White, beige and black
Issued: 1994 in a special edition of 1,000
Series: Cricket

| Back | | Price | | |
Stamp	USD	CAD	GBP	AUD
BK-Exc	300.00	475.00	200.00	500.00

DB145
BOWLER BUNNYKINS™

Designer: Denise Andrews
Modeller: Warren Platt
Height: 4", 10.1 cm
Colour: White, beige and black
Issued: 1994 in a special edition of 1,000
Series: Cricket

| Back | | Price | | |
Stamp	USD	CAD	GBP	AUD
BK-Exc	300.00	475.00	200.00	500.00

DB146
CHRISTMAS SURPRISE BUNNYKINS™

Designer: Graham Tongue
Modeller: Warren Platt
Height: 3 ½", 8.9 cm
Colour: Cream and red
Issued: 1994 - 2000
Varieties: Also called Santa's Helper
             Bunnykins, DB192

| Back | | Price | | |
Stamp	USD	CAD	GBP	AUD
BK-5a	35.00	55.00	20.00	60.00

Note: All-over white models exist.

DB147
RAINY DAY BUNNYKINS™

Designer:	Graham Tongue
Modeller:	Warren Platt
Height:	4", 10.1 cm
Colour:	Yellow coat and hat, blue trousers, black boots
Issued:	1994 - 1997

Back Stamp	Price			
	USD	CAD	GBP	AUD
BK-5a	40.00	60.00	25.00	65.00

DB148
BATHTIME BUNNYKINS™

Designer:	Graham Tongue
Modeller:	Warren Platt
Height:	4", 10.1 cm
Colour:	White bathrobe with grey trim, yellow towel and duck
Issued:	1994 - 1997

Back Stamp	Price			
	USD	CAD	GBP	AUD
BK-5a	40.00	60.00	25.00	65.00

DB149
EASTER GREETINGS BUNNYKINS™

Designer:	Graham Tongue
Modeller:	Warren Platt
Height:	4 ½", 11.9 cm
Colour:	Yellow, white and green
Issued:	1995 - 1999
Varieties:	Also called Easter Surprise Bunnykins, DB225

Back Stamp	Price			
	USD	CAD	GBP	AUD
BK-5a	45.00	65.00	25.00	70.00

DB150
WICKETKEEPER BUNNYKINS™

Designer:	Denise Andrews
Modeller:	Amanda Hughes-Lubeck
Height:	3 ½″, 8.9 cm
Colour:	White, beige and black
Issued:	1995 in a special edition of 1,000
Series:	Cricket

WICKETKEEPER BUNNYKINS
DB 150
PRODUCED EXCLUSIVELY
FOR U.K.I CERAMICS LTD
IN A SPECIAL EDITION OF 1,000
© 1994 ROYAL DOULTON

Back		Price		
Stamp	USD	CAD	GBP	AUD
BK-Exc	300.00	475.00	200.00	500.00

DB151
PARTNERS IN COLLECTING™

Designer:	Walter Hayward
Modeller:	Albert Hallam
Height:	3″, 7.6 cm
Colour:	Red, white and blue
Issued:	1995 - 1995
Varieties:	Also called Storytime Bunnykins, DB9, DB59
Series:	ICC Members Exclusive (15th Anniversary of ICC)

PARTNERS IN COLLECTING
DB 151
R.D. I.C.C. 15th ANNIVERSARY 1980-1995
EXCLUSIVELY FOR COLLECTORS CLUB
© 1995 ROYAL DOULTON

Back		Price		
Stamp	USD	CAD	GBP	AUD
BK-Special	100.00	150.00	70.00	175.00

DB152
BOY SKATER BUNNYKINS™
First Variation

Designer:	Graham Tongue
Modeller:	Martyn Alcock
Height:	4 ¼″, 10.8 cm
Colour:	Blue coat, brown pants, yellow hat, green boots and black skates
Issued:	1995 - 1998
Varieties:	DB187

BOY SKATER
BUNNYKINS
DB 152
© 1995 ROYAL DOULTON

Back		Price		
Stamp	USD	CAD	GBP	AUD
BK-5a	40.00	60.00	25.00	65.00

DB153
GIRL SKATER BUNNYKINS™

Designer:	Graham Tongue
Modeller:	Martyn Alcock
Height:	3 ½", 8.9 cm
Colour:	Green coat, with white trim, pink dress, blue books, yellow skates
Issued:	1995 - 1997

GIRL SKATER
BUNNYKINS
DB 153
© 1995 ROYAL DOULTON

Back Stamp	Price			
	USD	CAD	GBP	AUD
BK-5a	40.00	60.00	25.00	65.00

DB154
FATHER BUNNYKINS™
Style One

Designer:	Martyn Alcock
Modeller:	Martyn Alcock
Height:	4", 10.1 cm
Colour:	Red and white stripped blazer, creamy yellow trousers
Issued:	1996 - 1996
Series:	1. Bunnykins of the Year
	2. Holiday Outing

FATHER BUNNYKINS
DB 154
BUNNYKINS OF THE YEAR 1996
© 1995 ROYAL DOULTON

Back Stamp	Price			
	USD	CAD	GBP	AUD
BK-Special	50.00	75.00	30.00	80.00

DB155
MOTHER'S DAY BUNNYKINS™

Designer:	Graham Tongue
Modeller:	Shane Ridge
Height:	3 ½", 8.9 cm
Colour:	Brown and blue
Issued:	1995 - 2000

MOTHER'S DAY
BUNNYKINS
DB 155
© 1995 ROYAL DOULTON

Back Stamp	Price			
	USD	CAD	GBP	AUD
BK-5a	35.00	50.00	20.00	55.00

DB156
GARDENER BUNNYKINS™

Designer: Warren Platt
Modeller: Warren Platt
Height: 4 ¼", 10.8 cm
Colour: Brown jacket, white shirt, grey trousers, light green wheelbarrow
Issued: 1996 - 1998

Back Stamp	USD	Price CAD	GBP	AUD
BK-5a	40.00	60.00	25.00	65.00

DB157
GOODNIGHT BUNNYKINS™

Designer: Graham Tongue
Modeller: Shane Ridge
Height: 3 ¾", 9.5 cm
Colour: Pink nightgown, reddish brown teddy, blue and white base
Issued: 1995 - 1999

Back Stamp	USD	Price CAD	GBP	AUD
BK-5a	35.00	55.00	20.00	60.00

DB158
NEW BABY BUNNYKINS™

Designer: Graham Tongue
Modeller: Graham Tongue
Height: 3 ¾", 9.5 cm
Colour: Blue dress with white trim, white cradle, pink pillow, yellow blanket
Issued: 1995 - 1999

Back Stamp	USD	Price CAD	GBP	AUD
BK-5a	35.00	55.00	20.00	65.00

DB159
MAGICIAN BUNNYKINS™
Second Variation

Designer: Graham Tongue
Modeller: Warren Platt
Height: 4 ½", 11.9 cm
Colour: Black suit, yellow shirt, yellow table
            cloth with red border
Issued: 1998 in a special edition of 1,500
Varieties: DB126

| Back | | Price | | | |
Stamp		USD	CAD	GBP	AUD
BK-Exc		250.00	400.00	175.00	475.00

Note: Three different varieties of backstamps exist.

DB160
OUT FOR A DUCK BUNNYKINS™

Designer: Denise Andrews
Modeller: Amanda Hughes-Lubeck
Height: 4", 10.1 cm
Colour: White, beige and green
Issued: 1995 in a special edition of 1,250
Series: Cricket

| Back | | Price | | | |
Stamp		USD	CAD	GBP	AUD
BK-Exc		350.00	500.00	200.00	500.00

DB161
JESTER BUNNYKINS™

Designer: Denise Andrews
Modeller: Shane Ridge
Height: 4 ½", 11.9 cm
Colour: Red, green and yellow
Issued: 1995 in a special edition of 1,500

| Back | | Price | | | |
Stamp		USD	CAD	GBP	AUD
BK-Exc		400.00	600.00	225.00	650.00

DB162
TRICK OR TREAT BUNNYKINS™

Designer:	Denise Andrews
Modeller:	Amanda Hughes-Lubeck
Height:	4 ½", 11.9 cm
Colour:	Red dress, black hat, shoes and cloak, white moons and stars
Issued:	1995 in a special edition of 1,500

Back Stamp	Price			
	USD	CAD	GBP	AUD
BK-Exc	600.00	950.00	425.00	1,000.00

DB163
BEEFEATER BUNNYKINS™

Designer:	Denise Andrews
Modeller:	Amanda Hughes-Lubeck
Height:	4 ½", 11.9 cm
Colour:	Red, gold, black and white livery, black hat with red, blue and white band
Issued:	1996 in a special edition of 1,500

Back Stamp	Price			
	USD	CAD	GBP	AUD
BK-Exc	300.00	450.00	175.00	500.00

DB164
JUGGLER BUNNYKINS™

Designer:	Denise Andrews
Modeller:	Warren Platt
Height:	4 ½", 11.9 cm
Colour:	Blue suit, black pompons, white ruff
Issued:	1996 in a special edition of 1,500

Back Stamp	Price			
	USD	CAD	GBP	AUD
BK-Exc	250.00	400.00	175.00	425.00

DB165
RINGMASTER BUNNYKINS™

Designer:	Denise Andrews
Modeller:	Warren Platt
Height:	4 ½", 11.9 cm
Colour:	Black hat and trousers, red jacket, white waistcoat and shirt, black bowtie
Issued:	1996 in a special edition of 1,500

Back Stamp	Price			
	USD	CAD	GBP	AUD
BK-Exc	200.00	325.00	150.00	350.00

DB166
SAILOR BUNNYINS™

Designer:	Graham Tongue
Modeller:	Shane Ridge
Height:	2 ½", 6.4 cm
Colour:	White and blue
Issued:	1997 - 1997
Series:	1. Bunnykins of the Year
	2. Holiday Outing

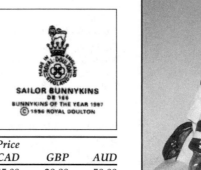

Back Stamp	Price			
	USD	CAD	GBP	AUD
BK-Special	30.00	45.00	20.00	50.00

DB167
MOTHER AND BABY BUNNYKINS™
Style One

Designer:	Shane Ridge
Modeller:	Shane Ridge
Height:	4 ½", 11.9 cm
Colour:	Brown, light pink dress, red shoes, yellow blanket
Issued:	1997 - 2001

Back Stamp	Price			
	USD	CAD	GBP	AUD
BK-5a	35.00	55.00	25.00	60.00

BUNNYKINS

DB209

DB210

DB211

DB212

DB213

DB214

DB215

DB216

DB217

DB218

DB219

DB220

BUNNYKINS

DB221

DB222

DB223

DB224

DB225

DB226

DB227

DB229

DB230

DB231

DB233

DB234

Note: DB228 Sandcastle Money Box; DB 232 not issued

BUNNYKINS

DB235

DB236

DB237

DB239

DB240

DB242

DB243

DB244

DB245

DB246

DB247

DB248

Note: DB238 Online Bunnykins; DB241 Bath Time Tableau

BUNNYKINS

DB249

DB250

DB251

DB252

DB253

DB254

DB255

DB256

DB257

DB258

DB259

DB260

BUNNYKINS

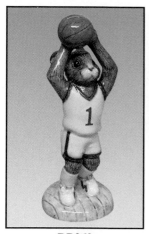

DB262

DB264

DB265

DB266

DB268

DB270

DB238

PROTOTYPE BUNNYKINS

Birthday Surprise
Early 1990's
4" high
Not put into
production

Scottish Dancer
Early 1990's
3¹/₂" high
Not put into
production

Note: DB261, 263, 267, 269 not assigned

TABLEAUS AND MONEY BOX

DB194 Merry Christmas

DB200 Happy Millennium

DB228 Sandcastle Money Box

DB241 Bath Time

BUNNYKINS MUSIC BOXES

DB33

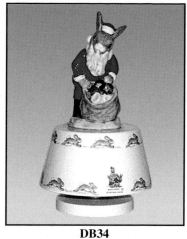

DB34

DB35

DB36

DB37

DB38

DB39

DB53

Note: DB33 has a colour variation

BUNNYKINS AND FINE BONE CHINA

Rex Mug, HW12

Small Baby Plate, HW14

China Plate, LFd

Cereal Bowl, SF10

Tea Cup, HW11

10½ inch Plate, SF13/EC2

BUNNYKINS AND SILVER DEPOSIT

Large Baby Plate with deposit, LF6

Don Mug with deposit, HW8

DB168
WIZARD BUNNYKINS™

Designer:	Denise Andrews
Modeller:	Shane Ridge
Height:	5", 12.7 cm
Colour:	Brown rabbit, purple robe and hat
Issued:	1997 in a special edition of 2,000

Back Stamp	Price			
	USD	CAD	GBP	AUD
BK-Exc	325.00	500.00	225.00	550.00

DB169
JOCKEY BUNNYKINS™

Designer:	Denise Andrews
Modeller:	Martyn Alcock
Height:	4 ½", 11.9 cm
Colour:	Green, white and yellow jockey suit, black shoes
Issued:	1997 in a special edition of 2,000

Back Stamp	Price			
	USD	CAD	GBP	AUD
BK-Exc	175.00	275.00	125.00	300.00

DB170
FISHERMAN BUNNYKINS™
Style Two

Designer:	Graham Tongue
Modeller:	Shane Ridge
Height:	4", 10.1 cm
Colour:	Blue hat and trousers, light yellow sweater, black wellingtons
Issued:	1997 - 2000

Back Stamp	Price			
	USD	CAD	GBP	AUD
BK-5a	45.00	65.00	30.00	75.00

DB171
JOKER BUNNYKINS™

Designer:	Denise Andrews
Modeller:	Martyn Alcock
Height:	5", 12.7 cm
Colour:	Yellow jacket, orange and white trousers, black hat
Issued:	1997 in a special edition of 2,500

Back Stamp	Price			
	USD	CAD	GBP	AUD
BK-Exc	150.00	250.00	100.00	275.00

DB172
WELSH LADY BUNNYKINS™

Designer:	Denise Andrews
Modeller:	Warren Platt
Height:	5", 12.7 cm
Colour:	Light pink and yellow dress, black hat, maroon shawl
Issued:	1997 in a special edition of 2,500

Back Stamp	Price			
	USD	CAD	GBP	AUD
BK-Exc	150.00	250.00	100.00	275.00

Note: Models exists with a white shawl.

DB173
BRIDESMAID BUNNYKINS™

Designer:	Graham Tongue
Modeller:	Amanda Hughes-Lubeck
Height:	3 ¾", 9.5 cm
Colour:	Light yellow dress, darker yellow flowers
Issued:	1997 - 1999

Back Stamp	Price			
	USD	CAD	GBP	AUD
BK-5a	45.00	65.00	30.00	75.00

DB174
SWEETHEART BUNNYKINS™
Second Variation - I Love Bunnykins

Designer:	Graham Tongue
Modeller:	Warren Platt
Height:	3 ¾", 9.5 cm
Colour:	White and blue, pink heart
Issued:	1997 in a special edition of 2,500
Varieties:	DB130

Back		Price		
Stamp	USD	CAD	GBP	AUD
BK-Exc	150.00	250.00	100.00	275.00

DB175
UNCLE SAM BUNNYKINS™
Second Variation

Designer:	Harry Sales
Modeller:	David Lyttleton
Height:	4 ½", 11.9 cm
Colour:	Red jacket, yellow shirt, blue and white striped trousers, red white and blue hat, platinum bowtie
Issued:	1997 in a special edition of 1,500
Varieties:	DB50
Series:	American Heritage

Back		Price		
Stamp	USD	CAD	GBP	AUD
BK-Exc	150.00	250.00	100.00	275.00

DB176
BALLERINA BUNNYKINS™

Designer:	Graham Tongue
Modeller:	Graham Tongue
Height:	3 ½", 8.9 cm
Colour:	Pink dress, yellow footstool
Issued:	1998 - 2001

Back		Price		
Stamp	USD	CAD	GBP	AUD
BK-6a	55.00	55.00	25.00	60.00

DB177
SEASIDE BUNNYKINS™

Designer: Martyn Alcock
Modeller: Martyn Alcock
Height: 3", 7.6 cm
Colour: Blue bathing costume, white and blue bathing cap, yellow sandy base
Issued: 1998 - 1998
Series: 1. Bunnykins of the Year
2. Holiday Outing

Back Stamp	USD	Price CAD	GBP	AUD
BK-Special	35.00	55.00	25.00	60.00

DB178
IRISHMAN BUNNYKINS™

Designer: Denise Andrews
Modeller: Martyn Alcock
Height: 5", 12.7 cm
Colour: Green waistcoat with shamrocks, white shirt, tan hat and trousers, white socks and black shoes
Issued: 1998 in a special edition of 2,500

Back Stamp	USD	Price CAD	GBP	AUD
BK-Exc	150.00	250.00	100.00	275.00

DB179
CAVALIER BUNNYKINS™

Designer: Graham Tongue
Modeller: Graham Tongue
Height: 4 ½", 11.9 cm
Colour: Red tunic, white collar, black trousers and hat, yellow cape, light brown boots
Issued: 1998 in a special edition of 2,500

Back Stamp	USD	Price CAD	GBP	AUD
BK-Exc	200.00	325.00	125.00	350.00

DB180
SCOTSMAN BUNNYKINS™

Designer:	Denise Andrews
Modeller:	Graham Tongue
Height:	5", 12.7 cm
Colour:	Dark blue jacket and hat, red-yellow kilt, white shirt, sporran and socks, black shoes
Issued:	1998 in a special edition of 2,500

Back Stamp	Price			
	USD	CAD	GBP	AUD
BK-Exc	125.00	200.00	90.00	225.00

DB181
DOCTOR BUNNYKINS™

Designer:	Martyn Alcock
Modeller:	Martyn Alcock
Height:	4 ¼", 10.8 cm
Colour:	White lab coat and shirt, dark blue trousers, black shoes, white and blue striped tie
Issued:	1998 - 2000

Back Stamp	Price			
	USD	CAD	GBP	AUD
BK-6a	35.00	55.00	25.00	60.00

DB182
BANJO PLAYER BUNNYKINS™

Designer:	Kimberley Curtis
Modeller:	Shane Ridge
Height:	5", 12.7 cm
Colour:	White and red striped blazer, black trousers, yellow straw hat
Issued:	1999 in a limited edition of 2,500
Series:	Bunnykins Jazz Band

Back Stamp	Price			
	USD	CAD	GBP	AUD
BK-Exc	125.00	200.00	90.00	225.00

DB183
FIREMAN BUNNYKINS™
Second Variation

Designer:	Graham Tongue
Modeller:	Martyn Alcock
Height:	4 ¼", 10.8 cm
Colour:	Red jacket and helmet, black, trousers, yellow boots
Issued:	1998 in a special edition of 3,500
Varieties:	DB75; Also called American Firefighter Bunnykins, DB268

Back Stamp	USD	Price CAD	GBP	AUD
BK-Exc	100.00	175.00	65.00	200.00

DB184
CLARINET PLAYER BUNNYKINS™

Designer:	Kimberley Curtis
Modeller:	Shane Ridge
Height:	5", 12.7 cm
Colour:	Blue and white striped jacket, grey trousers, yellow straw hat
Issued:	1999 in a limited edition of 2,500
Series:	Bunnykins Jazz Band

Back Stamp	USD	Price CAD	GBP	AUD
BK-Exc	125.00	200.00	90.00	225.00

DB185
DOUBLE BASS PLAYER BUNNYKINS™

Designer:	Kimberley Curtis
Modeller:	Shane Ridge
Height:	5", 12.7 cm
Colour:	Green and yellow striped jacket, green trousers, yellow straw hat
Issued:	1999 in a limited edition of 2,500
Series:	Bunnykins Jazz Band

Back Stamp	USD	Price CAD	GBP	AUD
BK-Exc	125.00	200.00	90.00	225.00

DB186
SAXOPHONE PLAYER BUNNYKINS™

Designer: Kimberley Curtis
Modeller: Shane Ridge
Height: 5", 12.7 cm
Colour: Navy and white striped shirt,
blue vest, black trousers
Issued: 1999 in a limited edition of 2,500
Series: Bunnykins Jazz Band

Back Stamp	Price			
	USD	CAD	GBP	AUD
BK-Exc	125.00	200.00	90.00	225.00

DB187
BOY SKATER BUNNYKINS™
Second Variation

Designer: Graham Tongue
Modeller: Martyn Alcock
Height: 4 ¼", 10.8 cm
Colour: Blue jacket, white trousers, red boots
Issued: 1998 in a limited edition of 2,500
Varieties: DB152

Back Stamp	Price			
	USD	CAD	GBP	AUD
BK-Exc	35.00	55.00	25.00	60.00

DB188
JUDGE BUNNYKINS™

Designer: Caroline Dadd
Modeller: Shane Ridge
Height: 4 ¼", 10.8 cm
Colour: Red and white
Issued: 1999 - 1999
Series: ICC Membership Gift

Back Stamp	Price			
	USD	CAD	GBP	AUD
BK-Special	35.00	55.00	25.00	60.00

Note: White unfinished models exist on which the final red glaze was not applied.

DB189
MOTHER BUNNYKINS™

Designer:	Caroline Dadd
Modeller:	Martyn Alcock
Height:	4", 10.1 cm
Colour:	Blue, white and red
Issued:	1999 - 1999
Series:	1. Bunnykins of the Year
	2. Holiday Outing

Back Stamp	Price			
	USD	CAD	GBP	AUD
BK-Special	35.00	55.00	25.00	60.00

DB190
TOURIST BUNNYKINS™

Designer:	Caroline Dadd
Modeller:	Martyn Alcock
Height:	5", 12.7 cm
Colour:	Blue, yellow, ICC on hat
Issued:	1999 in a limited time offer.
Series:	1. Holiday Outing
	2. ICC Members Exclusive

Back Stamp	Price			
	USD	CAD	GBP	AUD
BK-Special	65.00	100.00	45.00	125.00

DB191
PIPER BUNNYKINS™

Designer:	Martyn Alcock
Modeller:	Martyn Alcock
Height:	4 ¼", 10.8 cm
Colour:	Green, brown and black
Issued:	1999 in a special edition of 3,000

Back Stamp	Price			
	USD	CAD	GBP	AUD
BK-Exc	100.00	150.00	70.00	175.00

DB192
SANTA'S HELPER BUNNYKINS™

Designer:	Graham Tongue
Modeller:	Warren Platt
Height:	3 ½", 8.9 cm
Colour:	Brown, green, red and yellow
Issued:	1999 in a limited edition of 2,500
Varieties:	Also called Christmas Surprise Bunnykins, DB146

Back Stamp	Price			
	USD	CAD	GBP	AUD
BK-Exc	35.00	55.00	25.00	60.00

Note: All over white model exists.

DB193
DETECTIVE BUNNYKINS™

Designer:	Kimberley Curtis
Modeller:	Warren Platt
Height:	4 ¾", 12.1 cm
Colour:	Brown, green, white and tan
Issued:	1999 in a limited edition of 2,500

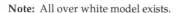

Back Stamp	Price			
	USD	CAD	GBP	AUD
BK-Exc	125.00	200.00	90.00	225.00

DB194
MERRY CHRISTMAS BUNNYKINS TABLEAU™

Designer:	Caroline Dadd
Modeller:	Shane Ridge
Height:	7 ¼" x 5 ½", 18.4 x 14.0 cm
Colour:	Brown, green, red, white and black
Issued:	1999 in a limited edition of 2,000
Series:	Tableau

Back Stamp	Price			
	USD	CAD	GBP	AUD
BK-Special	350.00	550.00	250.00	600.00

DB195
SYDNEY BUNNYKINS™

Designer:	Dalglish, Bryant, Bartholomeucz
Modeller:	Amanda Hughes-Lubeck
Height:	5", 12.7 cm
Colour:	Blue, white, black and brown
Issued:	1999 in a special numbered edition of 2,500
Series:	Australian Heritage

Back Stamp	Price			
	USD	CAD	GBP	AUD
BK-Exc	150.00	250.00	100.00	275.00

DB196
ANGEL BUNNYKINS™

Designer:	Caroline Dadd
Modeller:	Martyn Alcock
Height:	4", 10.1 cm
Colour:	Brown, yellow and white
Issued:	1999 - 2001

Back Stamp	Price			
	USD	CAD	GBP	AUD
BK-6a	35.00	55.00	25.00	60.00

DB197
MYSTIC BUNNYKINS™

Designer:	Martyn Alcock
Modeller:	Martyn Alcock
Height:	4 ¾", 12.1 cm
Colour:	Brown, yellow, green and purple
Issued:	July to December 1999

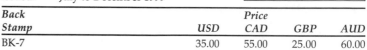

Back Stamp	Price			
	USD	CAD	GBP	AUD
BK-7	35.00	55.00	25.00	60.00

DB198
STATUE OF LIBERTY BUNNYKINS™

Designer:	Caroline Dadd
Modeller:	Amanda Hughes-Lubeck
Height:	5", 12.7 cm
Colour:	Red, white and blue
Issued:	1999 in a special edition of 3,000
Series:	American Heritage

| Back | | Price | | |
Stamp	USD	CAD	GBP	AUD
BK-Exc	75.00	125.00	50.00	150.00

DB199
AIRMAN BUNNYKINS™

Designer:	Caroline Dadd
Modeller:	Shane Ridge
Height:	4 ¼", 10.8 cm
Colour:	Brown, black and yellow
Issued:	1999 in a numbered limited edition of 5,000

| Back | | Price | | |
Stamp	USD	CAD	GBP	AUD
BK-6b	75.00	125.00	50.00	150.00

DB200
HAPPY MILLENNIUM BUNNYKINS™
TABLEAU

Designer:	Caroline Dadd
Modeller:	Shane Ridge
Height:	Unknown
Colour:	Blue, pink, red and black
Issued:	2000

*Photograph not
available
at press time*

| Back | | Price | | |
Stamp	USD	CAD	GBP	AUD
BK-Special		See below		

Note: 1. Only two produced.
2. One sold at the Bunnykins Millennium Exhibition Auction for
£9,800.00, $15,000.00 U.S. with the proceeds going to charity.
The other is held in the Royal Doulton Archives.

DB201
COWBOY BUNNYKINS™

Designer:	Kimberley Curtis
Modeller:	Martyn Alcock
Height:	4 ½", 11.9 cm
Colour:	Brown, red and cream
Issued:	1999 in a special edition of 2,500

Back Stamp	Price			
	USD	CAD	GBP	AUD
BK-Exc	175.00	275.00	100.00	325.00

DB202
INDIAN BUNNYKINS™

Designer:	Kimberley Curtis
Modeller:	Martyn Alcock
Height:	4 ½", 11.9 cm
Colour:	Brown, cream, red, white and blue
Issued:	1999 in a special edition of 2,500

Back Stamp	Price			
	USD	CAD	GBP	AUD
BK-Exc	175.00	275.00	100.00	325.00

DB203
BUSINESSMAN BUNNYKINS™

Designer:	Caroline Dadd
Modeller:	Martyn Alcock
Height:	4 ¾", 12.1 cm
Colour:	Brown, grey, black and red
Issued:	1999 in a numbered limited edition of 5,000

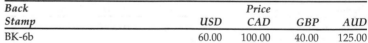

Back Stamp	Price			
	USD	CAD	GBP	AUD
BK-6b	60.00	100.00	40.00	125.00

DB204
MORRIS DANCER BUNNYKINS™

Designer: Caroline Dadd
Modeller: Shane Ridge
Height: 4 ½", 11.9 cm
Colour: Brown, cream, black, red and green
Issued: 2000 - 2000
Series: 1. Dancers of the World
             2. Special Events

Back Stamp	Price			
	USD	CAD	GBP	AUD
BK-Special	35.00	55.00	25.00	60.00

DB205
RUNNER BUNNYKINS™

Designer: Romanda Groom
Modeller: Shane Ridge
Height: 4", 10.1 cm
Colour: Brown, black, white, red and yellow
Issued: 1999 in a limited edition of 2,500
Series: Bunnykins Games

Back Stamp		Price		
	USD	CAD	GBP	AUD
BK-Special	125.00	175.00	75.00	200.00
DB205 - 209; 5 pce set	500.00	800.00	375.00	1,000.00

DB206
SWIMMER BUNNYKINS™

Designer: Romanda Groom
Modeller: Shane Ridge
Height: 3", 7.6 cm
Colour: Brown, blue, green, yellow and black
Issued: 1999 in a limited edition of 2,500
Series: Bunnykins Games

Back Stamp	Price			
	USD	CAD	GBP	AUD
BK-Special	125.00	175.00	75.00	200.00

Note: There is only one individually numbered certificate for the complete set of Bunnykins Games.

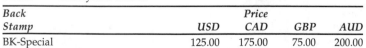

DB207
GYMNAST BUNNYKINS™

Designer:	Romanda Groom
Modeller:	Shane Ridge
Height:	4″, 10.1 cm
Colour:	Brown, red and yellow
Issued:	1999 in a limited edition of 2,500
Series:	Bunnykins Games

Back Stamp	Price			
	USD	CAD	GBP	AUD
BK-Special	125.00	175.00	75.00	200.00

DB208
BASKETBALL BUNNYKINS™
Style One

Designer:	Romanda Groom
Modeller:	Shane Ridge
Height:	5″, 12.7 cm
Colour:	Brown, blue, red and white
Issued:	1999 in a limited edition of 2,500
Series:	Bunnykins Games

Back Stamp	Price			
	USD	CAD	GBP	AUD
BK-Special	125.00	175.00	75.00	200.00

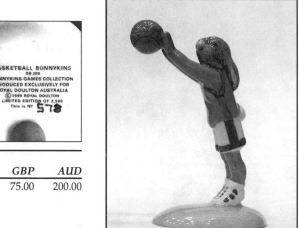

DB209
SOCCER BUNNYKINS™

Designer:	Romanda Groom
Modeller:	Shane Ridge
Height:	4″, 10.1 cm
Colour:	Brown, blue, white, green black and red
Issued:	1999 in a limited edition of 2,500
Series:	Bunnykins Games

Back Stamp	Price			
	USD	CAD	GBP	AUD
BK-Special	125.00	175.00	75.00	200.00

DB210
TRUMPET PLAYER BUNNYKINS™

Designer:	Kimberley Curtis
Modeller:	Shane Ridge
Height:	5", 12.7 cm
Colour:	Light blue and white striped jacket black trousers, yellow straw hat
Issued:	2000 in a limited edition of 2,500
Series:	Bunnykins Jazz Band

Back Stamp	Price			
	USD	CAD	GBP	AUD
BK-Exc	125.00	200.00	90.00	225.00

DB211
MINSTREL BUNNYKINS™

Designer:	Kimberley Curtis
Modeller:	Martyn Alcock
Height:	4 ½", 11.9 cm
Colour:	Green, red yellow and brown
Issued:	1999 in a numbered limited edition of 2,500

Back Stamp	Price			
	USD	CAD	GBP	AUD
BK-Exc	150.00	250.00	100.00	275.00

DB212
PILGRIM BUNNYKINS™

Designer:	Caroline Dadd
Modeller:	Amanda Hughes-Lubeck
Height:	4 ½", 11.9 cm
Colour:	Dark green, brown, white, black and pale blue
Issued:	1999 in a special numbered edition of 2,500
Series:	American Heritage

Back Stamp	Price			
	USD	CAD	GBP	AUD
BK-Exc	150.00	250.00	100.00	275.00

DB213
SUNDIAL BUNNYKINS™

Designer:	Martyn Alcock
Modeller:	Martyn Alcock
Height:	4 ½", 11.9 cm
Colour:	Pale blue, white and brown
Issued:	2000 - 2000
Series:	1. Bunnykins of the Year
	2. Time

Back Stamp	Price			
	USD	CAD	GBP	AUD
BK-Special	45.00	70.00	30.00	75.00

DB214
LAWYER BUNNYKINS™

Designer:	Martyn Alcock
Modeller:	Martyn Alcock
Height:	4", 10.1 cm
Colour:	Brown, black, grey and white
Issued:	2000 - 2000
Series:	ICC Membership Gift

Back Stamp	Price			
	USD	CAD	GBP	AUD
BK-Special	45.00	70.00	30.00	75.00

DB215
SIGHTSEER BUNNYKINS™

Designer:	Caroline Dadd
Modeller:	Martyn Alcock
Height:	4 ½", 11.9 cm
Colour:	Pink, light and dark brown
Issued:	From January to April, 2000
Series:	ICC Members Exclusive

Back Stamp	Price			
	USD	CAD	GBP	AUD
BK-Special	50.00	75.00	35.00	80.00

DB216
ENGLAND ATHLETE BUNNYKINS SYDNEY 2000™

Designer: Kimberley Curtis
Modeller: Shane Ridge
Height: 5 ½", 14.0 cm
Colour: Brown, white, blue and red
Issued: 2000 in a numbered limited edition of 2,500

Back Stamp		Price		
	USD	CAD	GBP	AUD
BK-Exc	150.00	250.00	85.00	275.00

DB217
OLD BALLOON SELLER BUNNYKINS™

Designer: From a design by Leslie Harradine
Modeller: Amanda Hughes-Lubeck
Height: 4", 10.1 cm
Colour: Brown, black shawl and skirt, white apron, pink shirt, multicoloured balloons
Issued: 2000 in a special numbered edition of 2,000

Back Stamp		Price		
	USD	CAD	GBP	AUD
BK-Exc	175.00	275.00	125.00	300.00

DB218
FORTUNE TELLER BUNNYKINS™

Designer: Warren Platt
Modeller: Warren Platt
Height: 4 ½", 11.9 cm
Colour: Brown, pink, yellow and dark green
Issued: April to September 2000

Back Stamp		Price		
	USD	CAD	GBP	AUD
Bk-7	45.00	70.00	30.00	75.00

DB219
BRITANNIA BUNNYKINS™

Designer: Kimberley Curtis
Modeller: Amanda Hughes-Lubeck
Height: 4 ¼", 10.8 cm
Colour: Brown, white, yellow, red and blue
Issued: 2000 in a numbered limited edition of 2,500

Back Stamp	Price USD	CAD	GBP	AUD
BK-Exc	150.00	250.00	95.00	300.00

DB220
LITTLE BO PEEP BUNNYKINS™

Designer: Martyn Alcock
Modeller: Martyn Alcock
Height: 4 ¼", 10.8 cm
Colour: Brown, white and yellow
Issued: 2000 to the present
Series: Nursery Rhyme

Back Stamp	Price USD	CAD	GBP	AUD
BK-6a	60.00	110.00	37.00	109.00

DB221
LITTLE JACK HORNER BUNNYKINS™

Designer: Martyn Alcock
Modeller: Martyn Alcock
Height: 4 ¼", 10.8 cm
Colour: Brown, red suit and hat, black shoes
Issued: 2000 to the present
Series: Nursery Rhyme

Back Stamp	Price USD	CAD	GBP	AUD
BK-6a	60.00	110.00	34.00	100.00

DB222
JACK AND JILL BUNNYKINS™

Designer:	Martyn Alcock
Modeller:	Martyn Alcock
Height:	4 ¼", 10.8 cm
Colour:	Brown, white, black and yellow
Issued:	2000 to the present
Series:	Nursery Rhyme

Back Stamp	Price			
	USD	CAD	GBP	AUD
BK-6a	120.00	200.00	52.00	160.00

DB223
CHOIR SINGER BUNNYKINS™

Designer:	Martyn Alcock
Modeller:	Martyn Alcock
Height:	4", 10.5 cm
Colour:	Black, beige, red and white
Issued:	2001 - 2001
Series:	ICC Members Exclusive

Back Stamp	Price			
	USD	CAD	GBP	AUD
BK-Special	45.00	70.00	30.00	75.00

DB224
FEDERATION BUNNYKINS™

Designer:	Brian Dalglish and Bill Bryant
Modeller:	Shane Ridge
Height:	5", 12.7 cm
Colour:	Brown, blue, red and white
Issued:	2000 in a limited edition of 2,500
Series:	Australian Heritage

Back Stamp	Price			
	USD	CAD	GBP	AUD
BK-Exc	150.00	250.00	95.00	275.00

DB225
EASTER SURPRISE BUNNYKINS™

Designer: Graham Tongue
Modeller: Warren Platt
Height: 4 ½", 11.9 cm
Colour: Purple, yellow and black
Issued: 2000 in a limited edition of 2,500
Varieties: Also called Easter Greetings
           Bunnykins, DB149

Back Stamp	Price USD	CAD	GBP	AUD
BK-Exc	40.00	65.00	30.00	75.00

DB226
MOTHER AND BABY BUNNYKINS™
Style Two (Large Size)

Designer: Amanda Hughes-Lubeck
Modeller: Amanda Hughes-Lubeck
Height: 6 ¼", 15.9 cm
Colour: Blue, white and yellow
Issued: 2000 in a limited edition of 2,000
Series: The Bunnykins Family

Back Stamp	Price USD	CAD	GBP	AUD
BK-8b	80.00	135.00	50.00	150.00

DB227
FATHER BUNNYKINS™
Style Two (Large size)

Designer: Amanda Hughes-Lubeck
Modeller: Amanda Hughes-Lubeck
Height: 6 ¾", 17.1 cm
Colour: Cream, red, tan and yellow
Issued: 2000 in a limited edition of 2,000
Series: The Bunnykins Family

Back Stamp	Price USD	CAD	GBP	AUD
BK-8b	80.00	135.00	50.00	150.00

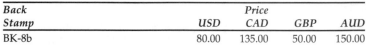

DB228
SANDCASTLE MONEY BOX

Designer: Warren Platt
Modeller: Warren Platt
Height: 4 ¼", 10.8 cm
Colour: Blue, green, pink, red, white and yellow
Issued: 2001 - 2002 in a limited edition of 2002
Series: Tableau

Back Stamp	Price			
	USD	CAD	GBP	AUD
BK-8b	225.00	295.00	120.00	325.00

DB229
SANDS OF TIME BUNNYKINS™

Designer: Martyn Alcock
Modeller: Martyn Alcock
Height: 3 ½", 9 cm
Colour: Yellow robe with suns and moons
Issued: 2001 - 2001
Series: 1. Bunnykins of the Year
2. Time

Back Stamp	Price			
	USD	CAD	GBP	AUD
BK-Special	60.00	85.00	35.00	100.00

DB230
LITTLE RED RIDING HOOD BUNNYKINS™

Designer: Martyn Alcock
Modeller: Martyn Alcock
Height: 4 ¼", 10.5 cm
Colour: Black, dark blue, green, red tan and white
Issued: 2001 in a limited edition of 2000
Series: 1. Fairy Tales
2. Special Events

Back Stamp	Price			
	USD	CAD	GBP	AUD
BK-Exc	150.00	250.00	100.00	275.00

DB231
CINDERELLA BUNNYKINS™

Designer:	Unknown
Modeller:	Martyn Alcock
Height:	4 ¼", 10.8 cm
Colour:	Pink and yellow
Issued:	2002 - 2002
Series:	1. ICC Members Exclusive
	2. Fairy Tales

Photograph not available at press time

Back Stamp	Price			
	USD	CAD	GBP	AUD
BK-Special	Price not established at press time			

Note: DB232 May Queen was not issued.

DB233
SHOPPER BUNNYKINS™

Designer:	Warren Platt
Modeller:	Warren Platt
Height:	4 ½", 11.5 cm
Colour:	Blue dress, beige coat, pink scarf, brown and white bag
Issued:	2001 to the present

Back Stamp	Price			
	USD	CAD	GBP	AUD
BK-8a	50.00	75.00	30.00	85.00

DB234
MR. PUNCH BUNNYKINS

Designer:	Kimberley Curtis
Modeller:	Martyn Alcock
Height:	4 ¾", 12 cm
Colour:	Blue, brown, orange, red and white
Issued:	2001 in a limited edition of 2,500
Series:	Punch and Judy

Back Stamp	Price			
	USD	CAD	GBP	AUD
BK-Exc	125.00	250.00	75.00	300.00

DB235
JUDY BUNNYKINS™

Designer:	Kimberley Curtis
Modeller:	Martyn Alcock
Height:	4¼", 11 cm
Colour:	Blue, brown and yellow
Issued:	2001 in a limited edition of 2,500
Series:	Punch and Judy

Back Stamp	USD	Price CAD	GBP	AUD
BK-Exc	125.00	250.00	75.00	300.00

DB236
WALTZING MATILDA BUNNYKINS™

Designer:	Wendy Boyce-Davies
Modeller:	Martyn Alcock
Height:	4", 10.1 cm
Colour:	Brown, blue, lemon, pink, white and yellow
Issued:	2001 in a limited edition of 2001
Series:	Australian Heritage

Back Stamp	USD	Price CAD	GBP	AUD
Bk-8b	150.00	250.00	100.00	300.00

DB237
FATHER CHRISTMAS BUNNYKINS™

Designer:	Warren Platt
Modeller:	Warren Platt
Height:	5", 12.7 cm
Colour:	Red, white, black, grey and silver
Issued:	2000 in a limited edition of 2,500

Photograph not available at press time

Back Stamp	USD	Price CAD	GBP	AUD
Bk-8b	100.00	175.00	65.00	200.00

DB238
ON LINE BUNNYKINS™

Designer:	Shane Ridge
Modeller:	Shane Ridge
Height:	2 ¾", 7.0 cm
Colour:	Brown, light blue trousers, blue and white shirt, red vest
Issued:	2001 in a special edition of 2,500

Back Stamp	Price			
	USD	CAD	GBP	AUD
BK-Exc	200.00	350.00	150.00	375.00

DB239
LITTLE BOY BLUE BUNNYKINS™

Designer:	Caroline Dadd
Modeller:	Shane Ridge
Height:	3 ¾", 9.5 cm
Colour:	Pale blue and white
Issued:	2002 to the present
Series:	Nursery Rhyme

Back Stamp	Price			
	USD	CAD	GBP	AUD
BK-8a	60.00	110.00	35.00	120.00

DB240
LITTLE MISS MUFFET BUNNYKINS™

Designer:	Caroline Dadd
Modeller:	Warren Platt
Height:	3 ½", 8.9 cm
Colour:	Pale blue, white and green
Issued:	2002 to the present
Series:	Nursery Rhyme

Back Stamp	Price			
	USD	CAD	GBP	AUD
BK-8a	60.00	110.00	35.00	120.00

DB241
BATH NIGHT BUNNYKINS™

Designer: After a design by Barbara Vernon
Modeller: Martyn Alcock
Height: 4 ¼", 10.8 cm
Colour: Beige, blue, brown, grey and white
Issued: 2001 in a limited edition of 5,000
Series: Tableau

Back		Price		
Stamp	USD	CAD	GBP	AUD
Bk-8b	125.00	200.00	85.00	225.00

DB242
TYROLEAN DANCER BUNNYKINS™

Designer: Shane Ridge
Modeller: Shane Ridge
Height: 4", 10.1 cm
Colour: White, black and grey
Issued: 2001 - 2001
Series: 1. Dancers of the World
            2. Special Events

Back		Price		
Stamp	USD	CAD	GBP	AUD
BK-Special	70.00	100.00	40.00	100.00

DB243
LITTLE JOHN BUNNYKINS™

Designer: Martyn Alcock
Modeller: Martyn Alcock
Height: 5", 12.5 cm
Colour: Brown, tan and yellow
Issued: 2001 to the present
Series: Robin Hood

Back		Price		
Stamp	USD	CAD	GBP	AUD
BK-8a	60.00	110.00	30.00	95.00

Note: A castle-like stand is available for the eight Bunnykins of the Robin Hood Collection.

DB244
ROBIN HOOD BUNNYKINS™

Designer:	Martyn Alcock
Modeller:	Martyn Alcock
Height:	4 ½", 11.9 cm
Colour:	Beige, brown, forest green, red and yellow
Issued:	2001 to the present
Series:	Robin Hood

Back Stamp	Price			
	USD	CAD	GBP	AUD
BK-8a	60.00	110.00	30.00	95.00

DB245
MAID MARION BUNNYKINS™

Designer:	Martyn Alcock
Modeller:	Martyn Alcock
Height:	4 ¼", 10.8 cm
Colour:	Pink, purple, green and gold
Issued:	2001 to the present
Series:	Robin Hood

Back Stamp	Price			
	USD	CAD	GBP	AUD
BK-8a	60.00	110.00	30.00	100.00

DB246
FRIAR TUCK BUNNYKINS™

Designer:	Martyn Alcock
Modeller:	Martyn Alcock
Height:	4 ½", 11.9 cm
Colour:	Brown, green, yellow and grey
Issued:	2001 to the present
Series:	Robin Hood

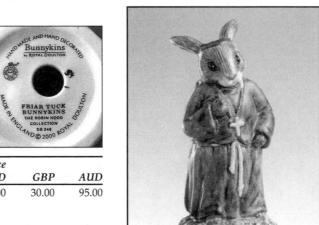

Back Stamp	Price			
	USD	CAD	GBP	AUD
BK-8a	60.00	110.00	30.00	95.00

DB247
MARY MARY QUITE CONTRARY BUNNYKINS™

Designer:	Caroline Dadd
Modeller:	Shane Ridge
Height:	3 ½″, 8.9 cm
Colour:	Pink and white
Issued:	2002 to the present
Series:	Nursery Rhyme

Back Stamp	*USD*	*Price CAD*	*GBP*	*AUD*
BK-8a	60.00	110.00	35.00	120.00

DB248
DIGGER BUNNYKINS™

Designer:	Dalglish, Bryant, Bartholmeucz
Modeller:	Warren Platt
Height:	5 ½″, 14 cm
Colour:	Khaki, beige, brown, silver and navy blue
Issued:	2001 in a limited edition of 2,500
Series:	Australian Heritage

Back Stamp	*USD*	*Price CAD*	*GBP*	*AUD*
BK-Exc	150.00	275.00	100.00	300.00

DB249
DODGEM BUNNYKINS™

Designer:	After a design by Barbara Vernon
Modeller:	Martyn Alcock
Height:	3″ x 4″, 7.6 x 10 cm
Colour:	Black, red, white and yellow
Issued:	2001 in a limited edition of 2,500
Series:	Travel

Back Stamp	*USD*	*Price CAD*	*GBP*	*AUD*
BK-Exc	150.00	275.00	100.00	300.00

DB250
DRUMMER BUNNYKINS™
Style Two

Designer:	Kimberley Curtis
Modeller:	Shane Ridge
Height:	4 ¼", 10.8 cm
Colour:	Black, white, pink and blue
Issued:	2002 in a limited edition of 2,500
Series:	Bunnykins Jazz Band

Back Stamp	Price			
	USD	CAD	GBP	AUD
BK-Exc	125.00	200.00	70.00	250.00

DB251
CAPTAIN COOK BUNNYKINS™

Designer:	Wendy Boyce-Davies
Modeller:	Warren Platt
Height:	4 ½", 10.1 cm
Colour:	Blue coat, yellow trousers, blue and yellow hat
Issued:	2002 in a limited edition of 2,500
Series:	Australian Heritage

Photograph not
available
at press time

Back Stamp	Price			
	USD	CAD	GBP	AUD
BK-Exc	125.00	200.00	80.00	200.00

DB252
MANDARIN BUNNYKINS™

Designer:	Caroline Dadd
Modeller:	Martyn Alcock
Height:	4 ¼", 10.8 cm
Colour:	Yellow robe; grey dragon; purple
Issued:	2001 in a limited edition of 2,500
Series:	Bunnykins of the World (1 of 15)

Back Stamp	Price			
	USD	CAD	GBP	AUD
BK-Exc	125.00	200.00	70.00	250.00

DB253
STOP WATCH BUNNYKINS™

Designer: Martyn Alcock
Modeller: Martyn Alcock
Height: 3 ¾", 9.5 cm
Colour: Green
Issued: 2002 - 2002
Series: 1. Bunnykins of the Year
2. Time

Back Stamp	Price			
	USD	CAD	GBP	AUD
BK-Special	60.00	110.00	32.00	110.00

DB254
VICAR BUNNYKINS™

Designer: Shane Ridge
Modeller: Shane Ridge
Height: 4 ½", 11.9 cm
Colour: Black and white
Issued: 2002 - 2002
Series: ICC Membership Gift

Photograph not available at press time

Back Stamp	Price			
	USD	CAD	GBP	AUD
BK-Special	50.00	85.00	32.00	100.00

DB255
GOLFER BUNNYKINS™

Designer: Shane Ridge
Modeller: Shane Ridge
Height: 5 ¼", 13.3 cm
Colour: Black, brown, green, grey, white and yellow
Issued: 2001 to the present

Back Stamp	Price			
	USD	CAD	GBP	AUD
Bk-8a	60.00	110.00	35.00	120.00

Note: Issued in the UK August 2001, in Australia March 2002 and Worldwide December 2002. Figure was exclusive to Royal Doulton outlets worldwide.

DB256
FLAMENCO BUNNYKINS™

Designer:	Shane Ridge
Modeller:	Shane Ridge
Height:	4 ½", 11.9 cm
Colour:	Yellow dress with black ruffles
Issued:	2002 - 2002
Series:	1. Dancers of the World
	2. Special Events

Back Stamp	Price			
	USD	CAD	GBP	AUD
BK-Special	60.00	110.00	35.00	120.00

DB257
LIBERTY BELL BUNNYKINS™

Designer:	Shane Ridge
Modeller:	Shane Ridge
Height:	5", 12.7 cm
Colour:	Black, blue, beige, grey and white
Issued:	2001 in a limited edition of 2,000
Series:	American Heritage

Back Stamp	Price			
	USD	CAD	GBP	AUD
BK-8a	150.00	275.00	90.00	300.00

DB258
KING RICHARD BUNNYKINS™

Designer:	Martyn Alcock
Modeller:	Martyn Alcock
Height:	4 ½", 11.5 cm
Colour:	Dark blue, grey, white, red and brown
Issued:	2002 to the present
Series:	Robin Hood

Photograph not available at press time

Back Stamp	Price			
	USD	CAD	GBP	AUD
BK-8a	60.00	110.00	32.00	95.00

DB259
TOWN CRIER BUNNYKINS™

Designer:	Caroline Dadd
Modeller:	Martyn Alcock
Height:	4 ½", 11.9 cm
Colour:	Black, red, yellow and grey
Issued:	2002 in a limited edition of 2,500

Photograph not available at press time

Back Stamp	Price			
	USD	CAD	GBP	AUD
BK-Exc	125.00	200.00	70.00	250.00

DB260
DAY TRIP BUNNYKINS™

Designer:	Caroline Dadd
Modeller:	Martyn Alcock
Height:	3 ½", 9.0 cm
Colour:	Green, blue, red, yellow and brown
Issued:	2002 in a limited edition of 2,500
Series:	Travel

Photograph not available at press time

Back Stamp	Price			
	USD	CAD	GBP	AUD
BK-Exc	125.00	200.00	70.00	250.00

DB261 NOT ALLOCATED

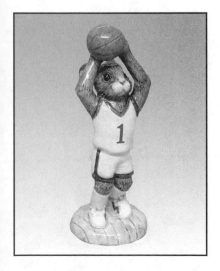

DB262
BASKETBALL PLAYER BUNNYKINS™
Style Two

Designer:	Shane Ridge
Modeller:	Shane Ridge
Height:	5", 12.7 cm
Colour:	Beige, brown, yellow and purple
Issued:	2002 in a limited edition of 2,000

Photograph not available at press time

Back Stamp	Price			
	USD	CAD	GBP	AUD
BK-Exc	100.00	150.00	50.00	175.00

DB263 NOT ALLOCATED.

DB264
WILL SCARLET BUNNYKINS™

Designer:	Martyn Alcock
Modeller:	Martyn Alcock
Height:	3 ½", 9.0 cm
Colour:	Light and dark green, red, yellow, brown and beige
Issued:	2002 to the present
Series:	Robin Hood

Back Stamp	USD	Price CAD	GBP	AUD
BK-8a	60.00	110.00	32.00	95.00

DB265
SHERIFF OF NOTTINGHAM BUNNYKINS™

Designer:	Martyn Alcock
Modeller:	Martyn Alcock
Height:	4 ½", 11.5 cm
Colour:	Brown, grey, black, dark yellow
Issued:	2002 to the present
Series:	Robin Hood

Back Stamp	USD	Price CAD	GBP	AUD
BK-8a	60.00	110.00	32.00	95.00

DB266
PRINCE JOHN BUNNYKINS™

Designer:	Martyn Alcock
Modeller:	Martyn Alcock
Height:	4 ½", 11.5 cm
Colour:	Brown, dark green, yellow and pink
Issued:	2002 to the present
Series:	Robin Hood

Back Stamp	USD	Price CAD	GBP	AUD
BK-8a	60.00	110.00	32.00	95.00

DB267 CHOCKS AWAY BUNNYKINS™ to be issued 2002

DB268
AMERICAN FIREFIGHTER BUNNYKINS™
Third Variation

Designer:	Shane Ridge
Modeller:	Shane Ridge
Height:	4 ¼", 10.5 cm
Colour:	Tan, black, light brown, yellow, grey and red
Issued:	2002 in a limited edition of 2,001
Varieties:	Also called Fireman Bunnykins, DB75, DB183
Series:	American Heritage

Photograph not available at press time

Back Stamp	Price			
	USD	CAD	GBP	AUD
BK-8b	Price not established at press time			

DB269
WITH LOVE BUNNYKINS™

Designer:	Shane Ridge
Modeller:	Shane Ridge
Height:	4 ¼", 10.5 cm
Colour:	Pale yellow, yellow, white, pink, green and brown
Issued:	2002 to the present

Photograph not available at press time

Back Stamp	Price			
	USD	CAD	GBP	AUD
BK-8a	Price not established at press time			

DB270
WEE WILLIE WINKLE BUNNYKINS™

Designer:	Caroline Dadd
Modeller:	Shane Ridge
Height:	4 ½", 11.5 cm
Colour:	White, yellow and brown
Issues:	2002 to the present
Series:	Nursery Rhyme

Photograph not available at press time

Back Stamp	Price			
	USD	CAD	GBP	AUD
BK-8a	Price not established at press time			

RESIN ISSUES
1996-1997

DBR1
HARRY BUNNYKINS
A LITTLE BUNNY AT PLAY™

Designer:	Unknown
Modeller:	Unknown
Height:	1 ¾", 4.5 cm
Colour:	Pale blue pyjamas, red and dark blue toys
Issued:	1996 - 1997

Royal Doulton
Harry Bunnykins
"a little bunny at play"
DBR1/ 491
© 1996 Royal Doulton
Made in China

Doulton Number		Price		
	USD	CAD	GBP	AUD
DBR1	15.00	20.00	10.00	20.00

DBR2
HARRY BUNNYKINS
PLAYTIME™

Designer:	Unknown
Modeller:	Unknown
Height:	2", 5.0 cm
Colour:	Pale blue pyjamas, yellow toys, pink, yellow and green pillow
Issued:	1996 - 1997

Royal Doulton
Harry Bunnykins
Playtime
DBR2/ 3605
© 1996 Royal Doulton
Made in China

Doulton Number		Price		
	USD	CAD	GBP	AUD
DBR2	15.00	20.00	10.00	20.00

DBR3
REGINALD RATLEY
UP TO NO GOOD™

Designer:	Unknown
Modeller:	Unknown
Height:	2 ¼", 5.7 cm
Colour:	Black jacket, hat and shoes, yellow shirt, red tie
Issued:	1996 - 1997

Royal Doulton
Reginald Ratley
Up to no good
DBR3/ 3530
© 1996 Royal Doulton
Made in China

Doulton Number		Price		
	USD	CAD	GBP	AUD
DBR3	15.00	20.00	10.00	20.00

DBR4
SUSAN BUNNYKINS
THE HELPER™

Designer:	Unknown
Modeller:	Unknown
Height:	3", 7.6 cm
Colour:	White and blue dress
Issued:	1996 - 1997

*Photograph not
available
at press time*

Doulton Number		Price		
	USD	CAD	GBP	AUD
DBR4	15.00	20.00	10.00	20.00

DBR5
WILLIAM BUNNYKINS
ASLEEP IN THE SUN™

Designer:	Unknown
Modeller:	Unknown
Height:	2 ¼", 5.7 cm
Colour:	White shirt, red jacket, brown trousers
Issued:	1996 - 1997

Doulton Number		Price		
	USD	CAD	GBP	AUD
DBR5	15.00	20.00	10.00	20.00

DBR6
LADY RATLEY
HER LADYSHIP EXPLAINS™

Designer:	Unknown
Modeller:	Unknown
Height:	3 ¼", 8.3 cm
Colour:	Light and dark purple dress black shoes and handbag
Issued:	1996 - 1997

Doulton Number		Price		
	USD	CAD	GBP	AUD
DBR6	20.00	30.00	15.00	30.00

DBR7
MRS. BUNNYKINS
A BUSY MORNING SHOPPING™

Designer:	Unknown
Modeller:	Unknown
Height:	3 ½", 8.9 cm
Colour:	White dress with blue flowers, pale yellow apron and hat, brown basket
Issued:	1996 - 1997

Doulton Number		Price		
	USD	CAD	GBP	AUD
DBR7	20.00	30.00	15.00	30.00

DBR8
FATHER BUNNYKINS
HOME FROM WORK™

Designer:	Unknown
Modeller:	Unknown
Height:	3 ¾", 9.5 cm
Colour:	Crean trousers, green jacket and black shoes
Issued:	1996 - 1997

Doulton Number		Price		
	USD	CAD	GBP	AUD
DBR8	20.00	30.00	15.00	30.00

DBR9
WILLIAM BUNNYKINS
A BUNNY IN A HURRY™

Designer:	Unknown
Modeller:	Unknown
Height:	2 ¼", 5.7 cm
Colour:	Brown trousers, white shirt and red jacket
Issued:	1996 - 1997

Doulton Number		Price		
	USD	CAD	GBP	AUD
DBR9	15.00	20.00	10.00	20.00

DBR10
SUSAN BUNNYKINS
WILDLIFE SPOTTING™

Designer:	Unknown
Modeller:	Unknown
Height:	2 ¾", 7.0 cm
Colour:	White dress with blue flowers, brown basket
Issued:	1996 - 1997

Royal Doulton
Susan Bunnykins
Wildlife spotting
DBR10/ 3548
© 1996 Royal Doulton
Made in China

Doulton Number	USD	Price CAD	GBP	AUD
DBR10	15.00	20.00	10.00	20.00

DBR11
SUSAN AND HARRY BUNNYKINS
MINDING THE BABY BROTHER™

Designer:	Unknown
Modeller:	Unknown
Height:	2 ½", 6.4 cm
Colour:	Susan - white dress with blue flowers
	Harry - pale blue pyjamas, multicoloured toys
Issued:	1996 - 1997

Royal Doulton
Susan and Harry Bunnykins
Minding the baby brother
DBR11/ 2850
© 1996 Royal Doulton
Made in China

Doulton Number	USD	Price CAD	GBP	AUD
DBR11	30.00	45.00	17.00	45.00

DBR12
FATHER BUNNYKINS AND HARRY
DECORATING THE TREE™

Designer:	Unknown
Modeller:	Unknown
Height:	4", 10.1 cm
Colour:	Father - blue trousers, white shirt and red pullover
	Harry - white pyjamas, green tree
Issued:	1996 - 1997

Royal Doulton
Father Bunnykins and Harry
Decorating the tree
DBR12/ 2667
© 1996 Royal Doulton
Made in China

Doulton Number	USD	Price CAD	GBP	AUD
DBR12	30.00	45.00	20.00	45.00

DBR13
MRS. BUNNYKINS AND WILLIAM
THE BIRTHDAY CAKE™

Designer:	Unknown
Modeller:	Unknown
Height:	3 ¼", 8.3 cm
Colour:	White dress with blue flowers, light yellow apron, red jacket, white shirt and brown trousers
Issued:	1996 - 1997

Doulton Number		*Price*		
	USD	CAD	GBP	AUD
DBR13	30.00	45.00	17.00	40.00

DBR14
HAPPY CHRISTMAS FROM THE
BUNNYKINS FAMILY™

Designer:	Unknown
Modeller:	Unknown
Height:	6", 15.0 cm
Colour:	Multi-coloured
Issued:	1996 - 1997
Series:	Music Box

Doulton Number		*Price*		
	USD	CAD	GBP	AUD
DBR14	110.00	150.00	75.00	150.00

DBR15
PICNIC TIME WITH THE
BUNNYKINS FAMILY™

Designer:	Unknown
Modeller:	Unknown
Height:	5", 12.7 cm
Colour:	Multi-coloured
Issued:	1996 - 1997
Series:	Music Box

Doulton Number		*Price*		
	USD	CAD	GBP	AUD
DBR15	90.00	150.00	75.00	150.00

DBR16
BIRTHDAY GIRL™

Designer:	Unknown
Modeller:	Unknown
Height:	1 ½", 4 cm
Colour:	Pink and white dress
Issued:	1997 - 1997

Doulton		Price		
Number	U.S.$	CAD	GBP	AUD
DBR16	15.00	20.00	10.00	20.00

Royal Doulton
Bunnykins
Birthday Girl
DBR16/ **874**
©1996 Royal Doulton
Made In China

DBR17
BIRTHDAY BOY™

Designer:	Unknown
Modeller:	Unknown
Height:	1 ½", 4 cm
Colour:	Blue pyjamas, white bib
Issued:	1997 - 1997

Royal Doulton
Bunnykins
Birthday Boy
DBR17/ **1456**
©1996 Royal Doulton
Made In China

Doulton		Price		
Number	U.S.$	CAD	GBP	AUD
DBR17	15.00	20.00	10.00	20.00

DBR18
THE NEW BABY™

Designer:	Unknown
Modeller:	Unknown
Height:	3 ½", 8.9 cm
Colour:	Mother - white, lilac and rose
	Baby - light blue
Issued:	1997 - 1997

Royal Doulton
Bunnykins
The New Baby
DBR18/ **101**
©1996 Royal Doulton
Made In China

Doulton		Price		
Number	USD	CAD	GBP	AUD
DBR18	20.00	30.00	15.00	30.00

DBR19
THE ROCKING HORSE™

Designer:	Unknown
Modeller:	Unknown
Height:	2 ¾", 7.0 cm
Colour:	Brown bunny, red and white dress, white horse
Issued:	1997 - 1997

Royal Doulton
Bunnykins
The Rocking Horse
DBR19/ 180
©1996 Royal Doulton
Made In China

Doulton Number	Price			
	USD	CAD	GBP	AUD
DBR19	15.00	20.00	10.00	20.00

WHAT IS IT?

INDICES

ALPHABETICAL INDEX TO BUNNYKINS TABLEWARE

NUMERICAL INDEX TO BUNNYKINS TABLEWARE

ALPHABETICAL INDEX TO
BUNNYKINS EARTHENWARE FIGURINES

NUMERICAL INDEX TO BUNNYKINS
EARTHENWARE FIGURINES

ALPHABETICAL INDEX TO BUNNYKINS RESIN FIGURINES

ROYAL DOULTON
Outlet Stores

Visit any of our Royal Doulton Outlet Stores where you will find a wide selection of collectibles. Also, your International Collector's Club membership may be renewed at any of our stores listed below.

Cabazon, CA.............(909) 849-4222	Smithfield, NC......... (919) 934-0101
Camarillo, CA...........(805) 987-6208	Flemington, NJ ....(908) 788-5677
Carlsbad, CA.............(760) 804-0159	Las Vegas, NV......... (702) 260-4192
Gilroy, CA...............(408) 842-1653	Central Valley, NY.....(845) 928-2434
Lake Elsinore, CA......(909) 674-5884	Riverhead, NY......... (631) 369-6940
Vacaville, CA............(707) 448-2793	Jeffersonville, OH..... (740) 948-9200
Clinton, CT..............(860) 669-3496	Lincoln City, OR.........(541) 996-5065
Rehoboth, DE........... (302) 226-9335	Lancaster, PA........... (717) 291-9370
Ellenton, FL............. (941) 729-2076	Grove City, PA ....(724) 748-4990
Estero, FL...............(941) 947-5200	Tannersville, PA ....(570) 619-4020
Orlando, FL..............(407) 352-5578	Myrtle Beach, SC....... (843) 236-5703
St. Augustine, FL.......(904) 824-9700	Pigeon Forge, TN ....(865) 428-0977
Calhoun, GA.............(706) 602-2066	Conroe, TX ....(936) 856-7383
Dawsonville, GA ....(706) 216-1480	San Marcos, TX......... (512) 754-0555
Michigan City, IN.......(219) 872-7916	Prince William, VA..... (703) 497-6845
Kittery, ME...............(207) 439-4770	Williamsburg, VA....... (757) 565-0752
Birch Run, MI........... (989) 624-1011	Burlington, WA.......... (360) 757-6660
Blowing Rock, NC...... (828) 295-9230	

ROYAL DOULTON

Visit our web site at: www.royal-doulton.com

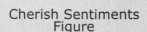

318